Dummies 101™: Netscape® Navigator™

S0-BYV-295

CHEAT SHEET

Accessing the CD-ROM Files

Note: If you don't already have Netscape Navigator, see Unit 1 for how to get it.

Follow the instructions in Units 1 and 8 and Appendix B of this book to install and access the files on the CD-ROM.

Browsing the World Wide Web

To See . . .	Click . . .
The preceding page	The Back button
Your starting page	The Home Button
A link's Web page	The link (underlined text)
A page at a Web address (URL)	The Location box; then type the URL and press Enter
A list of pages you've visited	Go on the menu
A list of bookmarks	Bookmarks on the menu
A page that lets you search the Web	The Net Search button
A printout of a Web page	The Print button
The *Dummies 101: Netscape Navigator* home page	The Location box; then type **net.dummies.com/ netscape101** and press Enter
Information about *The Internet For Dummies* and related books	The Location box; then type **net.dummies.com** and press Enter
Information about other *. . .For Dummies* and *Dummies 101* books	The Location box; then type **www.dummies.com** and press Enter

(Refer to Units 1, 2, 3, and 4 for how to use the Netscape browser.)

Reading Usenet Newsgroups

To Do This . . .	Click . . .
Open the Netscape News window	Window⇨Netscape News
Get the articles in a newsgroup	The newsgroup name
See the text of an article	The article header
See only subscribed newsgroups	Options⇨Show Subscribed Newsgroups
See all available newsgroups	Options⇨Show All Newsgroups
Subscribe to a newsgroup	The box in the Subscribe column (with a yellow check as the column heading)
Reply to an article by e-mailing its author	The article and then the Re:Mail button
Reply to an article by posting a response to the newsgroup	The article and then the Re:News button

(Refer to Unit 7 for how to use the Netscape News window.)

CHEAT SHEET

How Netscape Sends and Receives Your Mail

(See Table 5-1 in Lesson 5-1 for where to get this information.)

Location of your Netscape program directory (for example, C:\Program Files\Netscape\Navigator or C: \Netscape):_____

_____

Your Internet provider's POP server (for storing your incoming mail):

_____

Your Internet provider's SMTP server (for passing your outgoing mail along to the Internet): _____

Your Internet provider's NNTP server (for getting Usenet newsgroup articles):_____

Your e-mail user name: _____

Your e-mail password (write on a separate piece of paper and store in a safe place)

Dealing with E-mail

To Do This . . .	Click . . .
Open the Netscape Mail window	The Mail icon (the envelope in the lower-right corner of the Netscape window)
Send a new message	The To:Mail button
Reply to a message	The message and then the Re:Mail button
Delete a message	The message and then the Delete button
Forward a message	The message and then the Forward button
Print a message	The message and then the Print button
Get your new messages	The Get Mail button
Close the Netscape Mail window	File⇨Close
See your Address Book	Window⇨Address Book
Add an Address Book entry	Item⇨Add User
Change an Address Book entry	The entry; then choose Item⇨Properties
Delete an Address Book entry	The entry; then press Del
Attach a file to a message	The Attach button
Save an attached file	The image or the attachment box by using the right mouse button; then choose Save Image As

(Refer to Units 5 and 6 for how to use the Netscape Mail window.)

IDG BOOKS WORLDWIDE™

References for the Rest of Us!®

COMPUTER BOOK SERIES FROM IDG

Are you intimidated and confused by computers? Do you find that traditional manuals are overloaded with technical details you'll never use? Do your friends and family always call you to fix simple problems on their PCs? Then the ...*For Dummies*® computer book series from IDG Books Worldwide is for you.

...*For Dummies* books are written for those frustrated computer users who know they aren't really dumb but find that PC hardware, software, and indeed the unique vocabulary of computing make them feel helpless. ...*For Dummies* books use a lighthearted approach, a down-to-earth style, and even cartoons and humorous icons to diffuse computer novices' fears and build their confidence. Lighthearted but not lightweight, these books are a perfect survival guide for anyone forced to use a computer.

> "I like my copy so much I told friends; now they bought copies."
>
> **Irene C., Orwell, Ohio**

> "Thanks, I needed this book. Now I can sleep at night."
>
> **Robin F., British Columbia, Canada**

> "Quick, concise, nontechnical, and humorous."
>
> **Jay A., Elburn, Illinois**

Already, hundreds of thousands of satisfied readers agree. They have made ...*For Dummies* books the #1 introductory level computer book series and have written asking for more. So, if you're looking for the most fun and easy way to learn about computers, look to ...*For Dummies* books to give you a helping hand.

DUMMIES 101™: NETSCAPE® NAVIGATOR™

by Margaret Levine Young and Hy Bender

IDG Books Worldwide, Inc.
An International Data Group Company

Foster City, CA ◆ Chicago, IL ◆ Indianapolis, IN ◆ Southlake, TX

Dummies 101™: Netscape® Navigator™

Published by
IDG Books Worldwide, Inc.
An International Data Group Company
919 E. Hillsdale Blvd.
Suite 400
Foster City, CA 94404
www.idgbooks.com (IDG Books Worldwide Web Site)
http://www.dummies.com (Dummies Press Web Site)

Library of Congress Catalog Card No.: 96-77277

ISBN: 0-7645-0034-1

Printed in the United States of America

10 9 8 7 6 5 4 3 2 1

1B/TR/RQ/ZW/IN

Distributed in the United States by IDG Books Worldwide, Inc.

Distributed by Macmillan Canada for Canada; by Contemporanea de Ediciones for Venezuela; by Distribuidora Cuspide for Argentina; by CITEC for Brazil; by Ediciones ZETA S.C.R. Ltda. for Peru; by Editorial Limusa SA for Mexico; by Transworld Publishers Limited in the United Kingdom and Europe; by Academic Bookshop for Egypt; by Levant Distributors S.A.R.L. for Lebanon; by Al Jassim for Saudi Arabia; by Simron Pty. Ltd. for South Africa; by Pustak Mahal for India; by The Computer Bookshop for India; by Toppan Company Ltd. for Japan; by Addison Wesley Publishing Company for Korea; by Longman Singapore Publishers Ltd. for Singapore, Malaysia, Thailand, and Indonesia; by Unalis Corporation for Taiwan; by WS Computer Publishing Company, Inc. for the Philippines; by WoodsLane Pty. Ltd. for Australia; by WoodsLane Enterprises Ltd. for New Zealand. Authorized Sales Agent: Anthony Rudkin Associates for the Middle East and North Africa.

For general information on IDG Books Worldwide's books in the U.S., please call our Consumer Customer Service department at 800-762-2974. For reseller information, including discounts and premium sales, please call our Reseller Customer Service department at 800-434-3422.

For information on where to purchase IDG Books Worldwide's books outside the U.S., please contact our International Sales department at 415-655-3172 or fax 415-655-3295.

For information on foreign language translations, please contact our Foreign & Subsidiary Rights department at 415-655-3021 or fax 415-655-3281.

For sales inquiries and special prices for bulk quantities, please contact our Sales department at 415-655-3200 or write to the address above.

For information on using IDG Books Worldwide's books in the classroom or for ordering examination copies, please contact our Educational Sales department at 800-434-2086 or fax 817-251-8174.

For authorization to photocopy items for corporate, personal, or educational use, please contact Copyright Clearance Center, 222 Rosewood Drive, Danvers, MA 01923, or fax 508-750-4470.

is a trademark under exclusive license to IDG Books Worldwide, Inc., from International Data Group, Inc.

About the Authors

Margaret Levine Young

Unlike her peers in that 30-something bracket, Margaret Levine Young was exposed to computers at an early age. In high school, she got into a computer club known as the R.E.S.I.S.T.O.R.S., a group of kids who spent Saturdays in a barn fooling around with three antiquated computers. She stayed in the field through college against her better judgment and despite her brother's presence as a graduate student in the Computer Science department. Margy graduated from Yale and went on to become one of the first microcomputer managers in the early 1980s at Columbia Pictures, where she rode the elevator with Paul Newman, Bill Murray, and Jeff Goldblum.

Since then, Margy has coauthored over 15 computer books on the topics of the Internet, UNIX, WordPerfect, Microsoft Access, and (stab from the past) PC-File and Javelin, including *Dummies 101: The Internet for Windows 95, The Internet For Dummies,* 3rd Edition, *Internet FAQs: Answers to Frequently Asked Questions,* and *UNIX For Dummies,* 2nd Edition (all from IDG Books Worldwide). She met her future husband in the R.E.S.I.S.T.O.R.S., and her other passion is her children, Meg and Zac. She loves gardening, chickens, reading, and anything to do with eating, and lives near Middlebury, Vermont.

Hy Bender

Hy Bender is the author of *Excel Quick Reference* (Que, 1990), *PC Tools: The Complete Reference* (Osborne/McGraw-Hill, 1990), *PC Tools: The Complete Reference,* Second Edition (Osborne/McGraw-Hill, 1992), *Essential Software for Writers* (Writer's Digest Books, 1994), and *Getting Started with Windows 95* (WEKA, 1995). Most recently, Hy is the coauthor (with Margy Levine Young) of *Dummies 101: The Internet for Windows 95* (IDG Books Worldwide, 1996). *PC Tools: The Complete Reference* was selected as one of the "Best Books of the Year" by *Computer Currents* magazine. *Essential Software for Writers* was designated "Byte's Book of the Month" by Jerry Pournelle at *Byte Magazine,* praised as "exhaustive" and "lots of fun" by L. R. Shannon at *The New York Times,* and proclaimed "the best of its kind" by mega-selling author Peter McWilliams in his syndicated Personal Computers column.

Hy has also sold humor articles to *Mad Magazine, Spy, American Film,* and *Advertising Age* and has sold technical articles to *PC Magazine, PC Week,* and *PC World.*

ABOUT IDG BOOKS WORLDWIDE

VIII
WINNER
Eighth Annual
Computer Press
Awards ≥ 1992

IX
WINNER
Ninth Annual
Computer Press
Awards ≥ 1993

IDG
BOOKS
WORLDWIDE

Welcome to the world of IDG Books Worldwide.

IDG Books Worldwide, Inc., is a subsidiary of International Data Group, the world's largest publisher of computer-related information and the leading global provider of information services on information technology. IDG was founded more than 25 years ago and now employs more than 8,500 people worldwide. IDG publishes more than 270 computer publications in over 75 countries (see listing below). More than 90 million people read one or more IDG publications each month.

Launched in 1990, IDG Books Worldwide is today the #1 publisher of best-selling computer books in the United States. We are proud to have received eight awards from the Computer Press Association in recognition of editorial excellence and three from *Computer Currents'* First Annual Readers' Choice Awards. Our best-selling ...*For Dummies*® series has more than 25 million copies in print with translations in 30 languages. IDG Books Worldwide, through a joint venture with IDG's Hi-Tech Beijing, became the first U.S. publisher to publish a computer book in the People's Republic of China. In record time, IDG Books Worldwide has become the first choice for millions of readers around the world who want to learn how to better manage their businesses.

Our mission is simple: Every one of our books is designed to bring extra value and skill-building instructions to the reader. Our books are written by experts who understand and care about our readers. The knowledge base of our editorial staff comes from years of experience in publishing, education, and journalism — experience which we use to produce books for the '90s. In short, we care about books, so we attract the best people. We devote special attention to details such as audience, interior design, use of icons, and illustrations. And because we use an efficient process of authoring, editing, and desktop publishing our books electronically, we can spend more time ensuring superior content and spend less time on the technicalities of making books.

You can count on our commitment to deliver high-quality books at competitive prices on topics you want to read about. At IDG Books Worldwide, we continue in the IDG tradition of delivering quality for more than 25 years. You'll find no better book on a subject than one from IDG Books Worldwide.

John J. Kilcullen

John Kilcullen
President and CEO
IDG Books Worldwide, Inc.

IDG Books Worldwide, Inc., is a subsidiary of International Data Group, the world's largest publisher of computer-related information and the leading global provider of information services on information technology. International Data Group publishes over 276 computer publications in over 75 countries. Ninety million people read one or more International Data Group publications each month. International Data Group's publications include: **ARGENTINA:** Annuario de Informatica, Computerworld Argentina, PC World Argentina; **AUSTRALIA:** Australian Macworld, Client/Server Journal, Computer Living, Computerworld, Computerworld 100, Digital News, IT Casebook, Network World, On-line World Australia, PC World, Publishing Essentials, Reseller, WebMaster; **AUSTRIA:** Computerwelt Osterreich, Networks Austria, PC Tip; **BELARUS:** PC World Belarus; **BELGIUM:** Data News; **BRAZIL:** Annuário de Informática, Computerworld Brazil, Connections, Super Game Power, Macworld, PC Player, PC World Brazil, Publish Brazil, Reseller News; **BULGARIA:** Computerworld Bulgaria, Networkworld/Bulgaria, PC & MacWorld Bulgaria; **CANADA:** CIO Canada, Client/Server World, ComputerWorld Canada, InfoCanada, Network World Canada; **CHILE:** Computerworld Chile, PC World Chile; **COLOMBIA:** Computerworld Colombia, PC World Colombia; **COSTA RICA:** PC World Centro America; **THE CZECH AND SLOVAK REPUBLICS:** Computerworld Czechoslovakia, Elektronika Czechoslovakia, Macworld Czech Republic, PC World Czechoslovakia; **DENMARK:** Communications World, Computerworld Danmark, Macworld Danmark, PC Privat Danmark, PC World Danmark, PC World Danmark Supplements, TECH World; **DOMINICAN REPUBLIC:** PC World Republica Dominicana; **ECUADOR:** PC World Ecuador; **EGYPT:** Computerworld Middle East, PC World Middle East; **EL SALVADOR:** PC World Centro America; **FINLAND:** MikroPC, Tietoverkko, Tietoviikko; **FRANCE:** Distributique, Golden, Hebdo-Distributique, Info PC, Le Guide du Monde Informatique, Le Monde Informatique, Reseaux & Telecoms; **GERMANY:** Computer Partner, Computerwoche, Computerwoche Extra, Computerwoche Focus, I/M Information Management, Macwelt, PC Welt; **GREECE:** GamePro, Multimedia World; **GUATEMALA:** PC World Centro America; **HONDURAS:** PC World Centro America; **HONG KONG:** Computerworld Hong Kong, PCWorld Hong Kong, Publish in Asia; **HUNGARY:** ABCD CD-ROM, Computerworld Szamitastechnika, PC & Mac World Hungary, PC-X Magazine; **ICELAND:** Tolvuheimur/PC World Island; **INDIA:** Information Systems Computerworld, PC World India, Publish in Asia; **INDONESIA:** InfoKomputer PC World, Komputek Computerworld, Publish in Asia; **IRELAND:** ComputerScope, PC Live!; **ISRAEL:** People & Computers; **ITALY:** Computerworld Italia, Computerworld Italia Special Editions, Macworld Italia, Networking Italia, PC Shopping, PC World Italia, PC World/Walt Disney; **JAPAN:** DTP World, HP Open World Japan, Macworld Japan, Nikkei Personal Computing, Open World Japan, OS/2 World Japan, SunWorld Japan, Windows World Japan; **KENYA:** East African Computer News; **KOREA:** Hi-Tech Information/Computerworld, Macworld Korea, PC World Korea; **MACEDONIA:** PC World Macedonia; **MALAYSIA:** Computerworld Malaysia, PC World Malaysia, Publish in Asia; **MEXICO:** Computerworld Mexico, Macworld, PC World Mexico; **MYANMAR:** PC World Myanmar; **NETHERLANDS:** Computer! Totaal, LAN Magazine, LanWorld Buyers Guide, Macworld, Net Magazine, Totaal! Beurskrant; **NEW ZEALAND:** Absolute Beginner's Guide, Computer Buyer, Computer Industry Directory, Computerworld New Zealand, MTB, Network World, PC World New Zealand; **NICARAGUA:** PC World Centro America; **NIGERIA:** PC World Nigeria; **NORWAY:** Computerworld Norge, Computerworld Privat (Datamagasinet), CW Rapport Norge, IDG's KURSGUIDE, Macworld Norge, Multimediaworld, PC World Ekspress, PC World Nettverk, PC World Norge, PC World's Produktguide, Windows World Spesial; **PAKISTAN:** Computerworld Pakistan, PC World Pakistan; Panama: PC World Panama; **P. R. OF CHINA:** China Computer Users, China Computerworld, China Infoworld, China Telecom World Weekly, Computer & Communication, Electronic Design China, Electronics Today, Electronics Weekly, Game Camp, Game Soft, Network World China, PC World China, Popular Computer Weekly, Software Weekly, Software World, Telecom World; **PERU:** Computerworld Peru, PC World Profesional Peru, PC World Peru; **PHILIPPINES:** Computerworld Philippines, PC World Philippines, Publish in Asia; **POLAND:** Computerworld Poland, Computerworld Special Report, Macworld, Networld, PC World Komputer; **PORTUGAL:** Cerebro/PC World, Computerworld/Correio Informático, Dealer World Portugal, MacIn/PCIn, Multimedia World Portugal; **PUERTO RICO:** PC World Puerto Rico; **ROMANIA:** Computerworld Romania, PC World Romania, Telecom Romania; **RUSSIA:** Computerworld Russia, Mir PK, Sety; **SINGAPORE:** Computerworld Singapore, PC World Singapore, Publish in Asia; **SLOVENIA:** MONITOR; **SOUTH AFRICA:** Computing S.A., InfoWorld S.A., Network World S.A., Software World; **SPAIN:** Computerworld España, COMUNICACIONES WORLD, Dealer World, Macworld España, PC World España; **SWEDEN:** CAP&Design, Computer Sweden, Corporate Computing, MacWorld, Maxi Data, MikroDatorn, Nätverk & Kommunikation, PC/Aktiv, PC World, Windows World; **SWITZERLAND:** Computerworld Schweiz, Macworld Schweiz, PCtip; **TAIWAN:** Computerworld Taiwan, Macworld Taiwan, PC World Taiwan, Publish Taiwan, Windows World; **THAILAND:** Thai Computerworld, Publish in Asia; **TURKEY:** Computerworld Turkiye, MACWORLD Turkiye, PC WORLD Turkiye; **UKRAINE:** Computerworld Kiev, Computers & Software, Multimedia World Ukraine, PC World Ukraine; **UNITED KINGDOM:** Acorn User, Amiga Action, Amiga Computing, Appletalk, Computing, GamePro, Macworld, Network News, Parents and Computers, PC Advisor, PC Home, PSX Pro UK, The WEB; **UNITED STATES:** Cable in the Classroom, CD Review, CIO Magazine, Computerworld, Computerworld Client/Server Journal, Digital Video Magazine, DOS World, Federal Computer Week, GamePro, InfoWorld, I-Way, JavaWorld, Macworld, Multimedia World, Netscape World Online, Network World, PC Entertainment, PC World, Publish, SunWorld Online, SWATPro Magazine, Video Event, WebMaster; **URUGUAY:** PC World Uruguay; **VENEZUELA:** Computerworld Venezuela, PC World Venezuela; and **VIETNAM:** PC World Vietnam.   7/16/96

Dedications

Margy dedicates this book to Jordan, spouse extraordinaire. She also dedicates it to the marriage of Monica McKenna and Jim Arnold on September 28, 1996.

Hy dedicates this book, with gratitude and love, to his father.

Authors' Acknowledgments

First, we give our heartfelt thanks to Pam Mourouzis for the special care she provided as she expertly shepherded this book through the editing and production process. We also thank all the folks mentioned in the Publisher's Acknowledgments section that appears on the back of this page.

Margy thanks all the people who helped her family move to a new state right in the middle of writing this book: Susan, Jim, Don, and Kate Arnold; Monica McKenna; Sally Russell; Rodney Lowe, Evelyn May; Jessica, Ellen, and Norman Wright; Bob and Carol Caravana; Deb Bodeau; Doug Muder; Alison Barrows; Dave Kay; Katy Weeks; Dave Phoenix; and others whom she is too dazed to remember.

Hy thanks his beloved pal and fellow writer Tracey Siesser for 20 years of cherished friendship. Hy also thanks Tracey's cat Ossie for his inspiration and unique conversational style.

Publisher's Acknowledgments

We're proud of this book; please send us your comments about it by using the Reader Response Card at the back of the book or by e-mailing us at feedback/dummies@idgbooks.com. Some of the people who helped bring this book to market include the following:

Acquisitions, Development, and Editorial

Senior Project Editor: Pamela Mourouzis

Acquisitions Editor: Tammy Goldfeld

Assistant Acquisitions Editor: Gareth Hancock

Product Development Manager: Mary Bednarek

Permissions Editor: Joyce Pepple

Copy Editor: Christine Meloy Beck

Technical Editor: Dennis Cox

Editorial Manager: Kristin A. Cocks

Editorial Assistant: Chris H. Collins

Production

Project Coordinator: Valery Bourke

Layout and Graphics: Brett Black, Cameron Booker, Linda Boyer, J. Tyler Connor, Dominique DeFelice, Maridee V. Ennis, Angela F. Hunckler, Jane Martin, Drew R. Moore, Mark Owens, Brent Savage, Kate Snell

Proofreaders: Joel Draper, Rachel Garvey, Nancy Price, Robert Springer, Carrie Voorhis, Karen York

Indexer: Anne Leach

Special Help

Kevin Spencer, Associate Technical Editor; Access Technology, Inc.

General and Administrative

IDG Books Worldwide, Inc.: John Kilcullen, President & CEO; Steven Berkowitz, COO & Publisher

Dummies, Inc.: Milissa Koloski, Executive Vice President & Publisher

Dummies Technology Press & Dummies Editorial: Diane Graves Steele, Vice President and Associate Publisher; Judith A. Taylor, Brand Manager

Dummies Trade Press: Kathleen A. Welton, Vice President & Publisher; Stacy S. Collins, Brand Manager

IDG Books Production for Dummies Press: Beth Jenkins, Production Director; Cindy L. Phipps, Supervisor of Project Coordination; Kathie S. Schutte, Supervisor of Page Layout; Shelley Lea, Supervisor of Graphics and Design; Debbie J. Gates, Production Systems Specialist

Dummies Packaging & Book Design: Patti Sandez, Packaging Assistant; Kavish+Kavish, Cover Design

◆

The publisher would like to give special thanks to Patrick J. McGovern,
without whom this book would not have been possible.

◆

Files at a Glance

Here's a list of all the programs, plug-ins, exercise files, and document files that are stored on this book's CD-ROM, and where in the book you can find more information about them. For instructions on installing this software, see Appendix B.

Part I

Unit 1	Signing up for an Internet account	AT&T WorldNet sign-up program
Unit 1	Installing AT&T WorldNet Service for Windows 95	Wnet95.pdf document file
Unit 1	Installing AT&T WorldNet Service for Windows 3.1	Wnet31.pdf document file
Unit 2	Installing new bookmarks	Bookmark.htm exercise file
Unit 3	Decompressing files to make them useable	WinZip program

Part II

Unit 6	Attaching a file to an e-mail message	Meg.gif exercise file
Unit 7	Joining mailing list discussion groups	Maillist.pdf document file

Part III

Unit 8	Viewing animations on Web pages	Shockwave plug-in
Unit 8	Viewing video clips on Web pages	VDOLive plug-in
Unit 8	Viewing slide show presentations on Web pages	ASAP WebShow plug-in
Unit 8	Viewing Microsoft Word documents through Netscape	Word Viewer plug-in
Unit 8	Viewing and using spreadsheets on Web pages	Formula One/NET plug-in
Unit 8	Participating in live online chats through Netscape	Ichat plug-in
Unit 8	Spell-checking Netscape e-mail and newsgroup messages	CyberSpell plug-in
Unit 9	Viewing and manipulating picture files	Paint Shop Pro program
Unit 9	Placing a picture on a Web page	Mounts.gif, Ferns.gif, and Rainbow.gif exercise files

Appendixes

Appendix B	Reading pdf document files	Adobe Acrobat Reader program

Contents at a Glance

Table of Contents

Introduction

Welcome to *Dummies 101: Netscape Navigator,* part of the hands-on tutorial series from IDG Books Worldwide, Inc. Like our . . .*For Dummies* books, this book gives you lots of information in a form you can understand, without taking computers and software too seriously.

Netscape Navigator is the most popular program in the history of the Internet. You can use Netscape to browse the World Wide Web, the Internet's zoomiest and friendliest face. You've probably gotten awfully curious about those Web addresses at the bottom of every advertisement, article, and business card you come across these days. Well, by using Netscape, you can take a look at those Web pages and find out what all the fuss is about.

And Netscape doesn't just give you access to the World Wide Web. Netscape's Mail window provides an excellent e-mail program that you can use for sending, reading, replying to, forwarding, and storing e-mail messages. If you're interested in joining online conversations, the Netscape News window lets you join Usenet newsgroups, read articles by topic, and post your own articles.

One of the coolest things about Netscape is the way it can accept *plug-ins,* programs that add capabilities to Netscape. The CD-ROM in the back of this book has a bunch of plug-ins that you can install and use for free. You'll also learn how to find other plug-ins on the Internet.

If you're new to Netscape, the best way to learn about it is to take a course, with step-by-step instructions that build up your expertise as you go along. That's just what this book does. As opposed to a stuffy reference book with vague guidelines, this book provides a series of specific, detailed lessons that take you through getting and installing the latest version of Netscape, browsing the World Wide Web, sending and receiving e-mail, joining newsgroups, and more. The tutorials in this book take the place of a class, including lessons, exercises, quizzes, and tests.

This is the book for you if

- You want to use Netscape but are daunted by all the incomprehensible technical terms and different choices you need to make to get started.

- You've got an older version of Netscape Navigator and want to upgrade to the latest version and learn about all the new stuff it can do.

- You want to learn how to use Netscape's Web browser, e-mail, and newsgroups facilities, but you just don't have the time or the inclination to spend weeks going out to sit-down classes.

- You want to learn all the basic tasks of using Netscape so that you don't have to run for help every time you need to get some work done.

Unlike most of the other books in the *Dummies 101* series, this book does *not* assume that you already have the programs we describe. If you don't have Netscape, we'll tell you where to get it. If you don't even have an Internet account, the CD-ROM in the back of this book includes the AT&T WorldNet Service 2.0 sign-up software, which you can use to sign up for a new account. You'll learn about all the programs on the CD-ROM over the course of the book and in Appendix B.

Notes:

You, the Reader

Notes:

This book is designed for beginning and intermediate computer users who want more than just technical geekspeak about the Internet. We have to make some assumptions about you in order to make the course work for you. We assume that

- Windows 95 or Windows 3.1 is installed on your machine.

- You have a modem that communicates at 14,400 or 28,800 bps, and that modem is connected to your computer.

- You have a phone line connected to your modem.

- You have at least some understanding of how to use Windows 95 or Windows 3.1. (If you don't, consider checking out either *Dummies 101: Windows 95* or *Dummies 101: Windows 3.1,* both by Andy Rathbone and published by IDG Books Worldwide, Inc.)

If you already have Netscape Navigator installed on your computer, so much the better!

How the Book Works

This book contains a course in using Netscape, including how to upgrade to the latest version (if you have Version 1.*x* or Version 2.0) and how to sign up for an AT&T WorldNet Service account (if you don't have an Internet account yet). The step-by-step approach leads you through each Netscape feature by telling you exactly what to do and what your computer will do in response. Each unit has hands-on procedures to follow as you learn the basics, and then an additional exercise at the end of the unit to help you review what you learned.

After you cover the basics, you can skip to the units that discuss what you want to learn right away. Each unit indicates what you have to know before beginning the unit, in case you're skipping around, as well as what you'll learn in the unit. There's even a progress check at end of each lesson so that you can gauge how you're doing.

Best of all, we don't take Netscape, the Internet, or computers very seriously. After all, there's more to life than cruising the Net (or so we hear)!

Here's how to follow the lessons in this book:

- The course contains nine *units,* each starting with an introduction to the topic to be covered. Then you'll get to the *lessons* within the unit that delve into a topic and give step-by-step instructions on what to do.

- Topics that are more complicated or less widely used are covered in *Extra Credit* sidebars. These topics aren't critical for your learning, but they may contain just the information you need to make your Internet use more productive or more fun.

♦ When we tell you something important to remember, we summarize the information in a note in the margin (like the one in this margin).

♦ A *Recess* section indicates a good place to stop and take a breather (perhaps a walk around the block, or the block of cubicles, will clear your head). When you reach a Recess section, we tell you how to stop what you're doing and how to get started again when you come back.

♦ At the end of each unit, a quiz provides a way for you to review what you learned and adds some comic relief. If a question stumps you, flip back through the unit to find the point you missed. You'll also find an exercise that lets you practice what you learned. At the end of each part of the book is a review of all the units in that part, along with a grueling test. (Well, maybe it's not so grueling, considering that the answers are in the back of the book in Appendix A.)

a note in the margin summarizes an important point

In the text, stuff you need to type appears in **boldface**. When you have to press more than one key at a time, we show the names of the keys connected with a plus sign, like this: Ctrl+C. Hold down the first key (Ctrl, in this example), then press the second key (C), and then let them both up.

When we tell you to choose a command from the menu bar, a little arrow appears between the parts of the command, like this: File⇨Open. Click the first part of the command (File, in this example) on the menu bar, and then click the second part of the command (Open) on the menu that appears. The underlines under the letter F in File and O in Open indicate that you can press Alt+F and then O to choose the command if you don't feel like using your mouse.

A note about the Internet and moving targets: The Internet is in a perpetual state of flux. The ever-changing face of the Internet makes it an interesting place, but it also makes writing a book about it a little problematic. If you find that an electronic address in this book doesn't work, don't panic; the address simply may have changed. Luckily, we provide online updates to the book. See the section "Send Us E-mail" at the end of this Introduction to learn how to get updated information.

How the Book Is Organized

This book is divided into three parts plus two appendixes, as described in the following sections.

Part I: Browsing the World Wide Web

The first part of this book gets you up and running with Netscape Navigator. If you don't have Version 3.0 or later, you'll also find out how to get the latest version of Netscape. Then we describe the World Wide Web, the newest, zoomiest part of the Internet. You'll use the Netscape program to look at colorful Web pages, cruise links from one Web page to another, search the Web for just about any kind of information, and download all kinds of nifty programs, graphics, and sound files from the Web.

Part II: Reading E-mail and Usenet Newsgroups

In Part II, you'll learn to use the software you installed in Part I to read and compose e-mail. We also describe how to reply to messages you receive, keep an address book of the e-mail addresses of your friends and co-workers, and send all types of files by e-mail. Then you'll learn how to use the Netscape News window to participate in online discussions on Usenet newsgroups.

Part III: Multimedia, Plug-ins, and Creating Web Pages

The third part of the book describes how to give Netscape new capabilities by installing plug-in programs. You'll install and try out the plug-ins on the *Dummies 101* CD-ROM, giving your Netscape program the capability to make sounds, play movies, display interactive spreadsheets, and check the spelling of your e-mail messages. Finally, you'll learn how to use Netscape Navigator Gold to create and publish your own Web pages.

Appendixes

The back of the book offers two appendixes. Appendix A gives you the answers to the test questions that appear at the ends of Parts I, II, and III. Appendix B tells you how to install and use the various programs that are stored on the CD-ROM that comes in the back of this book.

Icons Used in This Book

We put one of the following four icons in the left margin when we want to point out important information:

on the CD

This icon tells you when you need to use a file that comes on the *Dummies 101* CD-ROM.

on the test

Here's an item you're going to need to know when you get to the quiz at the end of the unit or the test at the end of the part of the book. If it's on the test, it must be important!

extra credit

Descriptions of advanced or less common topics appear in sidebars highlighted with this icon.

heads up

Heads up! Here's a piece of information that can make your life easier or avert disaster.

About the Dummies 101 CD-ROM

on the CD

The *Dummies 101* CD-ROM that comes in the back of this book contains all the programs and files you'll need to do the lessons and exercises in this book. If you don't have an Internet account, it also includes the AT&T WorldNet software, which you can use to sign up for an Internet account (see Unit 1 and Appendix B). The CD-ROM also contains a bunch of plug-ins, which are programs you can install to increase the capabilities of Netscape Navigator. These plug-ins allow Netscape to do such things as play sounds, show movies, calculate spreadsheets, display word processing documents, and check your spelling (see Unit 8).

The CD-ROM comes with a handy installation program that installs the programs you decide to use — go to Appendix B for specific instructions, as well as a list of the programs and files that the CD-ROM contains.

If you have trouble with the CD-ROM (for example, if your computer can't read it or it arrives in three pieces), call IDG Books Customer Support at 800-762-2974.

Send Us E-mail

We love to hear from our readers. If you have questions or comments about the book, send us e-mail at `netscape101@dummies.com`. We can't answer all your questions about the Internet — after all, we're authors, not consultants — but we'd love to hear how the course worked for you.

If you want to know about other . . .*For Dummies* books, call 800-762-2974, send e-mail to `info@idgbooks.com`, or look at this page on the World Wide Web:

`http://www.dummies.com`

For more information about the Internet and updates to this book, look at this Web page:

`http://net.dummies.com/netscape101`

If you can't send e-mail, you can always send plain old paper mail by using the reader response card in the back of this book. You'll receive an IDG Books catalog in return. Don't worry — the authors will see your comments, too.

Browsing the World Wide Web

In this part . . .

Netscape Navigator can do a lot of cool things, but it's most famous for its capability to let you interact with the amazing World Wide Web. This part of the book first tells you how to sign up for an Internet account and get a copy of Netscape. It then steps you through using Netscape to cruise the World Wide Web and take advantage of the Web's many fabulous resources.

Getting Started with Netscape Navigator

Prerequisites

▶ Windows 95 or Windows 3.1 installed on your PC

▶ A CD-ROM drive connected to your PC

▶ A 14,400 bps or faster modem connected to your PC

Objectives for This Unit

✓ Preparing to go online

✓ Jumping onto the World Wide Web by using Netscape Navigator

✓ Moving around a Web page and identifying its links

✓ Using links to move to Web pages

✓ Switching among Web pages

The Internet has been popping up everywhere lately. Hundreds of articles about it appear regularly in newspapers and magazines, dozens of TV specials and videotapes are devoted to it, major motion pictures such as *The Net* are based on it — and there are even coffee shops springing up that let you cruise the Internet while you sip an espresso!

Does the Internet deserve all this hoopla? In a word, *yes*. The Internet's most famous component, the visually striking World Wide Web, lets you find information about any subject with a few keystrokes or mouse clicks. The Internet also enables you to send electronic mail (or *e-mail*) messages to friends and colleagues around the globe in seconds; participate in ongoing discussions about virtually any topic via Internet talk groups (called *newsgroups*); chat with people live through your keyboard by using Internet Relay Chat (or *IRC*); and freely copy thousands of programs, picture files, and other goodies that are just waiting for you to come and get them.

To take advantage of such Internet features, you need software that lets you access and interact with the Net. The best program for doing so is Netscape Navigator, which is published by Netscape Communications Corporation. Most people refer to Netscape Navigator as just *Netscape*, and that's what we'll do from now on, too.

Netscape is the Internet program of choice by an overwhelming margin — it's used by more than 80 percent of folks on the Net, or about *40 million* people! In fact, Netscape isn't simply the best-liked Internet program around; it's one of the two or three most popular programs of *any* kind in the history of computers. Netscape is packed with features that let you cruise the World Wide Web, send and receive e-mail, participate in newsgroup discussions, and much more.

> Netscape lets you cruise the Web, send and recieve e-mail, and join newsgroups

This book and the CD-ROM that comes with it are designed to teach you how to run Netscape and use it to take advantage of all the wonderful things on the Internet. By the time you finish this book, you'll have turned from a *newbie* (Internet newcomer) to a *Nethead* (Internet expert)!

In this book, we cover Netscape Navigator 3.0, which is the most current version at the time we write this book. However, because Netscape tends to keep its key features operating the same way across versions, most of the material in this book also applies to Netscape 2.0 (and is likely to apply to future versions of Netscape as well).

This first unit tells you what you need to know to get started. It then guides you through an initial look at the World Wide Web using Netscape.

Lesson 1-1   Preparing to Go Online with Netscape Navigator

Before you can cruise the Internet with Netscape, you have to prepare yourself for the journey. Specifically, you need to own the right equipment, set up an Internet account, have a recent copy of Netscape, and know a few basic terms.

Understanding what equipment you need

You need several pieces of equipment to make full use of this book.

First, you need a PC that runs Windows 95 (or its advanced sibling, Windows NT) or some version of Windows 3.1 (such as Windows 3.11 or Windows 3.11 for Workgroups).

You also need a CD-ROM drive so that you can transfer the terrific software on this book's CD-ROM to your hard disk.

In addition, you need a phone line that's available for use with your PC.

Finally, you need a device called a *modem*. This special piece of equipment requires some explanation.

> online = connected to other computers via a phone line

on the test

To *go online* means to get your PC to communicate with other computers over a phone line. (In fact, while on the Internet, your PC can access *millions* of other computers.) Talking over the phone isn't a capability built into your PC, however, so it needs help from your modem, which converts your PC's digital language into audio that can travel over phone wires and converts the audio signals from other computers back into digital data.

Not all modems are created equal. For example, if you have an internal modem, it's tucked away in a slot inside your PC, and you don't have to think much about it because it's always on and available. If you have an external modem, it resides outside your PC, has an on/off switch, and is connected to a socket in the back of your computer by a special cable. (If you ever encounter a problem getting online with an external modem, always start your trouble-shooting by making sure that the modem's power switch is turned on and that its cable is still tightly attached to your PC.)

Modems also have different speed capabilities, which are measured in bits per second, or *bps*. As we write this book, the current standard speed is 28,800 bps, which can transmit and receive data very quickly — for example, transferring the contents of a 1.44MB floppy disk at 28,800 bps takes about seven minutes. The next lower speed is 14,400 bps, which is about half as fast at 28,800 bps and is the bare minimum speed you need to use the Internet effectively.

To sum up, if you have a PC running Windows, a CD-ROM drive, a modem, and a phone line you can plug into your modem, you're set as far as equipment goes. Your next step is to decide how to connect to the Internet.

Getting an Internet account

One of the wonderful things about the Internet is that no one owns it — it's a resource that millions of people and companies around the world share. However, before you can go online, you need to sign up with a company that has the proper hardware and software to provide you with access to the Internet. Such a company is called, appropriately enough, an *Internet provider*, and it typically charges a monthly fee for its service. Thousands of such providers exist, so you have lots of choices.

For example, if you're running Windows 95, you can sign up for The Microsoft Network by doing little more than double-clicking (that is, clicking twice in rapid succession) the MSN icon on your desktop and then answering some questions (with credit card in hand).

Two other popular services are Netcom and Concentric, both of which provide hundreds of telephone numbers across the U.S. that let you dial into the Internet for the price of a local call.

Another excellent Internet provider is AT&T WorldNet Service. Among this provider's unique features is toll-free customer service that's available 24 hours a day, seven days a week; and, until at least the end of 1996, five *free* hours of use per month if you're an AT&T long-distance customer. We feel that AT&T WorldNet Service is an ideal choice for beginners, so we've included both the Windows 95 and Windows 3.1 versions of its software kit — which consists of a sign-up program and a customized edition of Netscape — on the CD-ROM that comes with this book. (For more information, see Appendix B and read the Wnet95.pdf or Wnet31.pdf file stored on the CD-ROM.)

You can also access the Internet through an online service, such as America Online or CompuServe. The advantage of an online service is that it provides a number of features *in addition to* Internet access, such as easy-to-use discussion areas and special databases that offer information that's not available on the Net. However, the disadvantage is that an online service is more expensive for long-term use. For example, at the time we write this book, most Internet providers let you cruise the Internet as long as you want for a flat fee of $20 to $25 a month. In contrast, both America Online's and CompuServe's standard

Notes:

AT&T WorldNet sign-up software is on the Dummies 101 CD-ROM

plans charge $9.95 per month for the first five hours and then $2.95 for each additional hour. If you plan to limit your time online, these deals are excellent; but if you're going to spend a lot of time on the Net, the hourly charges can quickly add up to stiff monthly bills.

Of course, if you use online resources as serious business tools, you can always sign up with more than one provider. (Personally, we belong to both America Online and CompuServe so that we can use their extra services, but we do all our Internet work through a dedicated Internet provider that charges a flat monthly rate.) If you'd like to contact any of the companies we just mentioned, see Table 1-1.

Table 1-1	Some Popular Internet Providers	
Company	*Telephone Number*	*Comments*
America Online	800-827-6364 or 703-448-8700	Online service that includes Internet access among its many features
AT&T WorldNet Service	800-400-1447	National Internet provider; we provide its sign-up software on this book's CD-ROM
CompuServe	800-848-8199	Online service that includes Internet access among its many features
Concentric	800-939-4262 or 408-342-2800	National U.S. Internet provider
The Microsoft Network	800-386-5550	Limited online service that primarily offers Internet access; you can join it by double-clicking the MSN icon on your Windows 95 desktop
Netcom	800-353-6600 or 408-983-5950	National U.S. Internet provider

Then again, you might consider hooking up with a small local service. Although such companies aren't able to provide local telephone numbers for connecting to the Net outside your area, you don't need such numbers unless you travel frequently, and local companies can sometimes provide a more personal touch (for example, offering beginner classes or organizing subscriber get-togethers) than their national competitors. You can locate Internet providers in your area by checking the *Internet* and/or *Computer Services* sections in your phone book's Yellow Pages, leafing through ads in your newspaper's *Science* or *Technology* section, or asking your friends and colleagues which providers they recommend. Alternately, if you have a friend who already knows how to use the Net and is willing to spare a few minutes, ask your friend to go to the World Wide Web location `thelist.iworld.com`. This location is the home of a search program named *The List* that lists Internet providers based on the criteria you specify (such as the name of your country, state, or area code).

Whether you select a large national Internet provider, a small local Internet provider, or an online service, the important thing is that you have an account with a company that can serve as your connection to the Internet. After you're signed up, you need just one more thing: a copy of Netscape itself.

Getting and installing Netscape

Before you can tackle the various exercises that teach you how to use Netscape, you need to *have* Netscape Version 3.0 or higher. (As mentioned previously, most of the material in this book also applies to Netscape 2.0; but if you're going to take the trouble of learning Netscape, you may as well do so with a recent version of the program.)

Netscape actually comes in two different editions: Standard and Gold. The only difference between them is that the Gold edition contains extra features that allow you to create and publish your own material on the World Wide Web. If this option intrigues you, see Unit 9 for more information.

You can get Netscape in a variety of ways. One approach is simply to buy the program directly from Netscape Communications Corporation by calling 415-937-3777 or 415-937-2555 with a credit card in hand. If you're upgrading from an older version of Netscape that you or your company paid for, be sure to say so when speaking to your salesperson, because that fact may entitle you to buy the current version at a lower price. After the Netscape installation software — which is typically stored on a CD-ROM — arrives in your mailbox, you can follow the instructions included in the package to copy the new version of Netscape to your hard disk.

Alternately, you can purchase Netscape from a local computer store or from a mail-order vendor that advertises in computer magazines and software catalogs, such as PC Connection (800-800-0004) or MicroWarehouse (800-367-7080). Such retailers typically charge less for a program than the actual publisher of the program, so buying Netscape from a third-party vendor is likely to save you money. Again, after you receive the software package, you can follow the instructions that are included to install Netscape on your hard disk.

Another option is to get Netscape directly from the Internet. When you signed up for an Internet account, your provider probably included a Web browser as part of your startup kit. (For example, if you used the software on this book's CD-ROM to subscribe to AT&T WorldNet Service, you now have a copy of Netscape Navigator Version 2.02 or 1.22.) The browser you have may not be the latest version of Netscape, but you can use it to connect to the Net and then copy, or *download,* the latest version of Netscape from any of hundreds of areas on the Web. (For example, we recommend the superb Tucows Internet software library at the Web location www.tucows.com.) You can skip to Lesson 3-2 for instructions for downloading software from the Web, or you can simply ask a friend who already knows her way around the Net to download Netscape for you.

After you download Netscape, you have a single installation file that contains dozens of program and data files in compressed form. To make Netscape useable, follow these steps:

1 **Save any documents that you have open and then exit all programs that are currently running.**

It's best to close all programs before installing a new one to ensure that no conflict between programs occurs during the installation process.

2 **Locate the file you just downloaded. If you're using Windows 95, open a My Computer or Windows Explorer window and then move to the folder that contains the file. If you're using Windows 3.1, use File Manager to locate the file.**

Notes:

Netscape Gold helps you publish information on the Web

buy Netscape, or download (copy) an evaluation version from the Web

double-click a
downloaded copy of
Netscape to install
the program

3 **Position your mouse pointer over the file and double-click — that is, click your left mouse button twice in rapid succession.**

If nothing happens, you may have paused too long between your two clicks, so just try again. When you've double-clicked successfully, a message asking you to confirm that you want to install Netscape appears.

4 **Click the Yes button to run the installation program, and then follow the instructions that appear on-screen.**

You have to answer a few questions, including which folder you want to use to store the Netscape program. After you select the folder, write down its full name on the Cheat Sheet in the front of this book so that you can refer to the folder in later exercises. (For example, if you choose to accept the default suggestion for Windows 95, write **C:\Program Files\Netscape\ Navigator**.) After you're done writing, click the Next button to continue with the installation.

5 **If you're asked whether you want to install CoolTalk, see the sidebar at the end of Unit 8 for information about this program that lets you make telephone calls by using the Internet. If you think that you might find this program useful, click the Yes button to install it; otherwise, click No.**

6 **Answer any additional questions to proceed with the installation.**

After you're done with its initial questions, the installation program decompresses and copies all its files to the Netscape folder you selected. You're then asked whether you want to go online to the Netscape Communications area on the World Wide Web to complete the installation. We suggest that you skip this step for now by clicking the No button. (You can explore this area after you learn more about the Web by going to the location `home.netscape.com/home/setup.html`.)

7 **Answer any additional questions to complete the installation.**

When the installation program has finished, you see a folder (or, under Windows 3.1, a Program Group) on your desktop that contains an icon for Netscape Navigator. If you're using Windows 95, you also see a Netscape Navigator icon on your desktop. Double-clicking either icon runs the Netscape program.

8 **Double-click the Netscape Navigator icon.**

A license agreement appears. This is the only time you see this agreement, so take a few minutes to examine it. You can move down and up in the window by pressing the PgDn and PgUp keys.

Notice that the agreement states that your downloaded copy of Netscape is an evaluation copy. If you decide that you like Netscape and want to keep using it, you're supposed to register the program by paying for it. Doing so entitles you to certain extra privileges, such as telephone technical support from Netscape Communications.

9 **If you accept the terms of the license agreement, click the Accept button. (If you don't click Accept, Netscape won't run.)**

After you click the Accept button, Netscape opens and is ready for use. In addition, you probably see an Internet dialer program (such as the Windows 95 Connect To dialog box) that allows you to connect to the Internet. You run both the dialer and the Netscape programs in the next lesson. For now, though, simply exit.

10 **Choose File➪Exit from Netscape's menu — that is, click the File heading on the Netscape menu bar and then click the Exit option that appears.**

The dialer and Netscape programs disappear.

Notes:

Fantastic! You're now set to use Netscape as your window on the Internet!

Note: Windows 95 includes an excellent dialer program as part of its software. Windows 3.1 doesn't come with a dialer program, but Internet providers typically supply a dialer program when Windows 3.1 users sign up for an account. In addition, the CD-ROM retail version of Netscape Navigator for Windows 3.1 includes a dialer program. If all else fails, though, you (or a friend with Net access) can simply download a Windows 3.1 dialer program from the Web.

You have just one more thing to do before you start running Netscape, and that's to become familiar with some key words and phrases related to using Windows and the Internet.

Understanding a few basic terms

We try to avoid jargon as much as possible, but explaining how to use a computer program requires throwing in some technical words. We introduce most new terms as they're needed over the course of the book (and, we hope, always clearly define them when they pop up!). However, you should know a few words and phrases right away, so here's a quick list:

- **Click:** Press your left mouse button.
- **Click the OK button:** Position your mouse pointer over the OK button and then press your left mouse button.
- **Double-click:** Press your left mouse button twice in rapid succession.
- **Right-click:** Press your right mouse button.
- **Dialog box:** A box that displays a message and/or various options.
- **Run, launch, or fire up a program:** Get a program going.
- **Dial in or log in:** Use your modem and phone line to call up an Internet provider and get connected to the Internet.
- **Go online:** Take steps to connect with other computers by using your modem and a phone line.
- **Go offline:** Disconnect from your online session.
- **The Net:** Short for the Internet.
- **Default option:** The option that's selected before you make any adjustments (sort of like the factory setting).
- **Character:** A single letter, number, punctuation mark, or other symbol that you can type on your keyboard. (For example, the word *cat* has three characters, and so does the date *5/9*.)
- **Extension:** The one to three characters following the final period in a filename. (For example, the filename *Letter.txt* has the extension *txt,* the filename *Program.exe* has the extension *exe,* and the Web page file *My Home Page.htm* has the extension *htm*.)
- **Filename:** The name of an electronic file. In Windows 95, a filename can be up to 255 characters and can include spaces and punctuation. In Windows 3.1, a filename can consist of up to 8 characters and a 3-character extension, with no spaces or punctuation. If you're using Windows 3.1 and see a long filename in this book (or on the Net), keep in mind that you need to use relatively short names for files.

the Net =
the Internet

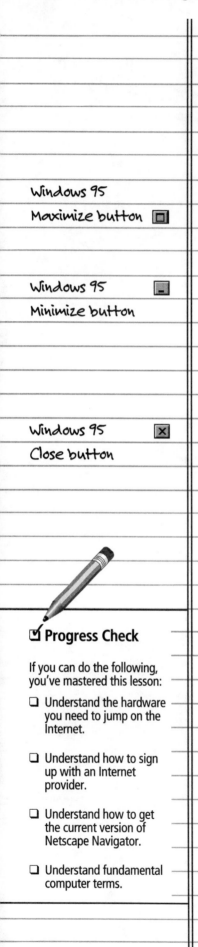

Windows 95
Maximize button 🔲

Windows 95
Minimize button 🔲

Windows 95
Close button ☒

✓ **Progress Check**

If you can do the following,
you've mastered this lesson:

❑ Understand the hardware
you need to jump on the
Internet.

❑ Understand how to sign
up with an Internet
provider.

❑ Understand how to get
the current version of
Netscape Navigator.

❑ Understand fundamental
computer terms.

on the test

▶ **Folder:** An area on your hard disk that is used to store files. Folders help keep your files organized in logical groups, just as physical folders help organize your papers in a filing cabinet.

▶ **Directory:** The term typically used for *folder* in Windows 3.1. *Directory* and *folder* mean the same thing, however, and this book simply uses the term *folder*.

▶ **Program Group:** Another area used to store files under Windows 3.1. Folders are used for this purpose under Windows 95.

▶ **Maximize a window:** Under Windows 95, click the middle button of the three buttons residing in the upper-right corner of every window. Under Windows 3.1, click the button that's in the upper-right corner of every window. Maximizing expands a window so that it fills the screen. (If the window already fills the screen, clicking the Maximize button shrinks the window back to its former size.)

▶ **Minimize a window:** Click the leftmost button of the buttons residing in the upper-right corner of every window. Clicking Minimize makes a window disappear from your screen but keeps it active (as indicated by the window being represented as a button on the Windows 95 Taskbar or as a small icon at the bottom of the Windows 3.1 desktop). You can restore a minimized window to your screen at any time by clicking its button on the Taskbar (under Windows 95) or double-clicking its icon (under Windows 3.1).

▶ **Click the window's Close button:** Under Windows 95, click the button directly to the right of the Maximize button. Under Windows 3.1, double-click the button that's in the upper-left corner of every window. This button closes the window — that is, it deactivates the window and makes it disappear.

▶ **Press Ctrl+D:** Hold down the Ctrl key and, while keeping it pressed, tap the D key.

▶ **Choose File⇨Save:** Click the File heading near the top of your window to display a menu of options and then click the Save option that appears on the menu. Alternately, hold down the Alt key, press F, and then press S.

If you don't memorize all these terms on the spot, don't worry; we'll go over their definitions again as needed. However, if most of these terms are entirely new to you, you may find it helpful to do some additional reading about Windows. Two (of many) fine books on this subject are *Dummies 101: Windows 95* and *Dummies 101: Windows 3.1*, both written by Andy Rathbone and published by IDG Books Worldwide.

Jumping onto the Web   Lesson 1-2

It's time that all the preparation work you did in Lesson 1-1 paid off. You're about to crawl onto the World Wide Web!

World Wide Web may sound like the title of a 1950s conspiracy movie involving radioactive Communist spiders. However, the *WWW,* or *Web* (as savvy Net users refer to it) is much cooler than that. Though it didn't even exist until 1990, the Web is rapidly becoming the most popular feature of the Internet.

The Web consists of electronic pages that display text and pictures, similar to the pages of a paper book or magazine (though some jazzier Web pages also can play sound and video clips). Well-designed Web pages are a visual treat, and they cover virtually every topic that you can think of — from the stock market to stock racing, from bass to baseball, and from Picasso to Prozac. The neatest thing about the Web, however, is that each page typically contains *links* to other pages, allowing you to jump from one page to another with a single mouse click.

For example, you might be reading a Web page about the life of William Shakespeare and notice that various phrases and pictures in the biography are underlined, are a different color, or are marked in some other special way. This usually means that clicking the phrase or picture (link) with your mouse takes you to another page covering that topic in more depth. At the William Shakespeare page, clicking the phrase *Romeo and Juliet* might take you to a page with the full text of that play, while clicking an image of the Globe Theatre could take you to a page with a series of detailed drawings of that famous Elizabethan playhouse.

Your voyage wouldn't have to end there, either. For example, the Globe Theatre page might contain a link to *modern theatre.* Clicking the phrase could offer you additional links to such disparate topics as Arthur Miller, movie adaptations, and Andrew Lloyd Webber's *Cats.* Clicking the latter might furnish — in addition to information about other Lloyd Webber hits, such as *Evita* and *The Phantom of the Opera* — links to Web pages about *real* cats. And any feline Web page worth its fur inevitably offers a link to pictures of Socks, the First Cat of the Clinton White House.

This hypothetical journey from Shakespeare to Socks shows you what jumping around the Web, also known as *cruising* or *surfing,* is all about. Because these electronic pages — which are created independently by thousands of individuals and organizations around the planet — are all linked together in various intricate ways, they truly form a World Wide Web of information.

In this unit, you get on the Web by using the Netscape *browser* window, which lets you browse through electronic pages. You first learn how to examine a Web page and use its links to move to other pages. You then learn how to use Netscape buttons to switch among a few pages and how to use Netscape's Go menu and History window to switch among many pages.

Figure 1-1: When you run Netscape, a Netscape browser window and your Internet dialer program appear.

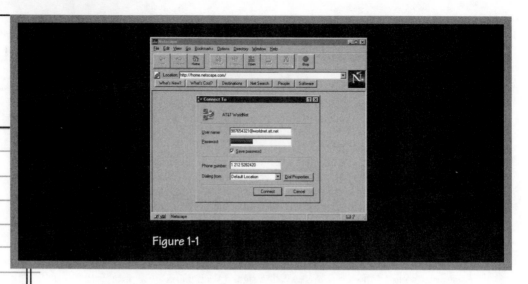

Figure 1-1

Opening Netscape and connecting to the Net

In Lesson 1-1, you signed up with an Internet provider and installed Netscape onto your hard disk. Now follow these steps to actually run Netscape and use it to browse the Web:

1 **Make sure that you're in Windows, that your modem is turned on, that you have a phone line connected to your modem, and that you don't have another telecommunications program running.**

2 **Double-click the Netscape Navigator icon on your Windows 95 desktop (or, under Windows 3.1, in your Program Group). Alternately, click the Windows 95 Start button, click Programs, click the Netscape Navigator option from the second menu that appears, and then click the Netscape Navigator icon from the third menu that appears.**

The Netscape browser window opens, and whatever Internet dialer program you're using appears. For example, if you're using the Windows 95 Dialer, a Connect To dialog box pops up in front of the Netscape window, as shown in Figure 1-1.

Note: Some Windows 3.1 dialer programs don't pop up automatically when you run Netscape. If that's true of your dialer program, simply run your dialer manually by double-clicking the program's icon.

3 **Click the appropriate button on your dialer program to connect to the Internet.**

For example, if you're using the Windows 95 Dialer, click the Connect button. After a few moments, your dialer program dials into the local phone number you're using to access your Internet provider, gets your modem talking to your provider's modem, and transmits the user name and password that identify you to your provider. If all goes well, you're then connected to the Internet, and your dialer program becomes minimized — that is, it disappears from your screen but stays active and is represented as a button on the Windows 95 Taskbar (or an icon in Windows 3.1).

Netscape Navigator icon

heads up

If your connection isn't successful, make sure that your PC, modem, and phone line are all securely attached. Also, make sure that you entered the phone number, user name, and password information correctly in your dialer program. If none of that helps, try again a little later; your Internet provider's

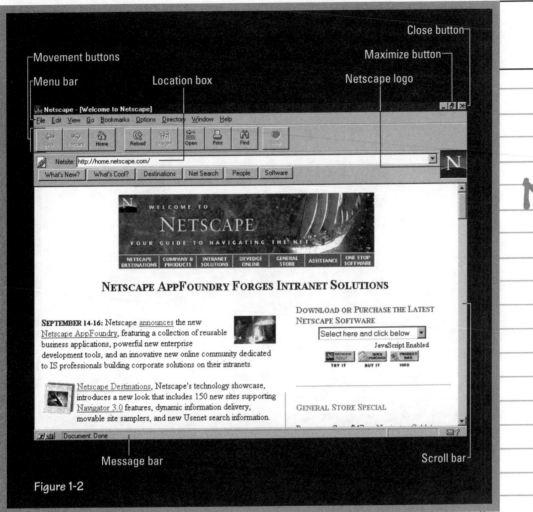

Figure 1-2: Netscape Communications's initial Web page.

Figure 1-2

Notes:

computers may be temporarily overloaded or experiencing a technical problem. If after several tries you're still having trouble, call your Internet provider for help identifying the difficulty.

Most versions of Netscape are set to start you on the Netscape Communications initial Web page, so you probably see a screen similar to the one in Figure 1-2.

Note: If you use Windows 3.1, you see a slightly different-looking window. (For example, instead of an X-shaped Close button in the upper-right corner that you can click to exit the window, you have a Control-menu box in the upper-left corner that you can double-click to exit the window.) The figures in this book display Windows 95 screens, but the explanations and exercises apply to Windows 3.1 as well as Windows 95.

If your window doesn't fill the screen, click the Maximize button (represented by a box symbol in Windows 95 and an upward-pointing triangle in Windows 3.1) in the window's upper-right corner.

Congratulations! You've successfully landed on the World Wide Web. (Now we're getting somewhere!)

The initial Netscape Communications Web page that you're on is called a *home page* because it's the place from which you set off on your Web journey. Every Web area, or *site,* has its own home page that contains links to other pages in the site (and elsewhere).

home page =
initial Web page
of a Web site

Figure 1-3: Click
Netscape's vertical
scroll bar to see more
of a Web page.

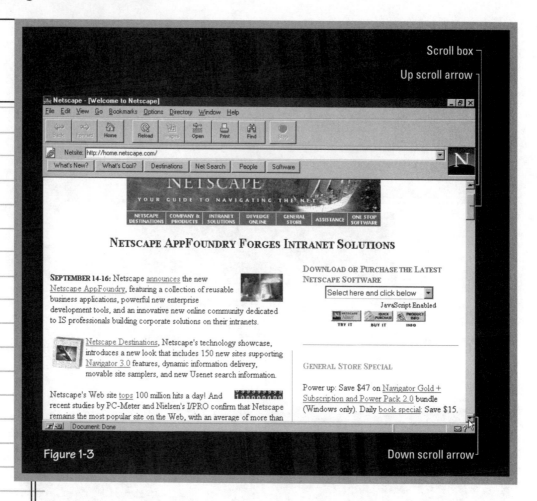

Figure 1-3

Scroll box

Up scroll arrow

Down scroll arrow

The text and pictures that you see on your screen will look different from the screen shots that appear in this book because Web page content is constantly being updated and improved. However, the basic skills on how to use the Web that we cover still apply.

Moving up and down a Web page

If you take a close look at the page displayed in your Netscape window, you see that only part of the page is visible. Web pages are almost always longer than a browser's window, so you typically must view pages a section at a time. One way to view different sections of a page is to use the vertical scroll bar — that is, the gray stripe along the right edge of your Netscape window.

The vertical scroll bar has three main elements: the down and up scroll arrows on its ends and the scroll box between them, which indicates by its position in the bar just how far down you are on the page (see Figure 1-3). Clicking the down or up arrow moves the page about a line at a time; clicking and dragging the scroll box, as described in the next exercise, moves you around the page more rapidly.

1 **Click the down arrow of your window's vertical scroll bar.**

The page scrolls down a bit in your window, allowing you to see more of the page's content.

2 **Click the down arrow repeatedly until the scroll box is at the bottom of the bar.**

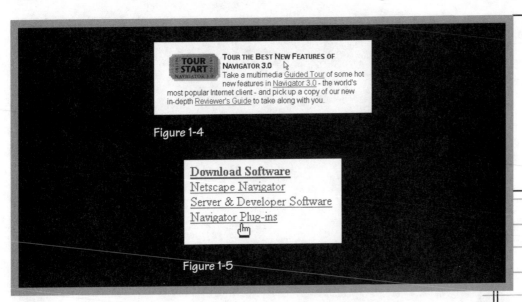

Figure 1-4

Figure 1-5

Figure 1-4: When you point to regular text on a Web page, your mouse pointer retains its arrowhead shape.

Figure 1-5: When you point to a Web page link, your mouse pointer changes to the shape of a pointing hand.

The page continues to scroll down until the end of its content appears in the window.

3 **Click the up arrow of the vertical scroll bar.**

The page scrolls up a bit in the window.

4 **Click the scroll box in the vertical scroll bar and, while keeping your mouse button pressed, drag the box to the top of the bar. (This procedure is called *clicking and dragging*.)**

The page jumps back to the top of the Web page.

Of course, if you get tired of using the scroll bar, you can press the PgDn and PgUp keys on your keyboard instead.

1 **Press PgDn.**

The page zips down, displaying its lower section in your window.

2 **Press PgUp.**

The page swooshes up to its top section again.

That's all there is to moving up and down in a Web page!

To sum up: Your browser window is almost always shorter than the Web page you're looking at. To see the whole page, simply use the vertical scroll bar or the PgDn and PgUp keys.

Finding links on a Web page

Notice that certain phrases and images on the Web page you're viewing are distinguished from the other text and pictures by underlines, different colors, or other effects. Such markings indicate that these areas are links that you can use to jump to other Web pages.

on the test

Finding out whether a highlighted phrase or image is really a link is easy. All you have to do is move your mouse.

clicking and dragging = clicking something and then holding down your mouse button while you move the mouse

click the vertical scroll bar arrows or press PgDn and PgUp to examine a Web page

Figure 1-6: Netscape's message bar shows the electronic address, or URL, associated with the link that you're pointing to.

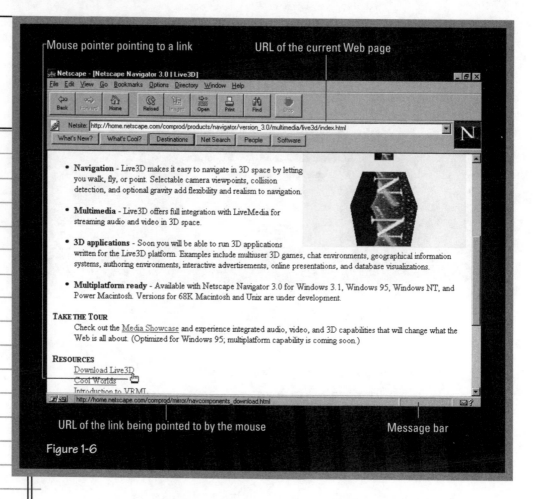

Mouse pointer pointing to a link   URL of the current Web page

URL of the link being pointed to by the mouse   Message bar

Figure 1-6

Notes:

URL = electronic
address of a
Web page or
other information
on the Net

1 **Move your mouse pointer over a word, phrase, or picture that you suspect is a link.**

If the area you choose is a link, your mouse pointer changes from its usual arrowhead shape to a hand with a pointing finger (see Figures 1-4 and 1-5).

2 **Move your mouse pointer slowly over every area of the Web page in your window.**

Your mouse pointer turns into a hand when it's over areas that are links, and the pointer reverts to its usual arrowhead shape when it's over areas that contain only normal text and pictures.

Identifying a link's electronic address

on the test

Another way to prove that you found a link is to keep an eye on the gray message bar at the bottom of your window (see Figure 1-6). When your mouse is pointing to a link, the message bar displays the Internet location, or electronic *address*, of the page to which the link takes you. This location is called a *URL*. (Actually, the official techie term is *Uniform Resource Locator* but, understandably, almost everybody just calls 'em URLs.) For example, the URL of the page that you're currently viewing is `http://home.netscape.com/`. That's why (in case you were wondering) the address `http://home.netscape.com/` appears in the Location box in the upper portion of your window.

Try displaying some other URLs now:

1 Move your mouse pointer over an area that you know is a link.

Your mouse pointer turns into a hand, and the address of the Web page associated with the link — that is, the page's URL — is displayed in the message bar at the bottom of the window.

2 Move your mouse pointer over a different area that you know is a link.

Your mouse pointer remains a hand, but the Web address in the message bar changes to reflect the URL of the new link that you're on.

3 Move your mouse pointer over an area that you know is *not* a link.

Your mouse pointer reverts to its arrowhead shape, and the message bar either goes blank or displays a previous message (such as `Document: Done`) because you're no longer pointing to an area associated with a URL.

extra credit

The wacky world of URLs

Some fun facts about Web page URLs:

- Web URLs usually have the format `http://www.name.com`.

- Web URLs usually begin with *http://*, which stands for *HyperText Transfer Protocol*. *HyperText* refers to the art of linking disparate sections of text together; *transfer* refers to the transmission of data; and *protocol* refers to the rules and standards that allow computers to communicate with each other.

- Following the double slash (*//*), Web URLs usually sport a *www* — which stands for World Wide Web, 'natch — and a period (also referred to as a *dot*).

- Following *www.*, URLs usually contain a name representing the organization affiliated with the Web site, plus another period; for example, *att.* for AT&T or *microsoft.* for — well, you know.

- U.S. Web sites have URLs that usually end with a three-letter code, such as *com* for a commercial organization, *gov* for a government department, *mil* for a military site, *edu* for an educational institution, *net* for groups running a network (that is, a bunch of connected computers), and *org* for miscellaneous others (such as nonprofit organizations).

- Non-U.S. Web sites have URLs that usually end in a two-letter country code, such as *au* for Australia, *ca* for Canada, *fr* for France, *jp* for Japan, and *se* for Sweden.

- URLs can also refer to other areas of the Internet. Non-Web codes include *ftp://* for FTP file transfers and *news://* for newsgroups (see Unit 7).

You don't really need to remember any of this stuff. Then again, the info may prove handy for impressing people at parties.

☑ Progress Check

If you can do the following, you've mastered this lesson:

❏ Connect to a Web page.

❏ Move up and down a Web page.

❏ Locate links on a Web page.

❏ Identify the URL associated with a link.

Lesson 1-3

Cruising the Web by Using Links

to use a link,
click it

Notes:

Now that you know how to move around a Web page and identify its links, you're ready for the big step — jumping to another Web page.

To perform this incredible technical feat, you need to do two things: point to a link and click. It's that simple!

After you click, Netscape uses the Web address associated with the link to connect you to the page to which you want to jump. If the page is available (for example, if it isn't tied up by too many other people trying to access it at the same time you are), Netscape connects to the page and copies its text, pictures, and other data to your browser window. When that process is complete, you're all set to explore the new page.

Sound good? Then go for it!

1 **If you aren't still online, repeat the steps at the beginning of Lesson 1-2 to run Netscape and connect to the Internet.**

Your Netscape browser window should be maximized and displaying a Web page.

2 **Point to a link that interests you on the current Web page.**

Your mouse pointer turns into a hand, and the URL of the link — that is, the address of the Web page that the link is associated with — appears in the message bar.

3 **Click (that is, press your left mouse button).**

In the Netscape logo in your window's upper-right section (which consists of a large N hovering over a planet), you see comets begin to shoot past the planet. This eye-catching activity is a cool way of letting you know that Netscape is operating to fulfill your request for new data.

At the same time, several notices appear in the message bar, though some may flash by too quickly for you to read. First, you see `connect host`, which indicates that Netscape is trying to connect to the URL you selected. Next — if you connect to the page successfully — you see a `transferring data` message, which means that Netscape is transmitting the text and graphics of the new Web page to your PC. As bits of the new page appear, Netscape continuously flashes what percentage of the data has been transferred and — if it's an especially long transfer — how many more seconds it will take to complete the process. Finally, you see the message `Document: Done`, which means that Netscape successfully copied all the new Web page's data to your computer. Also, comets stop flying over the planet in the Netscape logo to show that the attempt to make a new connection is complete. (If the connection was *not* successful for some reason, simply try again by clicking a different link.)

4 **Read the new page.**

Skim through the page. When you're done, pick out a link on this new page that interests you.

5 **Point to a link on the page you want to explore and then click your left mouse button.**

Once again, the message bar displays `connect host` and `transferring data` notices. A short time after that, the page you selected appears on your screen.

Forward button — Home button

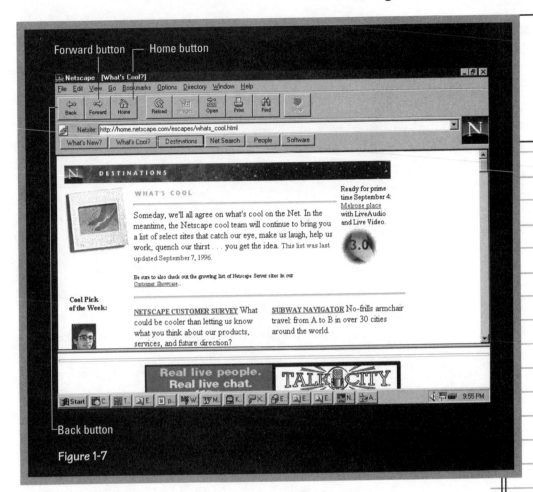

Figure 1-7

Back button

Figure 1-7: Netscape's Back, Forward, and Home buttons make jumping back and forth between Web pages that you visit in the same session a snap.

6 Read the new page.

Notice that this page contains links leading to additional Web pages.

7 Point to a link on the page you want to explore and then click your left mouse button.

Again, the message bar displays `connect host` and `transferring data` notices. A short time after that, the page that you selected appears on your screen.

Clearly, you could go on and on like this, jumping from Web page to Web page. (Indeed, we've lost more people that way. . . .) However, for now you should push on to the next exercise.

heads up

Typically, you receive all a Web page's data within a minute or two. However, occasionally a page requires more time. In such a case, the page may have many pictures (which take much longer to transmit than text), or numerous other people may be trying to access the page at the same time you are, or the Web site may be experiencing technical problems. If you become impatient, you can abort a transfer by clicking the Stop button in the upper-left section of the Netscape window. You can then read whatever information and use whatever links on the page were transmitted before you clicked Stop.

heads up

Another way to avoid long waits is to prevent Netscape from automatically transferring pictures at all. For more information about this option, see Lesson 4-1.

Netscape's
Stop button

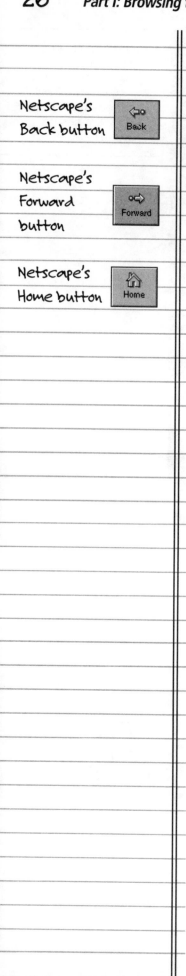

Netscape's
Back button

Netscape's
Forward
button

Netscape's
Home button

Moving back and forth on the Web

Constantly leaping to new Web pages is all well and good, but what if you want to go back to a previous page? No problem! All you've gotta do is click Netscape's cleverly named Back button, which is located in the top-left section of the window (see Figure 1-7).

Similarly, if you want to move forward again, you can click — you guessed it! — Netscape's Forward button. (Who says that computers are complicated?)

Finally, if you want to jump directly to your starting point, you can click Netscape's Home button. This button instantly returns you to the place where you began your session (in this case, the Netscape Communications home page).

But don't take our word for it; check it out for yourself. (You should still be connected to the Internet from the preceding exercise.)

1 **Click the Back button in the upper-left section of the Netscape window.**

The current Web page is quickly replaced in your window by the preceding page you viewed.

2 **Click the Back button again.**

Again, the current page is replaced by the preceding page.

3 **Click the Back button again.**

Your current page is replaced by the preceding page. If you scrupulously followed the steps in the preceding exercise, this page is also the page you started on. (And if you didn't, simply click the Back button a few more times until you return to the page where you started.) The Back button is now dim, or *grayed out,* indicating that you can't move back any farther.

4 **Click the Back button again.**

Nothing happens because you returned to your starting point.

5 **Click the Forward button, which is directly to the right of the Back button.**

Your initial Web page is quickly replaced by the second page you visited during this session.

6 **Click the Forward button again.**

Your current page is replaced by the third page you moved to during this session.

7 **Click the Forward button again.**

Again, your current page is replaced by the next page you visited during this session. If you scrupulously followed the steps in the preceding exercise, this page is also the last page you visited. (And if you didn't, simply click the button a few more times until you arrive at your last page.) The Forward button dims to indicate that you can't move forward any farther.

8 **Click the Forward button again.**

Nothing happens because you reached the end of the sequence of Web page links that you selected.

9 **Click the Home button.**

You immediately jump back to your starting point, the Netscape Communications home page.

We're tempted to note that the last step of this exercise proves that, through the wonders of technology, you *can* go home again. However, we're worried that you'd want to hit us if we did, so we won't.

on the test

Remember, click Netscape's Back button to move to the preceding Web page, click the Forward button to move to the next Web page, and click Home to return immediately to your initial Web page.

heads up

Netscape's Back, Forward, and Home buttons keep track of only the Web pages that you select during your *current* Internet session. When you exit Netscape, these buttons "forget" the Web pages you just visited; when you reopen Netscape for a new session, the buttons start from a clean slate, paying attention only to the Web pages that you visit during your new session.

Using the Go menu and History window

The Back and Forward buttons are all you need for moving among a few Web pages. However, if you're using ten or more Web pages during a session, you may find it a nuisance to click through lots of intermediate pages to reach the one you want. In such cases, you can use Netscape's Go menu, which lists the URL of each page you've visited and lets you move directly to whichever URL you select. For a demonstration, follow these steps:

1 Click the Go menu.

A menu pops down, listing the URL of each Web page you've visited during this session. Also, a check mark appears next to the URL of the page you're currently on.

2 Click a URL without a check mark next to it.

You move to the Web page located at the URL you selected.

3 Click the Go menu again.

The menu pops down, and the check mark now appears next to the URL you selected.

4 Click a URL without a check mark next to it.

You move to the Web page located at the new URL you selected. (And so on.)

That's all there is to using the Go menu. The only other thing to know is that if you visit too many pages during a session to be listed on the menu, you may have to choose Window⇨History to get at the URL you want. Doing so opens a History window that can display a virtually unlimited number of URLs. Try it!

1 Choose Window⇨History.

A window like the one in Figure 1-8 appears. It both lists the name and the URL of each Web page you've visited during this session and highlights the name and URL of the page you're currently on. It also provides Go to and Close buttons (which you use shortly) and a button for creating bookmarks (a topic you learn about in the next section).

2 Click a listed Web page that isn't highlighted.

The highlighting shifts to the page you selected.

3 Click the window's Go to button.

The Web page you highlighted appears in the Netscape window. (If this isn't evident because the Netscape window is hidden, move the History window by clicking its title bar and dragging it off to the side a bit.)

Notes:

click the Go menu to see recently visited URLs

choose Window→ History to list all the Web pages you've visited this session

Figure 1-8: The History window shows you all the Web pages you've visited during a session. You can move to any listed page by double-clicking it.

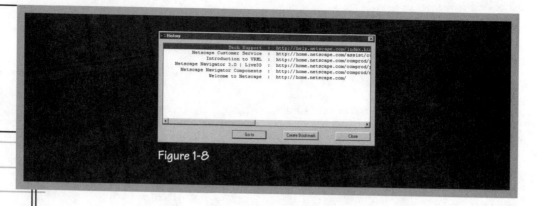

Figure 1-8

☑ Progress Check

If you can do the following, you've mastered this lesson:

❏ Move to a new Web page by using a link.

❏ Move to the preceding page, the next page, or your home page by using Netscape buttons.

❏ Move directly to a page by using the Go menu.

❏ Move directly to a page by using the History window.

4 **Double-click a listed Web page (which has the same effect as highlighting it and clicking the Go to button).**

The highlighting shifts to the page you selected, and the page appears in the Netscape window. (And so on.)

5 **Click the History window's Close button.**

The History window disappears.

Unlike the Go menu, the History window doesn't close until you tell it to. When you need to switch among many Web pages frequently, you may find it convenient to leave the History window open, resize it so that it takes up less room on your screen, and then quickly move to each page you want by double-clicking it in the window.

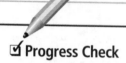

heads up

Like the Netscape Back, Forward, and Home buttons, the Go menu and History window keep track of only the Web pages you select during your *current* Internet session. Every time you restart Netscape for a new session, the Go menu and History window begin with a clean slate, paying attention only to the Web pages you visit during your new session.

Recess

Well, all right! There's much more to know about cruising the Web, but you just mastered the basics. (And performed brilliantly!) Give yourself a reward (we favor chocolate ourselves), and then tackle the following tricky quiz questions.

Unit 1 Quiz

For each of the following questions, circle the letter of the correct answer or answers. Remember, there may be more than one right answer for each question.

1. **Before you can start using Netscape, you need:**

   A. Nerves of steel.

   B. A 14,400 or 28,000 bps modem.

Notes:

C. An account with an Internet provider.

D. A recent version of the Netscape program.

E. Happy feet.

2. **Examples of national Internet providers include:**

   A. AT&T WorldNet Service and The Microsoft Network.

   B. McDonald's and Burger King.

   C. America Online and CompuServe.

   D. Coke and Pepsi.

   E. Concentric and Netcom.

3. **The World Wide Web:**

   A. Was created by the U.S. military during the height of the Cold War in the 1950s.

   B. Is currently funded by evil alien spiders.

   C. Consists of electronic pages created by thousands of independent individuals and organizations from all over the globe.

   D. Is often referred to as *the Wide W*.

   E. Is typically accessed with a special program called a *WoWWzer*.

4. **To determine whether a word, phrase, or image on a Web page is a link:**

   A. Ask it politely.

   B. Look for a chain icon to its left.

   C. Check whether it's surrounded by the colors of the rainbow.

   D. Move your mouse pointer over it and see whether the pointer changes to a hand.

   E. Move your hand over it and see whether your fingers change to mouse pointers.

5. **A URL is:**

   A. An address indicating the electronic location of something on the Internet, such as a Web page.

   B. The name of a hot Irish rock band.

   C. Internet shorthand for *URban Legend*, meaning a story that may sound plausible but isn't true.

   D. The title of episode 68 of *The X-Files*.

   E. What appears in Netscape's message bar when you point to a link.

6. **To return to a Web page you've visited during your current session, you can:**

   A. Click the Lost & Found button and then follow the prompts.

   B. Click the Back button until you return to the page.

   C. Click the page's name from the Go menu or double-click it from the History window.

D. Click a link that points to the page.

E. Act embarrassed and explain that you think you accidentally left your gloves behind.

Unit 1 Exercise

Notes:

If your setup is typical, you can run Netscape and your dialer program independently of each other. Try it!

1. Run both Netscape and your Internet dialer program at the same time. (**Hint:** Use the Netscape Navigator icon.)

2. Connect to the Internet.

3. Disconnect from the Internet without closing Netscape. (**Hint:** Start by clicking the dialer's button on the Windows 95 Taskbar, or double-clicking its icon in Windows 3.1, to pop up its dialog box and display a disconnect option.)

4. Because you're not being charged for online time now, spend a few leisurely minutes examining the Netscape browser window, including its various menus and buttons. (You'll find using Netscape offline especially helpful when you learn how to create and read e-mail in Unit 5.)

5. Fire up the dialer by itself. (**Hint:** Look for a dialer icon that you can double-click.)

6. Reconnect to the Internet. After you connect, Netscape automatically becomes your window on the Internet again.

7. Click the Netscape window's Close button. This action should exit Netscape but maintain your Internet connection (indicated by your dialer's button still appearing on the Windows 95 Taskbar or its minimized icon still appearing on your Windows 3.1 desktop). If you had another Internet program, you now could run it instead of Netscape. You learn how to get such programs directly from the Web in Lesson 3-2.

8. Log off from the Internet a second time using your dialer program.

•••••••••

Searching for Information on the Web

Objectives for This Unit

- ✔ Using bookmarks to move to Web pages
- ✔ Creating and deleting bookmarks
- ✔ Organizing bookmarks
- ✔ Typing in a URL
- ✔ Searching a Web page for information
- ✔ Searching the entire Web for information

Prerequisites

▶ Cruising the Web with Netscape Navigator (Lessons 1-2 and 1-3)

on the CD

▶ Exercise file (Bookmark.htm)

Cruising the Web by Using Bookmarks

Lesson 2-1

As you saw in Unit 1, links give you an intuitive, rambling way to explore the Web and discover information you didn't even know you wanted. When you find a Web page you consider especially useful, however, you may want some way of returning to it easily and repeatedly. The navigation tools you've learned about so far — such as Netscape's Back and Forward buttons and its Go menu — let you return to pages that you've visited during your current session, but they don't maintain a permanent record of those pages for future sessions.

Fortunately, Netscape also provides a nifty feature called *bookmarks.* Just as a physical bookmark helps you quickly go to a particular page in a book, Netscape's bookmarks let you jump to particular Web pages. These electronic bookmarks are stored on your hard disk, and they remain there until you explicitly delete them. Therefore, you can use a bookmark at any time during your Web session to move to a specific Web page.

bookmark = electronic marker that makes it easy to return to a Web page

Notes:

This lesson shows you how to use predefined bookmarks, create your own bookmarks, and delete bookmarks. By the time you're done, you'll be able to create a Web page library that's tailored to your personal tastes and needs.

Installing a bookmark file

Bookmarks are stored in your Netscape folder in a file named Bookmark.htm. The *htm* extension stands for *HyperText Markup Language,* which is the computer language that both Web pages and bookmarks are written in. (For more information about htm files, see Unit 9.)

on the CD

The Bookmark.htm file typically stays empty until you add bookmarks to it yourself by using a Netscape command. However, to jump-start your ability to get around the Web, we've created a substitute Bookmark.htm file containing bookmarks for what we consider to be some of the best sites on the Internet. To take advantage of this collection of bookmarks, follow these steps:

*bookmarks are
stored in a file
named
bookmark.htm*

1 Run Netscape (but don't connect to the Internet).

You see the Netscape browser window and your dialer program. For now, ignore your dialer program and notice that one of the menus in your Netscape window is named *Bookmarks.*

*to see your
bookmarks, choose
Bookmarks from
the menu*

2 Click the Bookmarks menu.

If the version of Netscape you're using is typical, you see only the two Bookmarks commands, which are Add Bookmark and Go to Bookmarks. When you actually have bookmarks, they are listed on this menu below the two commands.

heads up

If you *do* see bookmarks listed — for example, if bookmarks were supplied in your version of Netscape by your Internet provider — don't worry. Installing the substitute Bookmark.htm file won't destroy your current file but will simply rename it *Bookmark.old.* If you ever want to restore your original bookmarks file, you can move to your Netscape folder, rename Bookmark.htm to something else, and then change the name of Bookmark.old back to Bookmark.htm.

3 Choose File⇨Exit to close both Netscape and your dialer program.

Both programs exit. Now install the bookmark file we've created for you, which is stored on the CD-ROM that came with this book.

4 Insert the *Dummies 101* CD-ROM into your CD-ROM drive.

Be careful to touch only the edges of the CD-ROM, and be sure to insert the CD-ROM with its printed side up.

If you're using Windows 95, a *Dummies 101* Installer program that displays buttons for installing various programs on the CD-ROM should appear. If this occurs, skip to Step 9.

5 If the Installer program does *not* appear: If you've already created a *Dummies 101* Installer icon (by skipping ahead to either Appendix B or the "*Dummies 101* CD-ROM Installation Instructions" page at the back of this book), double-click the icon to bring up the Installer window and then skip to Step 9.

If you haven't created a *Dummies 101* Installer icon yet, simply follow the next few steps to bring up the Installer window manually.

6 If you're using Windows 95, click the Start button (that is, the button in the bottom-left corner of your screen). If you're using Windows 3.1, click the Program Manager's File menu.

A menu that includes a Run option pops up.

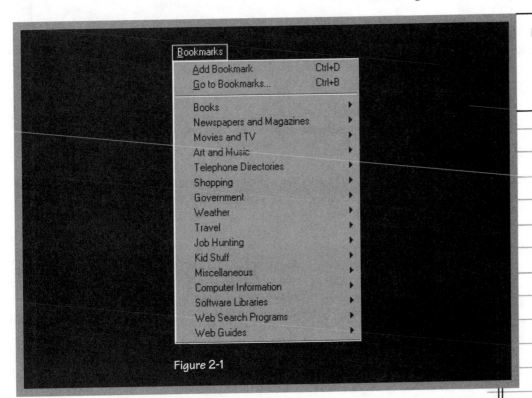

Bookmarks

Add Bookmark	Ctrl+D
Go to Bookmarks...	Ctrl+B

Books ▶
Newspapers and Magazines ▶
Movies and TV ▶
Art and Music ▶
Telephone Directories ▶
Shopping ▶
Government ▶
Weather ▶
Travel ▶
Job Hunting ▶
Kid Stuff ▶
Miscellaneous ▶
Computer Information ▶
Software Libraries ▶
Web Search Programs ▶
Web Guides ▶

Figure 2-1

Figure 2-1: The Bookmarks menu lets you create and use Web page pointers that are stored on your hard disk.

7   **Click the Run option.**

A Run dialog box appears.

8   **In the Run dialog box, type** d:\install **(that is, the letter *d,* a colon, a backslash, and the word *install*). If your CD-ROM drive isn't drive D, type the letter appropriate for your drive instead of D. When you're done, press Enter or click OK.**

The Run dialog box closes and, after a few moments, the *Dummies 101* Installer program appears. Notice that the Installer displays buttons for installing various programs on the CD-ROM.

9   **Click the Bookmarks button.**

Installation of the Bookmark.htm file begins. When you're asked to provide the name and location of your Netscape program folder, accept the displayed suggestion if it's accurate or type the correct name and location. (For example, if you used the default Netscape installation for Windows 95, your folder is **C:\Program Files\Netscape\Navigator**.) If you don't know or remember where the folder is located, you can search for it by using My Computer or Windows Explorer or by using the Windows 3.1 File Manager. Follow any additional prompts that appear on-screen to complete the installation.

10   **When the installation of the Bookmark.htm file is completed, click the Installer box's Exit button.**

The Installer program exits.

Note: If for some reason the Bookmark.htm installation doesn't work properly for you, try this instead: With the *Dummies 101* CD-ROM in your CD-ROM drive, press Ctrl+B to open a Bookmarks window, press Alt+F and then I to open an Import bookmarks file dialog box, type **d:\bookmark.htm** (if your CD-ROM drive isn't D, type the appropriate drive letter instead), and press Enter. This copies all the bookmarks from the CD-ROM into your existing bookmarks file.

You now have a bunch of interesting new bookmarks. Proceed to the next section to check 'em out!

Notes:

Leafing through bookmarks

To examine the new bookmarks you just installed, follow these steps:

1 Run Netscape and connect to the Internet.

Your Netscape browser window should be maximized and displaying a Web page.

2 Choose the Bookmarks menu.

You again see the commands Add Bookmark and Go To Bookmarks. This time, however, you also see a list of bookmark categories below the commands, as shown in Figure 2-1.

3 Move your mouse pointer over *Books*. (If you're using Windows 3.1, keep your mouse button held down.)

You see the names of book-related Web sites, including *The Internet Classics Archive* (offers full-text translations of nearly 400 classic Greek, Roman, and Italian works, such as *The Iliad* and *The Odyssey*), *The Complete Works of Shakespeare* (provides the complete works of William Shakespeare), *BookWire* (supplies book news, reviews, and handy guides to book resources on the Net), and *Amazon.com Bookstore* (an online bookstore with over one million titles in its searchable electronic catalog).

4 Move your mouse pointer over *Newspapers and Magazines*.

You see the names of more Web sites, including *The New York Times on the Web* (a searchable version of the daily "newspaper of record"), *USA Today* (a searchable version of the visually splashy daily newspaper), *The Wall Street Journal Money Interactive Edition* (a source for up-to-date stock prices, business news, and other timely financial information), and *Time Warner's Pathfinder* (which lets you search for and read articles from a variety of Time-Warner publications, including *Entertainment Weekly, Fortune, Money, People, Sports Illustrated,* and *Time Magazine*).

5 Move your mouse pointer over *Job Hunting*.

You see the names of additional Web sites, including *America's Job Bank* (lists over 250,000 jobs from 1,800 state Employment Service offices), *CareerPath.com* (lets you search through employment ads from nine major newspapers, including *The New York Times, The Washington Post,* and the *Los Angeles Times*), and the *Online Career Center* (lets you search for work by job category and region and lets you post your resume online).

6 Move your mouse pointer over *Travel*.

You see the names of yet more Web pages, including *City.Net* (provides extensive information on virtually any city or region in the world), *Virtual Tourist II World Map* (provides the same comprehensive information as City.Net, but lets you search for it visually via thousands of maps), and *Hotel Anywhere* (offers information on over 7,000 hotels worldwide, as well as links to hundreds of other travel-related Web sites).

7 Move your mouse pointer over *Hotel Anywhere* (but don't click).

The URL associated with the bookmark under your mouse pointer is displayed in the message bar (just as a URL is displayed when you point to a link on a Web page).

8 Choose the Bookmarks menu's Go To Bookmarks option.

You now see the names of the bookmarks within each folder, as shown in Figure 2-2. (If you don't, double-click every folder to display the Web page names it contains.) Because you have *scores* of bookmarks, you can't see them all in the window simultaneously.

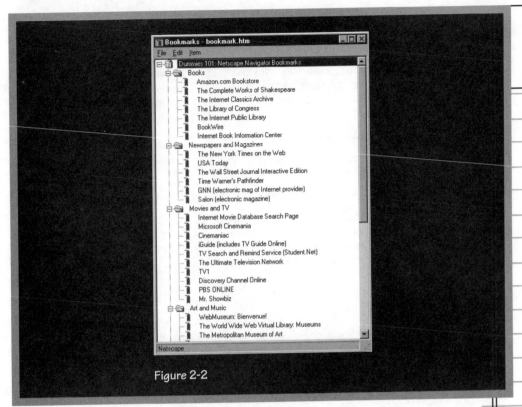

Figure 2-2

Figure 2-2: The Bookmarks
window makes
examining all your
bookmarks easy.

9 **Click the vertical scroll bar arrows or press the PgDn and PgUp keys to examine all your bookmarks.**

The window contains over 100 bookmarks covering a wide range of topics.

10 **Click a bookmark.**

The bookmark is highlighted, and its URL is displayed in the window's message bar.

11 **Click the Close button of the Bookmarks window to exit.**

The list of bookmarks closes, giving you an unobstructed view of the Netscape window again.

heads up

The Bookmarks window is one of the few options that you can select from more than one menu. In addition to choosing Bookmarks⇨Go To Bookmarks, you can open the Bookmarks window by choosing Window⇨Bookmarks. You can also open the window by pressing the keystroke shortcut Ctrl+B, which has the same effect as choosing the option from a menu.

Intrigued? Good! Because your next step is to use the bookmarks you just viewed to actually visit some of the best sites on the Web.

Using bookmarks to sample the best of the Web

Using a bookmark to visit a Web page is just as easy as using a link — you simply point to it and click (unless you're in the Bookmarks window, in which case you need to point and *double*-click).

Keep in mind, however, that everything on the Internet changes rapidly, including Web addresses. Therefore, if a bookmark you try in the following exercise no longer works, just select a different bookmark.

*to open the
Bookmarks window,
choose Bookmarks→
Go To Bookmarks,
choose Window→
Bookmarks, or press
Ctrl+B*

1 Choose Bookmarks⬦Books⬦The Complete Works of Shakespeare.

You're greeted with information about the bard and his works. If you're so inclined, delve deeper into this Web site by choosing to read scenes from a particular play. You don't have to rush; we'll wait for you. (After all, his work *is* timeless. . . .)

2 Choose Bookmarks⬦Newspapers and Magazines⬦USA Today.

You see the latest headline news from *USA Today* (complete with full-color photographs!).

3 Choose Bookmarks⬦Travel⬦Virtual Tourist II World Map.

You're met by a map of the world and an invitation to click the name of the area in which you're interested. Follow the prompts and click progressively more detailed maps until you zero in on information about the country, state, or city you're seeking.

Pretty cool, huh?

If you enjoyed visiting those Web sites, you may want to take some time to explore a few of the other pages linked to the predefined bookmarks. In each case, move to the page you want by choosing the Bookmarks menu, moving your mouse pointer over the appropriate category, and then clicking the bookmark. After you're done, go on to the next section, which explains how to create your own bookmarks.

Creating bookmarks

Using predefined bookmarks is a fun and easy way to get started exploring the Web. However, because nobody else can judge which Web pages are of the most interest to *you,* get in the habit of creating your *own* bookmarks. If you do so regularly and thoughtfully, you soon build up an extremely useful Web page library tailored to your particular tastes and needs.

on the test

Creating a bookmark involves two simple steps: moving to a Web page and then either choosing Bookmarks⬦Add Bookmark or pressing Ctrl+D.

You can use the bookmark you create yourself in exactly the same way you use a predefined bookmark — that is, by displaying it through the Bookmarks menu and clicking it.

1 If you aren't still connected to the Internet, log on again now.

Your Netscape browser window should be maximized and displaying a Web page.

2 Locate a link to a Web page that interests you.

When you point to the link, your mouse pointer turns into a hand and the link's URL appears in the message bar.

3 Click the link.

You move to the Web page associated with the link.

4 Repeat Steps 2 and 3 until you reach a page that you think you'd enjoy visiting repeatedly in the future.

You're on a Web page that you reached through a series of links.

5 Choose the Bookmarks menu.

You see the option Add Bookmark, as well as a list of bookmark categories. Make note of the last item on the menu's list.

to create a bookmark for the Web page you're on, choose Bookmarks→ Add Bookmark or press Ctrl+D

6 **Choose the Add Bookmark option.**

The menu closes, and (although you can't see it right now) a bookmark pointing to your current page is added to the bottom of the bookmarks list.

7 **Click the Home button.**

You return to the Netscape Communications home page.

8 **Choose Bookmarks.**

The menu drops down and shows that the last item on the bookmarks list is now the bookmark you created in Step 6.

9 **Select the bookmark you created.**

You move back to the Web page associated with the bookmark.

The bookmark you created remains on your bookmarks list until you explicitly delete it. You learn how to remove bookmarks that have outlived their usefulness in the next section.

Creating bookmarks is quick and easy. Therefore, as you continue to cruise the Internet and discover interesting Web pages, don't hesitate to take advantage of this great feature.

extra credit

Creating Web page shortcuts

Creating a bookmark isn't the only way you can set a pointer to a Web page. If you're using Windows 95, you can also create a *shortcut,* which is a file that you can keep directly on your desktop. To do so, simply move to a Web page you want to access frequently, click the "chain links" icon directly to the left of Netscape's Location box and, while keeping your mouse button held down, drag the icon to your desktop. Lastly, release your mouse button. The shortcut to the Web page appears as an icon on your desktop.

If you double-click the shortcut when Netscape is running, Netscape responds by moving to the page. More importantly, if you double-click the shortcut when Netscape *isn't* running, Netscape and your dialer program automatically open and, after you connect to the Internet, Netscape moves to the appropriate Web page. The latter is more efficient than double-clicking the Netscape Navigator icon, clicking the Bookmarks menu, and then clicking a bookmark. However, it's best to avoid cluttering your desktop with a lot of icons, so we suggest that you create shortcuts for no more than two or three Web pages that you access constantly.

Deleting bookmarks

As you add more and more bookmarks, your bookmark list may become too cluttered for you to use it easily. If this happens, you can reduce the muddle by eliminating bookmarks that have outlived their usefulness.

on the test

To remove a bookmark, highlight it in the Bookmarks window and then either choose Edit⇨Delete or press the Del key. For example, follow these steps to remove the bookmark you created in the preceding section:

1 **Press Ctrl+B (which has the same effect as choosing Book-marks⇨Go To Bookmarks).**

The Bookmarks window opens and displays all your bookmarks.

Notes:

to delete a bookmark, select it in the Bookmarks window and then choose Edit→ Delete or press the Del key

☑ **Progress Check**

If you can do the following, you've mastered this lesson:

❏ Install a Bookmark.htm file containing predefined bookmarks.

❏ Display bookmarks from the Bookmarks menu and Bookmarks window.

❏ Use a bookmark to move to a Web page.

❏ Create bookmarks.

❏ Delete bookmarks.

Notes:

2 Press Ctrl+End.

You move to the bottom of the window. Because the bookmark you created is the last one on the list, it is now highlighted. (If it isn't, click it now to highlight it.)

3 Press the Del key (or choose Edit⇨Delete).

The bookmark you selected is eliminated.

heads up
After you delete a bookmark, you can't bring it back. Therefore, think twice before deleting to ensure that you don't accidentally remove a bookmark you meant to keep.

Lesson 2-2   Organizing Bookmarks

Just as you should keep your hard disk organized by grouping your files into folders, you should keep your bookmarks organized by grouping *them* into folders. Doing so helps to ensure that you can always find the bookmark you need quickly and easily.

To put your bookmarks in order, first open the Bookmarks window. You can then use Item and Edit menu options to create new folders, cut or copy bookmarks from folders, and paste bookmarks to folders.

For example, to create a *Favorites* folder and then copy some of your favorite bookmarks into it, follow these steps:

1 Press Ctrl+B (or choose Bookmarks⇨Go To Bookmarks).

The Bookmarks window opens.

2 Press Ctrl+Home to move to the top of the window.

The main bookmark folder, which contains all the other bookmarks and folders, is highlighted.

3 Notice that the window has three menus: File, Edit, and Item. Choose Item.

Several menu options appear, including Insert Folder. This option creates a new folder.

4 Choose Insert Folder.

A dialog box like the one in Figure 2-3 appears. Near its top is a Name box that contains the highlighted text *New Folder*.

5 Type the name Favorites for your new folder.

The name you typed replaces the previous text in the Name box.

6 Click the OK button.

The dialog box closes, and a new folder named Favorites appears in the window. It's pictured as open to indicate that its contents are displayed automatically.

7 Select any listed bookmark that you consider a favorite by clicking it.

The bookmark is highlighted to indicate that it's selected.

choose Item→Insert Folder from the Bookmarks window to create a bookmark folder

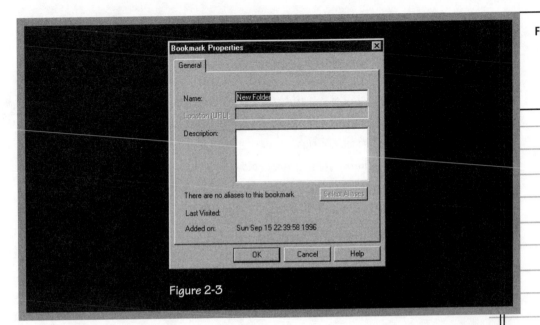

Figure 2-3

Figure 2-3: Use the
Bookmark Properties
dialog box to create new
folders for organizing
your bookmarks.

8 Choose Edit⇨Copy.

A copy of the bookmark is invisibly inserted in the Windows Clipboard, and the
original bookmark is unaffected.

9 Click your Favorites folder.

The folder is highlighted to indicate that it's selected.

10 Choose Edit⇨Paste.

A copy of the bookmark appears in the Favorites folder.

11 Select another favorite bookmark by clicking it.

The bookmark is highlighted.

12 Press Ctrl+C (which has the same effect as choosing Edit⇨Copy).

The bookmark is copied.

13 Click your Favorites folder.

The folder is highlighted.

14 Press Ctrl+V (which has the same effect as choosing Edit⇨Paste).

A copy of the bookmark appears in the Favorites folder.

If you like, you can continue repeating Steps 11 through 14 until all your
favorite bookmarks are grouped together in your Favorites folder.

Alternately, if you don't want to make copies of bookmarks but simply want to
move them to Favorites, you can press Ctrl+X or choose Edit⇨Cut in Steps 8
and 12. The latter command *removes* the selected bookmark from its current
location and stores it in the Windows Clipboard, allowing you to paste it into
a different location.

Creating and deleting subfolders and separator lines

You can further organize your bookmarks by creating subfolders (folders
within folders) and separator lines (lines that visually distinguish one group of
bookmarks or folders from another).

For example, follow these steps to create and mark off a Music subfolder within your Favorites folder:

1 **If you aren't still in the Bookmarks window, press Ctrl+B.**

2 **Click your Favorites folder to select it.**

The folder is highlighted.

3 **Choose Item⇨Insert Folder.**

A dialog box appears.

4 **Type Music.**

The name you typed replaces the previous text in the Name box.

5 **Click the OK button.**

The dialog box closes, and a new subfolder named Music appears in your Favorites folder.

6 **Choose Item⇨Insert Separator.**

The word *separator* enclosed in brackets (*<separator>*) is inserted following the Music folder to separate it visually from everything else in your Favorites folder.

Now assume you've decided that it would be better to change your Music subfolder into a distinct folder on the same level as Favorites and that you want to do away with the separator altogether. You can quickly make the revisions like this:

1 **If the Music folder isn't still highlighted, click it to select it.**

The folder is highlighted.

2 **Press Ctrl+X to cut the folder.**

The folder is deleted from the window and moved to the Clipboard.

3 **Press Ctrl+Home to move to the top of the window.**

The main bookmarks folder is selected.

4 **Press Ctrl+V to paste.**

The Music folder reappears, but it's now at the same level as the Favorites folder.

5 **Click the separator to select it.**

The separator is highlighted.

6 **Press the Del key.**

The separator is removed.

As you've seen throughout this lesson, you have a lot of freedom in choosing how to organize and reorganize your bookmarks. Play around with different options until you find an ordering scheme that works best for you.

heads up

If, despite your best organizational efforts, you occasionally have trouble locating a bookmark, choose Edit⇨Find. This action opens a dialog box that lets you find a bookmark based on a word or phrase contained in its name or URL.

☑ **Progress Check**

If you can do the following, you've mastered this lesson:

❑ Create bookmark folders.

❑ Copy, cut, and paste bookmarks.

❑ Create bookmark subfolders.

❑ Create bookmark separators.

❑ Move and delete bookmark folders and separators.

Recess

You've done a *fabulous* job of learning how to cruise the Web with bookmarks, so take some time to brag to your friends about the new skills you've mastered. When you're refreshed, forge ahead to the next lesson, which teaches you how to jump directly to *any* Web page.

Entering URLs   Lesson 2-3

Cruising the Web using links and bookmarks is fast and fun, but it takes you only so far. For example, if a friend tells you the addresses of some hot new Web pages or if a favorite magazine prints a list of great Web sites that you'd probably enjoy, how can you get to the Web pages unless you happen to have access to links or bookmarks that point to them? To take advantage of such recommendations, you need to know how to jump directly to a Web page by entering its URL (which, as we explained in Unit 1, is an electronic address that tells browsers like Netscape precisely where on the Internet a particular Web page is located). By typing a page's URL, you can move straight to the page without passing Go!

on the test

Fortunately, typing a URL isn't very hard. To begin, click anywhere inside Netscape's Location box, which is directly below the Home button (see Figure 2-4). Your click highlights the text in the box, which is typically the URL of your current Web page. Go ahead and type the URL of the new Web page that you want; the first letter you type automatically replaces the entire old URL. Finally, press Enter to activate your new URL. If you typed the URL correctly, Netscape jumps to the Web page you want.

The only tricky part is that URLs are about as easy to remember and type correctly as social security numbers. You must remember to type a URL *carefully*. If you get even one number, letter, or punctuation mark wrong, the URL won't work, and you end up with an error message instead of a new Web page.

Note: Whether you type the characters in a URL in lowercase or uppercase usually doesn't matter, but using the capitalization that you're provided is the safest way to go.

On the up side, though, you seldom need to type a particular URL more than once. After the URL takes you to the Web page that it's associated with, you can press Ctrl+D to create a bookmark for the page and then simply click your bookmark in the future to return to the page.

Typing a URL in the Location box

Maybe we're a tad biased, but the first URL we want you to type goes to our *Dummies 101: Netscape Navigator* home page, whose URL is `http:// net.dummies.com/netscape101`.

Tip: The first part of our Dummies 101 Web page URL, *http://,* is the prefix for *all* Web page URLs, so you can skip typing it; when you press Enter, Netscape fills in the *http://* prefix for you automatically.

Notes:

to type in a URL, click inside the Location box and then enter your text

Figure 2-4: When you learn about a hot new Web page, check it out by typing its URL in Netscape's Location box.

Figure 2-5: You can find the *Dummies 101: Netscape Navigator* home page at `http://net.dummies.com/netscape101/`.

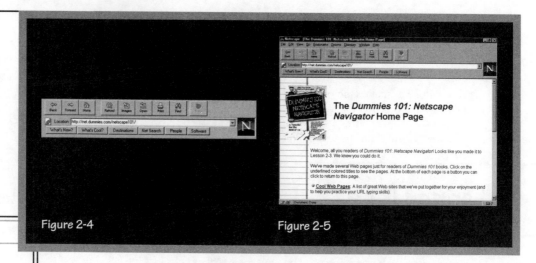

Figure 2-4   Figure 2-5

you can skip typing http:// for Web URLs because Netscape fills in that prefix for you

1 Run Netscape and connect to the Internet.

Your Netscape browser window should be maximized and displaying a Web page.

2 Click anywhere inside the Location box (that is, the box directly below the Home button).

The text inside the box — which is the URL of your current page — is highlighted by your click.

3 Type the letter n.

The first letter you type (*n*) immediately replaces the highlighted text.

4 Type et and a period.

The box contains *net.*, which is the beginning of the *Dummies 101: Netscape Navigator* URL (following the standard *http://* prefix, which you don't have to type). A URL can begin with anything, although many start with *www*, which, of course, stands for World Wide Web.

5 Type dummies and a period.

The box contains *net.dummies.* The word *dummies* provides the first clue that the page may be devoted to an IDG Books book (or to the musical group Crash Test Dummies).

6 Type com and a forward slash — that is, the / on the ? key.

Note: Be sure to not confuse / with the backslash (\ ), which you use to specify file locations on your hard disk.

The box contains *net.dummies.com/*. The *com* text is a three-letter code that tells you the page is published by a commercial organization. (A list of other three-letter codes used in URLs appears in "The wacky world of URLs" sidebar in Lesson 1-2.) You've now typed enough to specify the *Internet For Dummies Central* home page, which provides information about various . . .*For Dummies* books and their authors. This is a perfectly nice page and you should be sure to visit it later, but at the moment you want a different page, so you have one more piece of text to type.

7 **Type** netscape101.

The box contains *net.dummies.com/netscape101*. The *netscape101* text tells Netscape that you want the *Dummies 101: Netscape Navigator* home page, so you've completed typing the URL.

8 **Press Enter.**

You are on this book's home page, which looks similar to Figure 2-5. If you examine the Location box, you see that Netscape has automatically filled in the prefix and added a final slash so that the URL now reads `http://net.dummies.com/netscape101/`.

If you didn't connect properly, double-check your URL to make sure that you typed it correctly. If you did type the URL exactly as you see it in the book and you still don't reach the page, technical problems with the Dummies site may be blocking your progress — for example, the page may be too busy at the moment to accept your connection request — so just try again a little later until you access the page.

9 **Press Ctrl+D to create a bookmark for the page.**

You can't see it right now, but a bookmark pointing to the *Dummies 101: Netscape Navigator* page is added to the bottom of your bookmarks list.

10 **Choose the Bookmarks menu to verify that your bookmark has been created.**

The new bookmark appears at the bottom of the menu. If you've already created too many bookmarks to fit on the menu, choose Go To Bookmarks and press Ctrl+End to see the new bookmark. After you're done, press Ctrl+W to close the Bookmarks window.

Congratulations! You successfully typed a URL! You can now take advantage of any recommendation you receive about the latest and greatest Web pages.

Now that you're on the *Dummies 101: Netscape Navigator* home page, take a few moments to look it over. We use it quite a bit in subsequent exercises, so you may want to take some time to get to know it.

extra credit

Some popular Web pages

If you'd like to practice your newfound URL typing skills, try them on some of the cool Web sites listed on our *Dummies 101: Netscape Navigator* page! The list includes most of the Web sites in your bookmarks file (with up-to-date links!), as well as exciting new Web sites that have popped up since we created your bookmarks file. Flex your fingers and get typing!

Tip: If a Web URL begins with www and ends with com, you can simply type the middle portion of the URL to get to the appropriate page; Netscape fills in the rest of the URL for you automatically! For example, to jump to the first site on this list, www.amazon.com, you can just click in the Location box, type **amazon**, and press Enter. Try it!

☑ **Progress Check**

If you can do the following, you've mastered this lesson:

❑ Type a URL in Netscape's Location box.

❑ Use the URL you type to move to a Web page.

Copying URLs into the Location box

If a URL is printed on paper, you've gotta type it to use it. If a URL appears on your screen, though — say, as a result of a friend e-mailing it to you or the URL appearing in an article that you're reading online — you can simply copy the URL to the Windows Clipboard and then paste it into Netscape's Location box. Here's how:

1. **Click in front of the first character of the URL you want to copy.**

2. **While holding down your mouse button, drag the mouse's cursor over the URL until the entire electronic address is highlighted, and then release your mouse button.**

3. **Press Ctrl+C to copy the highlighted text to the (invisible) Windows Clipboard.**

4. **Click anywhere inside Netscape's Location box to highlight its current text.**

5. **Press Ctrl+V to paste in your URL.**

6. **Press Enter to activate the URL and jump to its Web page.**

Copying URLs saves your fingers a lot of energy that they can use to do more exploring on the Web.

Lesson 2-4   # Searching a Web Page for Information

When a Web page consists of only a few paragraphs, you can pick out the facts you want from it pretty easily. If a page is long and contains lots of text, though, you may appreciate some help locating the information you seek.

Netscape's Find button

That's why Netscape provides a Find command. Like the Find option in a word processor, it lets you search for a word or phrase in an electronic document. To summon the Find option, you can click Netscape's Find button, choose Edit⇨Find, or press the keystroke shortcut Ctrl+F. Any of these three actions pops up a Find dialog box. After you type your search text in the dialog box and press Enter, Netscape looks for occurrences of your text on the current Web page.

To try out the Find command, follow these steps to access and search through excerpts from William Shakespeare's classic play *Hamlet*:

1 If you aren't still connected to the Internet, dial in again now.

Your Netscape browser window should be maximized and displaying a Web page.

2 Move to the *Dummies 101: Netscape Navigator* home page by using the bookmark you created in Lesson 2-3.

You can also jump to the page by clicking inside Netscape's Location box, typing the URL **net.dummies.com/netscape101**, and pressing Enter.

3 Click Netscape's Find button (or choose Edit⇨Find or press Ctrl+F).

A Find dialog box like the one in Figure 2-6 appears. The dialog box contains a Find what box, where you type the word or phrase that indicates the subject you're looking for, and a Find Next button, to execute the search after you type

to search for a
word or phrase, click
the Find button,
choose Edit→Find,
or press Ctrl+F

Figure 2-6

Figure 2-6: Use the Find
dialog box to search for a
word or phrase on a Web
page.

Notes:

your search text. In addition, it has a Match case option that locates exact
uppercase and lowercase matches of your search text, and it has direction
buttons to specify whether to search Up or Down from your current position on
the page. For this exercise, leave the Match case box unchecked and leave the
Down button checked.

4. **Drag the Find dialog box to the bottom of the screen so that it
doesn't block your view of the page.**

   The Find what box and Find Next button should still be visible, but the rest of
   the dialog box can be hidden behind your Windows 95 Taskbar (or the bottom
   of your Windows 3.1 desktop).

5. **Type Hamlet in the Find what box and then press Enter to execute
the search.**

   The page jumps to the first (and, in this case, only) occurrence of the word
   Hamlet. This word is part of a link, so you can use it to move to a different
   page.

6. **Click the link associated with the word *Hamlet*.**

   The link is activated, and you move to a page containing excerpts from
   Shakespeare's immortal drama.

7. **Press Tab twice.**

   The text in the Find what box is highlighted.

8. **Type life to search for the various ways Shakespeare used this
word to weave poetic phrases in *Hamlet*.**

   The previous text in the Find what box *(Hamlet)* is replaced by the word *life.*

9. **Press Enter to execute the search.**

   The page jumps to the first occurrence of *life,* which is in Hamlet's bold
   proclamation concerning his pursuing a ghost: "I do not set my life at a pin's
   fee,/And for my soul, what can it do to that,/Being a thing immortal as itself?"

10. **Click Find Next to continue searching.**

    The page jumps to the second occurrence of *life,* which is in this terrible
    revelation by the ghost of Hamlet's father: "But know, thou noble youth,/The
    serpent that did sting thy father's life/Now wears his crown."

11. **Click Find Next to continue searching.**

    The page jumps to the third occurrence of *life,* which is in Hamlet's fearsome
    reply, "You cannot, sir, take from me anything that I will more willingly part
    withal — except my life, my life, my life."

12. **Continue clicking Find Next to locate more matches.**

    You should find *life* in several more places, including this section from Hamlet's
    most famous soliloquy: "To sleep, perchance to dream. Ay, there's the rub,/For
    in that sleep of death what dreams may come/When we have shuffled off this
    mortal coil/Must give us pause. There's the respect/That makes calamity of so
    long life."

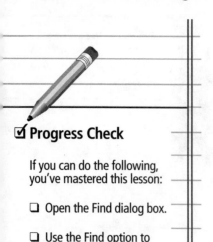

☑ **Progress Check**

If you can do the following, you've mastered this lesson:

❑ Open the Find dialog box.

❑ Use the Find option to locate a word or phrase on a Web page.

When you've found all the occurrences of life, a dialog box appears with the message `Search string not found`.

13 **Press the Esc key to close the dialog box and press Esc again to exit the Find box.**

The message box and Find dialog box disappear.

14 **Click Netscape's Back button.**

You return to the *Dummies 101: Netscape Navigator* home page.

That's all there is to searching for *any* type of text on a Web page. (We should probably add that you'll find most Web material to be considerably cheerier than *Hamlet* . . . though not nearly as well written.) The Find command can save you a lot of time, so make ample use of it when examining text-intensive Web pages.

Lesson 2-5

Searching the Entire Web for Information

on the test

Just as you can use Netscape's Find command to search a Web page for a word or phrase, you can use Internet search programs to scour the entire Web for pages dealing with a particular topic. Because literally *tens of millions* of Web pages exist — giving a whole new meaning to the phrase "information overload" — such search programs are indispensable for zeroing in on the data you need.

Happily, these *Web searchers* are available on the Web itself and can be accessed with just a few mouse clicks. Further, most of them are free! (The publishers of the Web searchers generate revenue by selling advertising space on their search sites or by selling related products.)

Because the Web is so enormous and ever-changing, no single search program can do a perfect job of finding the most appropriate pages dealing with your topic. A number of excellent Web searchers are available, though, so if you aren't satisfied with the results you get from one, you can simply turn to another.

Two different kinds of search programs exist. The first relies on human editors who attempt to bring order to the Web's chaos by organizing Web pages into large categories (for example, Government, Business, or Arts) and smaller subcategories (for example, Arts⇨Art History⇨Artists⇨da Vinci, Leonardo⇨ Leonardo da Vinci Drawings on Web page `http://banzai.msi.umn. edu/~reudi/leonardo.html`). This type of search program is best when you're researching a broad, popular topic that human editors are likely to have assigned a subcategory.

The second type of search program is *open-ended* — that is, it doesn't rely on any kind of predefined structuring or categorizing of Web pages. Instead, it depends entirely on its own intelligence to provide good matches for your search topic. Using an open-ended search program is best when you're researching a narrow or obscure topic. You learn more about the advantages and disadvantages of each approach shortly.

New Web searchers are constantly popping up on the Net. As we write this book, the following are some of the best search programs available:

on the test

- **AltaVista** (www.altavista.digital.com): Provides extremely fast, accurate searching of over 20 million Web pages. AltaVista comes the closest to being comprehensive, and it's one of our favorites.

- **Excite** (www.excite.com): Offers two fine services: a search program named NetSearch and a Web guide named NetDirectory that lists evaluations of sites organized by topic.

- **InfoSeek** (guide.infoseek.com): Produces highly accurate results within the confines of its database. InfoSeek is excellent at matching your search topic with relatively new Web pages, sometimes at the price of ignoring older Web sites.

- **Lycos** (www.lycos.com): Furnishes sophisticated search options (for example, letting you search for Web pages that mention Dean Martin but *don't* mention Jerry Lewis) and a huge Web page database. Lycos also offers a Web guide organized by category (a2z.lycos.com) and recommendations of top Web sites (www.pointcom.com).

- **Magellan Internet Directory** (www.mckinley.com): Gives you not only the names and URLs of the Web pages you're seeking but also reviews and ratings (from one to four stars) of many of the sites.

- **Yahoo!** (www.yahoo.com): The oldest major category-based search program and a great place to start when researching broad topics. Yahoo! isn't as comprehensive as some of the services in this list but, at the same time, it's likely to produce more targeted matches. Yahoo! also offers great features such as *Picks of the Week* (www.yahoo.com/picks), a savvy list of the best of the Web (www.yahoo.com/Entertainment/Cool_Links), a weekly listing of new Web sites (www.yahoo.com/weblaunch.html), and a search program devoted to finding Web sites for kids (www.yahooligans.com).

- **Savvy Search** (www.cs.colostate.edu/~dreiling/smartform.html): A high-level or "meta-search" program that, instead of scouring the Web directly, plugs your search word into several popular Web searchers and then gives you all the initial matches together on the same page, organized by search program! Use this tool to avoid the time and effort of entering text into each search program separately.

At this point, you're probably thinking, "Sounds great, but how can I easily get to all these different search programs?" Well, by an amazing coincidence, you can access them with a mouse click from our *Dummies 101: Netscape Navigator* home page!

heads up

Because there's no way to predict what may change on the Web, a Web searcher we discuss in this lesson may no longer be available (or available for free) when you try to access it. If this happens, don't sweat it — simply use a different search program instead. At the same time, keep an eye on our *Dummies 101: Netscape Navigator* Web site for links to fabulous new search programs as they become available.

Using a category-based Web searcher

To get started on your Web research skills, try using Yahoo! — a category-based Web searcher — to find Web sites dealing with movies.

Figure 2-7: Kick off your research from our Web search page, which lets you access many of the best Web search programs. To use a particular program, click in its search box, type your research topic, and press Enter.

Figure 2-8: Yahoo! generates a list of Web categories most relevant to your search topic. You can scan the list and select appropriate subcategories until you find at a list of pages on your specific topic.

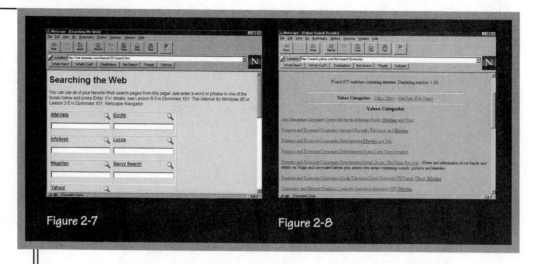

Figure 2-7   Figure 2-8

1 **If you aren't still connected to the Internet, dial in again now.**

Your browser window should be maximized and displaying a Web page.

2 **If you aren't on the *Dummies 101: Netscape Navigator* home page, move there by using the bookmark you created in Lesson 2-3.**

You can also jump to the page by clicking inside Netscape's Location box, typing the URL **net.dummies.com/netscape101**, and pressing Enter.

3 **Locate and click a link that contains the phrase *Web search*.**

You move to a page with text entry boxes linked to popular Web search programs (see Figure 2-7).

4 **Press Ctrl+D to create a bookmark for this Web search page.**

You can't see it right now, but a bookmark pointing to the Web search page is added to the bottom of your bookmarks list.

5 **Locate the Yahoo! search box and click inside the box.**

A blinking cursor appears inside the Yahoo! box to indicate that you can now enter your search text.

6 **Type *movies* to research movie-related Web sites; then press Enter.**

Your search request takes you to a Yahoo! page like the one in Figure 2-8. This page lists the first batch of categories in Yahoo!'s Web catalog that best match your search phrase *movies*. (You can display additional categories by clicking a link near the bottom of the page that says something like *Next 25 Matches*.)

7 **All the topics listed on the Yahoo Categories page are links. Locate the *Entertainment: Movies and Films* category and then click it. (If you don't see this topic, simply pick out and click a different broad movie category.)**

You move to a subgroup of categories within your selected category. Press PgDn once or twice to view the entire list.

8 **Pick out a listed category that interests you — for example, *Genres*, *Directors*, or *Actors and Actresses* — and then click it.**

You again move to a subgroup of categories within your selected category.

9 **Continue picking out and clicking categories that interest you until you work your way down to a list of specific Web sites.**

After you're done clicking through subcategories, you find yourself on a page listing the names and descriptions of Web sites that deal with the particular *movies* subtopic you selected. You can click the Web site names (which are links) to move to the pages they represent.

Notes:

As you just saw, a category-based guide to the Web such as Yahoo! (or, as another example, Excite's NetDirectory program) is especially useful for kicking off research on a broad topic. That's because the categories let you quickly see what kinds of information are available. Also, human editors make sure that the Web pages listed under each category are directly relevant, thus sparing you from wasting time with false leads.

However, this approach also has a few disadvantages. First, it forces you to do some work before arriving at a list of Web pages. Second, it's less likely to help you discover pages that aren't directly relevant but that you may find interesting anyway. Third, it's not as helpful for researching narrow or obscure topics, because category searchers tend to include fewer Web pages and center on popular subjects. That's why you should also use open-ended search programs. We discuss this method next.

Using an *open-ended* Web searcher

Open-ended Web searchers don't depend on human editors and don't list categories. Instead, these programs immediately present you with the names of Web sites related to your topic and ordered by relevance (based on such criteria as how often your search phrase appears on the Web page). Because they don't need Web pages to be preorganized into categories, these programs are free to include a lot more information; in fact, open-ended searchers such as AltaVista, InfoSeek, and Lycos typically cover tens of millions of Web pages, making them powerful tools for turning up raw information.

Because these programs can make only "intelligent guesses" about the relevance of a Web page to your search topic, they're likely to give you useful and useless sites mixed together, leaving you with the job of sifting through the list and identifying the pages that you really need. This approach is therefore best when you're looking for quick answers or a wide range of sites.

To get a feel for how open-ended searches work, use AltaVista to find Web sites devoted to Elvis Presley:

1 **Use the bookmark that you created in the preceding exercise (which is probably at the bottom of your bookmarks list) to return to the Web search page.**

You move back to the page you used to launch your Yahoo! search. (You can also reach this page by clicking inside Netscape's Location box, typing the URL **net.dummies.com/internet101/search.htm**, and pressing Enter.)

2 **Locate the AltaVista search box and then click inside the box.**

A blinking cursor appears inside the AltaVista box to indicate that you can now enter your search text.

3 **Type** Elvis Presley **to locate Web sites about the King of rock 'n' roll and then press Enter.**

You move to an AltaVista page, like the one in Figure 2-9, that lists an initial batch of Web pages it considers most relevant to your topic. Notice that each entry in the list includes the Web page's name and URL (both of which are links that you can use to jump to the page) and the first two lines of text from the page, which give you a sense of the page's contents.

4 **Use the PgDn key to read through the first batch of matches. To see more matches, click the number *2* or the word *Next* near the bottom of the page.**

Figure 2-9: AltaVista skips
Web categories by
directly generating a
list of Web pages it
considers the most
relevant to your search
topic.

Notes:

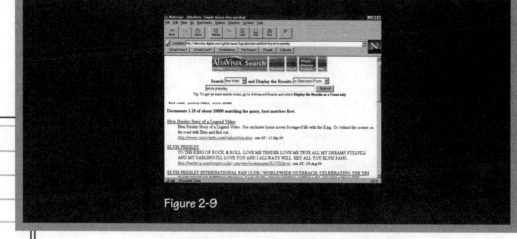

Figure 2-9

You move to the second set of matches. Similarly, you can move to the third, fourth, and fifth batch of matches by clicking the numbers or *Next* at the bottom of the page. You can go on like this for some time, because AltaVista has generated *thousands* of matches. Instead, try narrowing your search a bit by centering on Elvis's movie career.

5 **Use the bookmark you created in the preceding exercise to return to the Web search page, click in the AltaVista box following the *y* in your search phrase *Elvis Presley*, type a space and the additional word** movies, **and press Enter.**

You move to a new AltaVista screen that identifies Web pages dealing with Elvis Presley movies. This list of pages is a little more focused than the preceding list because it concerns a narrower topic.

6 **Click Netscape's Back button to return to the Web search page, use the Backspace key to delete the word *movies*, type the word** stamps **instead, and press Enter.**

You jump to a new AltaVista screen that lists Web pages dealing with Elvis stamps (such as the famous one issued in 1993). The results of this search are much more focused because this time your topic is quite narrow.

Using multiple Web searchers

Because every open-ended Web searcher has to *guess* at the relevance of a page to your interests, the quality of a program's matches can depend on luck. If you aren't satisfied with the sites that one search program generates, though, don't give up; simply run your search through one or two other programs.

1 **Use the last bookmark you created to return to the Web search page again, but this time choose a different search program (such as InfoSeek or Lycos). When you decide on the program to use, click in its search box, type** Elvis Presley, **and press Enter.**

You move to an initial list of Elvis Web pages generated by the program that you selected. Notice that the list is different from AltaVista's initial list (though you may see some overlap).

2 **Click Netscape's Back button to return to the Web search page, and again choose a different search program (such as Magellan or Excite). After you decide on the program to use, click in its search box, type** Elvis Presley, **and press Enter.**

Again, you move to an initial list of Elvis Web pages that's different from any of the others you've generated. You always get unique results from each Web searcher because each has its own methods of adding Web sites to its database, matching Web pages to a search phrase, and ranking the pages.

3 **Click the Back button to return to the Web search page, and this time use the meta-search program Savvy Search by clicking in its search box, typing** Elvis Presley, **and pressing Enter.**

You move to a list of initial matches from several different Web searchers (typically a mix of category-based and open-ended searchers), organized by program. If you want to delve further, you can click the link to the program that you feel produced the best matches. Doing a search in this way is more efficient than typing the search text yourself for each separate program.

extra credit

Narrowing your search

Your research results can be affected not only by which Web searcher you pick but also by the syntax you use to specify your topic! For example, in most search programs, the phrase *Princess Diana* matches Web pages that contain either *Princess* or *Diana*. To narrow the results, you can enclose the phrase in quotes *("Princess Diana")*, which forces the search to match only Web pages that contain the entire phrase *Princess Diana*.

on the test

To sum up, there's no one right way to search the Web. The program you use — and whether you use one Web searcher or several, or a meta-searcher like Savvy Search — depends on how general your search topic is, how comprehensive you need your research to be, how much work you want to do, and your personal tastes.

☑ Progress Check

If you can do the following, you've mastered this lesson:

❑ Research a subject by using a Web search program.

❑ Understand the difference between category-based and open-ended Web searchers.

❑ Use a variety of Web searchers.

❑ Avoid feeling overwhelmed by it all.

Unit 2 Quiz

For each of the following questions, circle the letter of the correct answer or answers. Remember, each question may have more than one right answer.

1. **To create a bookmark for a Web page, move to the page and:**

   A. Press Ctrl+D.

   B. Click the Bookmarks button.

   C. Choose Bookmarks⇨Add Bookmark.

   D. Fasten the page and the Bookmarks menu together by using the Glue command.

2. **To remove a bookmark:**

   A. Make it feel unwanted.

   B. Choose Bookmarks⇨Go To Bookmarks, click the bookmark, and choose Edit⇨Delete.

   C. Press Ctrl+B, click the bookmark, and press Del.

   D. Bookmarks are permanent and can't be removed.

Notes:

3. **To organize your bookmarks, you can:**

    A. Hold up a sign that says *Union!* in front of your screen.

    B. From the Bookmarks window, choose Item⇨Insert Folder to create folders for grouping the bookmarks.

    C. Automatically arrange them by color and pattern by using the Bookmarks⇨Auto Arrange option.

    D. Use the Cut, Copy, and Paste commands to move them to and from folders.

4. **If a newspaper article tells you about a great new Web page, you can check it out by:**

    A. Showing the article to Netscape and typing **Go fetch**.

    B. Clicking in the Location box, typing the Web page's URL, and pressing Enter.

    C. Closing your eyes, breathing deeply, and, like, letting your mind journey to the URL, man.

    D. Using a Web search program to locate the page and then clicking the page's link.

5. **To locate a word or phrase on a Web page:**

    A. Use the PgDn and PgUp keys to examine the page carefully.

    B. Use the Web Psychic program to make the desired text float to the front of your screen.

    C. Click Netscape's Find button, type your search text, and press Enter.

    D. Click in the Location box, type your search text, and press Enter.

Unit 2 Exercise

Apply what you've learned about using bookmarks and finding information on the Web by creating a mini-library of Web pages devoted to subjects that interest you.

1. Write down at least three topics that are dear to your heart.

2. Run Netscape and connect to the Internet.

3. Move to the AltaVista home page at `altavista.digital.com`.

4. Create a bookmark for the AltaVista page so you can return to it easily.

5. For each item on your list, search for Web pages devoted to the topic.

6. Whenever you locate a Web page that you feel is interesting, create a bookmark for it.

7. Repeat Steps 5 and 6 using the Yahoo! site at `www.yahoo.com`. (**Tip:** To move to the site, try typing just **yahoo** and letting Netscape fill in the rest of the URL.)

8. When you're done searching, create a new bookmark folder for each topic and then move each new bookmark into the appropriate folder.

9. Test your bookmarks by revisiting the Web pages you selected.

Saving Web Information and Downloading Files

Objectives for This Unit

✔ Printing Web pages

✔ Saving Web pages as text files

✔ Saving Web pages as HTML files

✔ Copying files from the Web

Prerequisites

▶ Cruising the Web with Netscape Navigator (Lesson 1-2)

▶ Creating bookmarks (Lesson 2-1)

▶ Entering URLs (Lesson 2-3)

▶ Searching for information on the Web (Lesson 2-5)

Printing and Saving Web Information   Lesson 3-1

In Unit 2, you learned how to use Netscape to locate information. If the information is complicated or important, though, you may want to preserve it in some way for further study offline.

Saving Web data allows you to examine the information you found at your leisure and to organize it, edit it, and reuse it. In addition, perusing text-heavy Web information from paper pages or your favorite word processor gives you the opportunity to mark up the text as you go along and saves you from racking up phone charges while you read.

You can preserve Web data by printing it to paper or by saving it to disk. Both methods are quick and easy.

on the test

You can print the contents of your current Web page by clicking Netscape's Print button, choosing File⇨Print, or pressing Ctrl+P. Doing any of these things pops up a Print dialog box with various options. To proceed with standard printing, just click OK.

Print

Netscape's Print button

Figure 3-1: Use the Print
dialog box to print the
contents of a Web
page.

Figure 3-1

Similarly, you can save the contents of your current Web page to disk by
choosing File⇨Save As or pressing Ctrl+S, which pops up a Save As dialog
box. After you type a filename (for example, **C:\WebData\NewFile**) and press
Enter, the file is saved to the hard disk location you specified.

To try out these convenient features — and also learn about various printing
and saving options — work through the next two exercises.

Printing the contents of a Web page

Although electronic mail and World Wide Web pages may ultimately save a
lot of trees, paper still has its uses. For example, paper pages are light,
portable, easy to read, and easy to mark up. They also can serve as a permanent record, as opposed to Web pages that can disappear overnight or even
computer file formats that can become obsolete after a number of years.
Finally, printing on paper lets you preserve the whole "look" of a Web page,
including its graphics, while saving to disk preserves a Web page's text but not
its graphics.

In Lesson 2-4, you searched through excerpts from Shakespeare's *Hamlet*.
Now follow these steps to print the text on the *Hamlet* Web page:

1   Run Netscape and connect to the Internet.

Your browser window should be maximized and displaying a Web page.

**2   Use the bookmark you created in Lesson 2-3 to move to the
    Dummies 101: Netscape Navigator home page.**

You can also move to the page by clicking inside Netscape's Location box,
typing the URL **net.dummies.com/netscape101**, and pressing Enter.

3   Locate and click the *Hamlet* link that you used in Lesson 2-4.

You move to the page containing the excerpts from *Hamlet*.

**4   Make sure that your printer is connected to your PC. Also, check
    that the printer is on, that its online light is on, and that it has at
    least ten pages in its paper tray.**

Your printer should be ready to print the contents of the Web page.

**5   Click Netscape's Print button (or choose File⇨Print, or press
    Ctrl+P).**

A Print dialog box like the one in Figure 3-1 appears. The dialog box contains a
Print range box that lets you print *A*ll the contents of the current Web page, a
range of paper Pages (for example, *from: 1 to: 2* prints only the first two paper

to print a Web page,
click the Print
button, choose
File→Print, or press
Ctrl+P

pages), or a Selection, which lets you print a highlighted section of the Web page. The box also lets you switch to a different printer; set the Number of copies to print; Collate your pages (meaning to print them in reverse order, or last page first); and Print to file, in case you want to save the output to disk (for example, if you're using a laptop and won't be able to print until later). Finally, the box provides a Properties button that lets you set such things as paper size and how fonts and graphics are handled. For now, accept the default settings by leaving the box as it is.

6 **Click the Print box's OK button.**

The Print box is replaced by a Printing Status box, which continually tells you what percentage of the Web page's contents have been processed for printing. When the processing is completed, the box closes and the actual printing of your Web page begins. (***Note:*** If the page does not print, double-check both your printer's status and the settings in the Print box.)

7 **After the page prints, check your pages against the contents of the Web page.**

The text and graphics on your paper pages should look the same as the text and graphics that appear on the electronic page.

extra credit

Changing print settings

If you ever need to adjust Netscape's standard print settings, you can do so in several ways:

▶ Choosing File⇨Page Setup lets you adjust such formatting features as page margins, page numbering, and headers and footers.

▶ Choosing File⇨Print⇨Properties (or, in Windows 3.1, File⇨Print⇨Setup) lets you switch to a different paper size, paper tray, and paper orientation (Portrait prints across the width of a page, and Landscape prints across the long side of a page). This option also lets you set how fonts and graphics are printed.

▶ Choosing File⇨Print Preview lets you see what your paper pages look like under the settings you've selected.

Although printing a Web page has many advantages, it also has drawbacks, such as the cost in paper and ink, the clutter that paper creates, and the difficulty of manipulating paper data (not to mention the possibility of nasty paper cuts). That's why Netscape also lets you save information to disk, which you can take on next.

Saving the contents of a Web page to disk

For long-term use, saving Web data to disk is often better than printing it because electronic text takes up much less space than paper and is significantly easier to search through and organize.

In addition, you can easily manipulate and reuse electronic data. For example, you can save stock prices from a Web page to a disk file and then import the file into a spreadsheet program or other analysis tool to crunch the numbers. As another example, you can periodically dump Web data that's pertinent to your job onto your hard disk and then edit the information in your word processor to produce savvy and timely office reports.

Notes:

You can save Web data in two file formats: text and HTML. Text format is understood by *all* PC programs, but it achieves that universality by ignoring formatting such as underlining, boldfacing, margins, fonts, and colors — basically, anything outside standard words, numbers, and punctuation. Saving information as text allows you to view and edit it in any program, but at the cost of the "look" of the Web page.

Conversely, saving a Web page as an HTML file preserves the look of the page (except for pictures, which are represented in the file by copies of a simple placeholder image). However, you can view HTML files properly only from a Web browser program such as Netscape. If you load them into another type of PC program instead, you see a messy jumble consisting of Web page text mixed together with confusing-looking formatting codes set in <brackets>. (For more information about HTML, see Unit 9.)

on the test

Because of these technical differences, you typically save Web information in text format so that you can view and edit the data by using other programs (such as your favorite word processor). You save in HTML format when you just want archival records of Web pages that you can re-examine at your convenience via Netscape.

Saving Web data as a text file

To save your data as a text file, turn once again to the *Hamlet* page.

1 **If you aren't still on the *Hamlet* Web page, move there now.**

If you need help finding the page, refer to Lesson 2-4.

2 **Choose File⇨Save As (or press Ctrl+S).**

A Save As dialog box like the one in Figure 3-2 appears. You use this box both to select the format you want to use for your disk file and to specify where on your hard disk you want to save the file.

If you're running Windows 95, the dialog box's large middle section is a File List that shows you the files in your current disk folder. To display the contents of a different folder, you can click inside the Save in box (above the File List) to display all your drives, click the drive you want, and then double-click the folder you want.

Alternately, you can click in the File name box (below the File List), type a new drive letter and folder name (for example, **C:\MyFolder**), and press Enter.

The dialog box also contains four buttons in its upper-right corner. You can use these buttons to move up one folder level (that is, to move from your subfolder to its parent folder); to create a new folder; to list files by name only (which lets you see more of them at a time); or to list each file followed by its size, type, creation date, and creation time.

Finally, you should notice the Save as type box at the bottom, which lets you specify both the type of files to appear in the File List and the format Netscape uses to save your Web page.

If you're running Windows 3.1, the file list appears on the left side of the Save As dialog box (under the File Name box). You can use the Drives box in the lower-right corner of the dialog box and the Directories box above it to move to the drive and folder in which you want to save the Web page.

3 **Move to a folder that is appropriate for storing Web data. For example, if you have a folder named *Data* on your C drive, double-click inside the File name box, type C:\Data, and press Enter.**

Your folder name appears in the Save in box.

to save the contents
of a Web page,
choose File→Save
As or press Ctrl+S

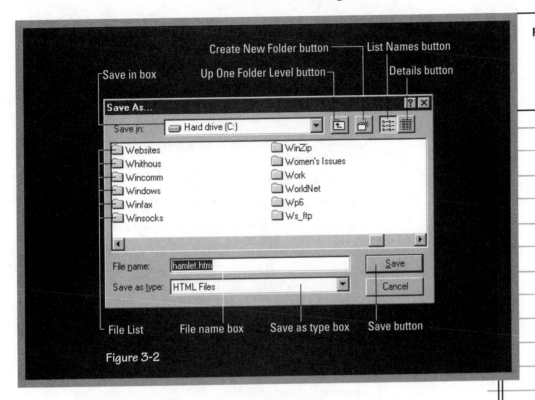

Figure 3-2

Figure 3-2: Use the Save As
dialog box to save the
contents of a Web page
as either a text file or an
HTML file.

4 Click anywhere inside the Save as type box.

Three options for displaying and saving files are listed: *HTML Files* for (you
guessed it!) HTML files, which all have filenames ending with the letters *htm*
or *html; Plain Text (*.txt)* for text files with names that happen to end with the
letters *txt;* and *All Files (*.*),* to display everything in the folder, including text
files that don't happen to end with the letters *txt.*

5 Click the All Files (*.*) option.

All the files in your current folder are listed.

**6 Click inside the Save as type box again, and this time click the
Plain Text (*.txt) option.**

Only files in your current folder with names ending in *txt* are listed. Use this
setting to save your Web page as a text document named Hamlet.txt.

**7 Double-click inside the File name box to highlight any text that is
already there and then type Hamlet.txt.**

Your filename Hamlet.txt is entered in the box.

8 Press Enter or click Save (or, if you're using Windows 3.1, click OK).

The text of your Web page is saved to the current drive and folder in the file
Hamlet.txt, and the Save As dialog box closes.

9 Again, choose File➪Save As or press Ctrl+S.

The Save As dialog box reopens.

**10 Click inside the Save as type box and click the Plain Text (*.txt)
option.**

You should now see the file Hamlet.txt listed, verifying that your text save was
successful.

Saving your data as an HTML file

Next, perform a similar operation to save your Web page as an HTML file.

Notes:

1 The Save As dialog box should still be open. Click inside the Save as <u>t</u>ype box and click the HTML Files option.

Only files with names ending in *htm* or *html* in your current folder are listed. Use this setting to save your Web page as an HTML document named Hamlet.htm.

2 Double-click inside the File <u>n</u>ame box to highlight any text that is there and then type Hamlet.htm.

Your filename Hamlet.htm is entered in the box.

3 Press Enter or click <u>S</u>ave (or, if you're using Windows 3.1, click OK).

Both the text and formatting of your Web page are stored to the current drive and folder in the file Hamlet.htm, and the Save As box closes.

Checking your saved text and HTML files

You've now finished saving your Web page in both text and HTML versions, so check out the files that you created.

1 Open Notepad, WordPad, or some other word processing program.

Both your word processor and Netscape should be running, with your word processor in the foreground.

2 Load the file Hamlet.txt into the word processor you're using. Specifically, for most Windows word processors, choose <u>F</u>ile⇨<u>O</u>pen; type the appropriate drive letter, folder name, and filename (for example, C:\Data\Hamlet.txt); and press Enter.

You should see a plain, all-text version of the current Web page. (If you notice any extraneous pieces of text, they're probably leftover HTML codes, which you should delete.) You can now use this Web data in the same way you would any other word processing document.

3 Save any revisions you made to the document (for example, by choosing <u>F</u>ile⇨<u>S</u>ave) and exit your word processor.

Both the document and the word processor close, returning the Netscape window to the front of your screen. Now examine the HTML file you created, which you can do by using Netscape's Open <u>F</u>ile option.

4 Choose <u>F</u>ile⇨Open <u>F</u>ile (if you're using the Standard edition of Netscape) or <u>F</u>ile⇨Open <u>F</u>ile in Browser (if you're using the Gold edition).

An Open dialog box (which has the same components as the Save As dialog box) appears.

to view an HTML file, choose <u>F</u>ile→Open <u>F</u>ile (Standard edition) or <u>F</u>ile→ Open <u>F</u>ile in Browser (Gold edition)

5 Type the appropriate drive letter, folder name, and filename (for example, C:\Data\Hamlet.htm), and then press Enter.

The HTML file you created appears in the Netscape window. The file looks very similar to the Web page that generated it. However, in place of the graphics on the Web page, the file has only copies of a simple placeholder image to represent the missing graphics.

6 Click the Back button.

You return to the Hamlet page out on the Web.

Whew! These file-saving exercises took a while to get through because they contain a lot of new material. Now that you have it all under your belt, though, you should have no trouble saving Web data. Typically, you press Ctrl+S to open the Save As box, set the format to Plain Text (*.txt), type an appropriate filename in the File name box, and press Enter. Easy as pie.

Saving a portion of a Web page

One other way that you can save Web data is by highlighting it and then copying it to the Windows Clipboard. This technique is handy when you're interested in only a portion of the Web page, because it spares you from having to save the entire document. Here's how to manage it:

1. **Click the beginning of the Web text that you want to copy.**

2. **While holding down your mouse button, drag over the section of text until all of it is highlighted, and then release your mouse button.**

3. **Press Ctrl+C to copy the highlighted text to the (invisible) Windows Clipboard.**

4. **Open a document in a word processor or other program in which you want to use the text.**

5. **Click the spot where you want to insert the text and then press Ctrl+V to paste it in.**

Keeping copyright issues in mind

As this lesson demonstrates, you can print or save to disk virtually any information you find on a Web page. However, that doesn't mean you're free to use the information without restraint. The text and pictures on Web pages are owned by the authors of those pages, and they are protected by U.S. copyright laws in the same way that the contents of books and magazines are protected. (This is true even if the pages don't display copyright notices.) For example, you can't publish large portions of text from a Web page without obtaining permission from the author, just as you can't publish long sections from a book or magazine article without permission.

If you need more information about U.S. copyright laws, a good place to start your research is the United States Copyright Office. To visit the Web home page of the Copyright Office, click inside Netscape's Location box, type **lcweb.loc.gov/copyright** and press Enter.

☑ Progress Check

If you can do the following, you've mastered this lesson:

❑ Print a Web page's contents.

❑ Save a Web page's contents as a text file.

❑ Save a Web page's contents as an HTML file.

❑ Open text and HTML files that you've created.

Using some discretion when preserving Web information is necessary, because cluttering up your desk or disk with nonessentials hinders your locating the facts you really need. (Comedian Steven Wright made this point succinctly when he observed, "You can't have everything. Where would you put it?") But as long as you restrict printing and saving to genuinely useful data, you'll find these features to be great aids on your journey along the Web.

Lesson 3-2

Downloading Files from the Web

In Lessons 2-5 and 3-1, you learned how to search Web pages for text information and save the data to disk. You can also search for and copy *files* from the Web to disk. The files may be programs (such as a new version of Netscape), pictures (ranging from the Mona Lisa to a Madonna poster), digital sounds (ranging from a Mozart sonata to the theme from *The Twilight Zone*), digital video (such as a clip of Neil Armstrong's famous first steps on the moon), or any other kind of data that you can use on your PC.

on the test

Getting files from another computer is called *downloading* because the data is typically loaded from a much larger computer system down to the hard disk of your PC. (Similarly, sending files from your PC to another computer is called *uploading*.)

To locate files to download, you can employ the same Web searchers you used in Lesson 2-5 for text research. Alternately, if you aren't sure what's available, you can cruise over to one of the many Web sites that specialize in distributing the latest and greatest program, picture, and sound files.

After you locate a file you want, you can initiate copying it to your PC by clicking its link. If the filename ends in a three-letter extension that Netscape recognizes — for example, *exe* for a program — a Save As dialog box appears. You can then specify the hard disk location and name for the file and press Enter to execute the download.

On the other hand, if the filename ends in a three-letter extension that Netscape does *not* recognize, you have to perform one extra step. Specifically, Netscape first displays an Unknown File Type dialog box that includes a Save File button. After you click the button, Netscape displays the Save As dialog box, which you can then use to download the file.

All that may seem complicated, but it really isn't — as we hope the next section demonstrates.

Searching for and downloading a file

You can find thousands of fun and useful files on the Internet. One of the most popular is WinZip, which is a data compression/decompression program — that is, it employs special tricks to shrink files by up to 90 percent of their usual size and then restores the files to normal size when needed. Many of the files stored online are compressed or *zipped* (as indicated by *zip* appearing as the last three letters of their filenames) to reduce the amount of time it takes to download them. After you copy the files, you need to run a program like WinZip to decompress them and make them useable.

Because WinZip is so handy, we feel that you should have a copy. We've already included it on this book's CD-ROM, just in case you don't feel like spending the time and phone charges to download the program. However, if you're willing to go the extra mile to learn about the downloading process — and get the guaranteed latest version of WinZip in the bargain — then follow these steps:

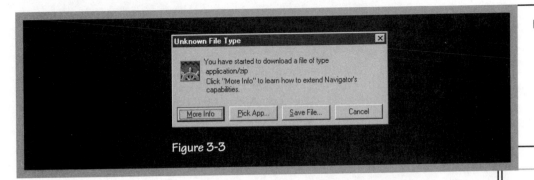

Figure 3-3

Figure 3-3: When you
activate a link leading to
a file type that Netscape
doesn't recognize, it
displays the Unknown
File Type dialog box.
Click the S̲ave File button
to download the file.

1 **Create a folder in advance for storing WinZip. If you're using Windows 95, click the Start button (in the bottom-left corner of the screen), click Programs, and click Windows Explorer; choose File➪New➪Folder to create the folder; type** WinZip **to name it; and click the Close button in Windows Explorer's upper-right corner to exit. If you're using Windows 3.1, run File Manager, choose File➪ Create Directory, type** WinZip **for the folder name, and press Enter.**

Your new folder is created. Make a note of its name and location (for example, C:\WinZip) because you'll use the folder shortly.

2 **If you aren't still connected to the Internet, dial in again now.**

Your browser window should be maximized and displaying a Web page.

3 **Move to the Web search page by using the bookmark you created in Lesson 2-5.**

You also can reach this page by clicking inside Netscape's Location box, typing the URL **net.dummies.com/netscape101/search.htm**, and pressing Enter.

4 **Locate the AltaVista search box and then click inside the box.**

A blinking cursor appears inside the box to indicate that you can enter your search text.

5 **Type** "winzip home page" **(including the quotation marks) and press Enter to find the Web site of the publisher of WinZip.**

You jump to an AltaVista list of Web pages that distribute — or, at minimum, *mention* — WinZip. The WinZip home page (which, at the time we're writing this book, has the URL www.winzip.com) should be listed at least once among the first batch of matches. (If you don't see the WinZip home page at first, try looking at additional matches by clicking the Next option near the bottom of the page.)

6 **When you locate a link to the WinZip home page, click the link.**

If you can't locate the link, click inside Netscape's Location box, type the URL **www.winzip.com**, and press Enter. You should move to the WinZip site.

7 **Locate the link that leads to the WinZip file (for example, a Download WinZip button or Download Evaluation Copy graphic) and click the link.**

You move to another page that offers narrower options leading to the file.

8 **Continue clicking appropriate options until you work your way to the link that lets you download the latest version of WinZip for Windows 95 (if you're using Windows 95) or WinZip for Windows 3.1 (if you're using Windows 3.1). After you find the link, click it.**

A Save As dialog box may appear. If it does, skip to Step 10.

If a Save As dialog box does not appear, an Unknown File Type dialog box like the one in Figure 3-3 appears. Notice that among its options is a S̲ave File button.

9 **Click the Save File button.**

A Save As dialog box (just like the one you used in Lesson 3-1 to save Web page data) appears. Notice that the name of the file you want has been entered for you automatically in the File name box.

10 **If the Save in box isn't already set to your WinZip folder, click inside the box to display your drives, click the drive on which your WinZip folder is stored (typically C), and then double-click folders until the folder you created to hold WinZip is selected.**

The name of the folder you created in Step 1 appears in the Save in box.

11 **Press Enter or click Save to initiate the download.**

The file is copied to your hard disk. A Saving Location box that continually tells you how much data has been transmitted and how much time is left for the transfer appears. After the entire file has been copied, the box closes.

12 **Open Windows Explorer (if you're using Windows 95) or File Manager (if you're using Windows 3.1) and switch to your WinZip folder.**

You should see a WinZip file in the otherwise empty folder. This file is actually a collection of many compressed files packaged with an installation program. To make WinZip useable, first run the current file.

13 **Double-click the WinZip file.**

The file runs a setup program. Follow the instructions that the program gives to complete your installation of WinZip, and/or see Appendix B for more information. Also see Appendix B for instructions for using WinZip to decompress files.

Congratulations! You successfully downloaded one of the hottest programs on the Internet! Just as important, you can use the same procedure to find and download thousands of *other* popular files. And when the files you download are zipped (and it's likely that lots of them will be), you can now use WinZip to decompress them quickly and make them useable.

Poking around Web sites for files

As efficient as Web searchers are, you shouldn't rely on them entirely to find files. That's because new kinds of files that you may not even dream exist, let alone think to search for, come out all the time. Therefore, you should also nose around Web sites devoted to program and data files occasionally and see if anything new catches your fancy. In fact, why not try that now?

1 **If you aren't still connected to the Internet, dial in again.**

Your browser window should be maximized and displaying a Web page.

2 **Click inside the Location box to highlight the current URL, type www.clicked.com/shareware, and press Enter.**

You move to the Top 20 Clicked Shareware Gallery, which provides what this site considers to be the best 20 programs in each of various categories such as the Internet, graphics, multimedia, and games. Explore the site at your leisure and download any files that you think would be genuinely useful (but avoid cluttering your disk with files that you don't really need).

use WinZip to decompress zipped files

3 **Click inside the Location box to highlight the current URL, type www.shareware.com, and press Enter.**

You move to the SHAREWARE.COM site, which offers thousands of different kinds of files, including word processors, electronic spreadsheets, database programs, picture files, sound files, and more. Snoop around the site's many different areas, including its This Week's Most Popular list.

4 **Click inside the Location box to highlight the current URL, type www.jumbo.com, and press Enter.**

You move to Jumbo!, a lighthearted site that also offers thousands of files (including lots of games). Poke around its nooks and crannies, and download any files that you feel may bring you joy.

5 **Click inside the Location box to highlight the current URL, type www.winsite.com, and press Enter.**

You move to WinSite, a site devoted to Windows programs. Again, look around until you're satisfied.

These four sites are by no means the only ones with interesting files available for downloading. For example, two others are listed in the *Software Libraries* category of your predefined bookmarks: The Ultimate Collection of Winsock Software (www.tucows.com) and Stroud's Consummate Winsock Applications (www.stroud.com or www.cwsapps.com), both of which let you download helpful Internet programs that work under Windows.

And if all those sites still don't fulfill your craving for data, you can use Web searchers, links, magazine articles, and the advice of friends to find more. In addition, be sure to check in periodically with our *Dummies 101: Netscape Navigator* home page (net.dummies.com/netscape101) for recommendations of new software distribution sites as they pop up!

heads up

As you download programs and other files, you should keep in mind that many of them — including WinZip — are *not* free. Instead, they're *shareware,* which means that they're available to you for an evaluation period (typically, anywhere from 30 to 90 days). If you decide that you like a shareware program and want to keep using it, you're expected to send a registration fee to its publisher, which entitles you to technical support and notifications about new versions.

Most shareware operates on an honor system, so the programs continue working even if you don't register them. However, it's a good idea to support the shareware concept and encourage the continued production of quality low-cost software by sending in your payment for the programs you use. For more information about paying for shareware, see the registration information that's contained in a text file included with each program.

heads up

One last thing to keep in mind when downloading a program is that there's a tiny risk that your running it will infect your hard disk with a computer virus. Contrary to the hype from the popular press, the odds of encountering a virus are very low, especially if you stick to well-maintained Web sites that test each program before offering it for downloading. Still, viruses that can infect and destroy your hard disk's data *do* exist, so it's sensible to run a virus detection program before launching any new software that you aren't certain is virus-free. You can buy a virus checker from a software store, or you can simply download one from the Web. For example, among the most popular antivirus programs are two shareware products named VirusScan and WebScan. You can download the most up-to-date versions of these programs from the McAfee Associates Web site at www.mcafee.com (see the exercise at the end of this unit).

Notes:

☑ **Progress Check**

If you can do the following, you've mastered this lesson:

❏ Find files on the Web.

❏ Download files from the Web.

❏ Understand the importance of paying for shareware you use regularly.

Unit 3 Quiz

Notes:

For each of the following questions, circle the letter of the correct answer or answers. Remember, each question may have more than one right answer.

1. **Printing a Web page is helpful because:**

   A. The Web is constantly changing, and there's always a chance that the information on a given Web page will disappear suddenly.

   B. Printing preserves the look of a Web page, including its graphics.

   C. Reading from paper pages is often easier on the eyes than reading from a computer screen.

   D. You can carry paper pages anywhere and read them at any time, even when you don't have access to a PC.

2. **To print a Web page:**

   A. You must first obtain a printing license.

   B. You press Ctrl+P and then Enter.

   C. You click the Print button and then click OK.

   D. You choose File➪Print and then click OK.

3. **Saving Web page information to disk is helpful because:**

   A. Limiting paper usage saves both money and trees.

   B. Electronic data is easier to analyze, edit, and reorganize than paper data.

   C. Storing electronic data requires less space than storing paper data.

   D. You can study the page in Netscape later when you're not online to avoid additional phone and/or connect charges.

4. **To save a Web page:**

   A. Pray for it nightly.

   B. Click the Save button and click OK.

   C. Choose File➪Save As, select a file type by using the Save as type box, type a filename in the File name box, and press Enter.

   D. Sock away a little bit of Web data every day and be patient.

5. **To get, or *download*, a file from the Web:**

   A. Swipe it when nobody's looking and hope that you don't get caught.

   B. Offer one of your own files to the Web and try to work out a trade.

   C. Choose File➪Download, enter a filename in the Download To box, and click OK.

   D. Click on the file's link, click the Save To Disk button on the Unknown File Type dialog box, select an appropriate folder by using the Save As dialog box, and press Enter.

Unit 3 Exercise

In this exercise, apply what you've learned about finding files and copying them from the Web by downloading an up-to-date version of the antivirus program named VirusScan.

1. Run Netscape and connect to the Internet.

2. Move to a page that lets you access a Web search program (for example, this book's Web search page at net.dummies.com/ internet101/search.htm).

3. Use a Web searcher (for example, AltaVista) to locate the McAfee Associates home page.

4. Find a Web page on the McAfee site that describes the VirusScan program.

5. Print the page.

6. Save the page's contents as a text file.

7. Locate the link that downloads the shareware version of the VirusScan program. At the time we write this, the page that contains the link is located at URL ftp://ftp.mcafee.com/pub/antivirus/, the VirusScan for Windows 95 link begins with the characters *v95* (for example, v95i205e.zip), and the VirusScan for Windows 3.1 link begins with the characters *wsc* (for example, wsci251e.zip). However, the URL and/or the names of the links may have changed by the time you read this. If you see a link named 00-index.txt, click it; doing so typically displays descriptions of each file on the page you're on.

8. Using the appropriate link, download the VirusScan program to your hard disk.

9. Disconnect from the Internet.

10. If the VirusScan file is zipped, use WinZip to decompress it and make its contents useable. (Information about using WinZip appears in Appendix B.)

11. Run VirusScan now to ensure that your hard disk is clear of viruses, and run it again before using any program for the first time that you think could possibly contain a virus.

Fine-Tuning the Browser

Prerequisites
▶ Cruising the Web with Netscape (Lesson 1-2)
▶ Using bookmarks (Lesson 2-1)
▶ Entering URLs (Lesson 2-3)
▶ Using Netscape Toolbar buttons (Lessons 1-2, 2-4, and 3-1)

Objectives for This Unit

✓ Cruising the Web without viewing pictures to speed up performance

✓ Using multiple Netscape windows to speed up performance

✓ Hiding Netscape window elements to expand Netscape's Web page display

✓ Using menu options in place of the Toolbar buttons and the Location box

✓ Changing the appearance of the Toolbar, links, and fonts

✓ Setting up a helper application

Now that you're an expert at getting around the Web, you're ready to take a closer look at the program you're using to do your cruising. This final unit on the Web therefore concentrates on special features of Netscape Navigator.

In this unit, you'll learn how to change Netscape's settings to help you get to Web pages more quickly. You'll also find out how to adjust Netscape's appearance to make it both more attractive and more efficient for your particular needs.

Enhancing Netscape's Performance   Lesson 4-1

If you haven't been frustrated by how *l-o-n-g* it takes for Web pages to be transferred to your screen, you're probably using a super-fast computer system and don't have much need for this lesson (though we recommend that you at least skim it to see whether any of the options discussed interest you).

However, if Web pages *do* take an awfully long time to appear on your screen, your system may have some limitations. For example, your modem may be slower than the current standard speed of 28,800 bits per second (or *bps*), which puts a ceiling on how rapidly your PC can receive data.

Notes:

to prevent Web page
pictures from being
transmitted, choose
Options→Auto Load
Images to turn off
the option

Netscape's Images
button

Another possibility is the amount of electronic memory in your system. Today's PCs tend to come with 16MB to 32MB of memory. If your system has less memory, your PC operates less efficiently, and that affects its performance on the Web.

A third factor is the speed of your computer's "brain," which is called a *central processing unit* chip or *CPU.* Modern CPUs include the Pentium and the Pentium Pro, which are faster than such older models as 486 and 386 CPUs.

Upgrading your computer system isn't your only option for boosting performance, though; you can choose to take advantage of some special Netscape features. The next two sections tell you how.

Cruising without pictures

If you don't care to spend lots of money making your computer system faster, you can still improve your cruising speed on the Web dramatically by making one simple adjustment to Netscape: Tell it to skip the pictures!

Specifically, you can choose Options⇨Auto Load Images to tell Netscape *not* to transmit any images that appear on a Web page and instead show only a simple placeholder graphic for each image. This setting makes transfers go a lot faster because text can move rapidly over the Web. Delays are caused almost entirely by graphics, which require much more data to be displayed on a computer than text does (proving once again that a picture is worth a thousand words).

When Auto Load Images is turned off, you still have the option of seeing the pictures on a Web page, but only when you explicitly *force* Netscape to get the data. You accomplish that by clicking Netscape's Images button, or choosing View⇨Load Images, or pressing Ctrl+I, which causes the graphics of the current Web page to be sent to your screen.

Follow these steps to see whether you prefer cruising the Web without pictures:

1 Run Netscape and connect to the Internet.

Netscape should be maximized and displaying a Web page. Notice that one of the Netscape buttons is named Images and is dimmed to indicate that it's unavailable. That makes sense because you're currently set to receive *all* Web page images automatically, so clicking the button right now to receive images would be redundant.

Also notice that one of the Netscape menus is named Options. This menu contains a number of settings that you can switch off and on.

2 Click the Options menu to open it.

Nearly a dozen options appear. One of them is Auto Load Images, which has a check mark to its left to indicate that it's currently turned on.

3 Click Auto Load Images to turn off the option.

The menu closes and the switch is turned off, meaning that Web pictures will now be blocked from your screen. Also, the Images button lights up to indicate that it's available for use.

4 Click the Options menu again to double-check your setting.

The Auto Load Images option no longer has a check mark next to it, showing that you've successfully turned it off. Now move to a Web page to try out your new setting.

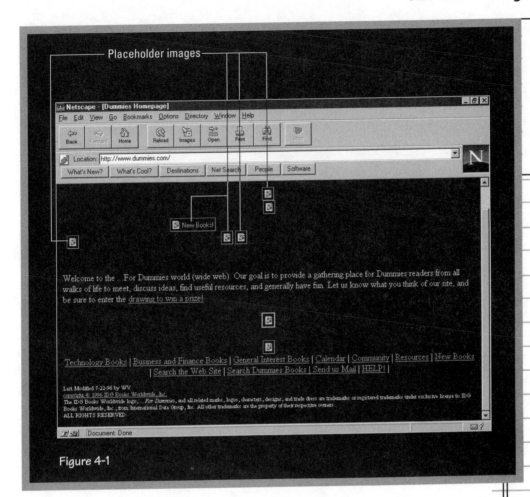

Figure 4-1

Figure 4-1: When you turn off the Auto Load Images switch, Netscape substitutes a placeholder image for a Web page's actual pictures. (Compare with Figure 4-2, which shows the page's pictures.)

5 **Click anywhere inside Netscape's Location box.**

The text inside the box is highlighted.

6 **Type the URL** www.dummies.com.

The highlighted text is replaced by your URL.

7 **Press Enter.**

You move to the . . .For Dummies home page of IDG Books Worldwide, a company that publishes many wonderful books (including, by a remarkable coincidence, the one you're reading!). Notice that the Web page was transferred to your PC unusually quickly. Also notice that no graphics are on the page except for a standard placeholder image that Netscape substitutes for the page's actual pictures (as shown in Figure 4-1).

8 **Click the Images button (or choose View⇨Load Images, or press Ctrl+I).**

The Web page is retransmitted, but this time with its pictures included. Unless you have a very fast system, the data transfer takes noticeably longer to complete this time. On the other hand, the Web page is now much more lively and attractive (see Figure 4-2).

9 **Explore the Dummies Web site by clicking links that interest you. Whenever you move to a page that you find especially intriguing, click the Images button to see the page's graphics.**

If you find that moving from page to page without having to wait for pictures to be copied over is a lot easier, consider keeping the Auto Load Images switch turned off in the future. To perform the remaining exercises in this unit, however, turn the switch back on.

Netscape's standard placeholder image

to force a Web page's images to be transmitted, click the Images button, choose View→Load Images, or press Ctrl+I

Figure 4-2: When you click the Images button, you force Netscape to retransmit a Web page with the page's pictures included.

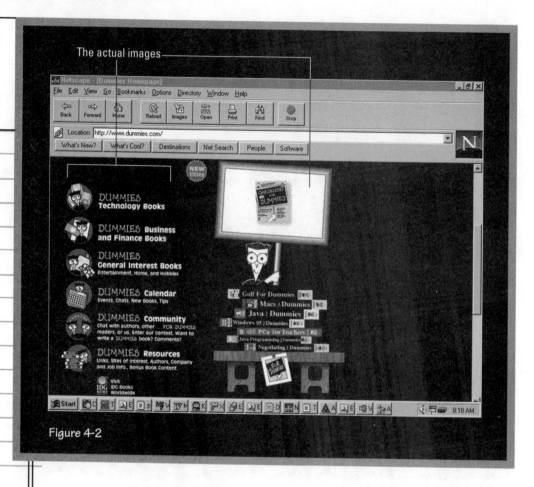

Figure 4-2

Notes:

10 **Choose Options⇨Auto Load Images to turn automatic picture loading back on.**

The menu closes, and the Images button dims to indicate that you're once again set to accept Web page pictures as well as text.

To sum up, the Auto Load Images switch lets you choose between the pleasure of Web graphics and the pleasure of speedy cruising. Which you opt for depends in part on the reason you're using the Web — for example, pictures aren't as important for research as they are for entertainment — and on just how exasperated you are by the amount of time it takes for Web pages to appear on your screen. If you *do* decide to run with the Auto Load Images switch turned off, don't forget that you can still display the pictures on a Web page by clicking the Images button.

extra credit

Displaying a single picture

Sometimes you aren't interested in seeing *all* the pictures on a Web page, but just a *particular* picture. Rather than click the Images button and wait for the whole page to be retransmitted, you can simply click the placeholder for the picture you're curious about. Doing so causes the data for that single picture to be transmitted, which typically takes much less time than reloading the entire page.

Figure 4-3

Figure 4-3: When you open two or more browsers, you can switch between them by clicking their windows or their buttons on the Windows 95 Taskbar.

Using multiple browsers

People say that two heads are better than one. After reading this section, you may decide that the same is true of browsers! That's because you can increase your efficiency by using two (or more) Netscape browser windows at the same time.

Running multiple browsers allows you to study the information on one Web page while Web data is transferring in the background to a different Netscape window. It also lets you switch between several Web pages without having to wait for any of the pages to reload.

on the test

Opening a new browser is a snap; just choose File⇨New Web Browser or press Ctrl+N. You can do so as often as you like (up to the limits of your PC's memory), but it's generally best to avoid running more than two or three browsers at a time to avoid confusion.

To explore the advantages of using multiple browser windows, follow these steps:

1 If you aren't still connected to the Internet, dial in again now.

Your Netscape browser window should be open and displaying a Web page. If you're running Windows 95, notice that the Netscape Navigator icon (a ship's navigation wheel) appears as a button on the Windows 95 Taskbar to represent your current window.

2 Choose File⇨New Web Browser (or press Ctrl+N).

A second browser window opens on top of your first one. If the second window is maximized (that is, completely covering your initial window), it may not be obvious that you have two browsers running. However, you can verify it by noticing that the Windows 95 Taskbar now has two Netscape Navigator buttons to represent the two browsers. Alternately, you can verify it by resizing the windows so that both are visible at the same time (as shown in Figure 4-3).

3 Access the home page of *USA Today* (which gives you the day's news) by clicking anywhere inside Netscape's Location box, typing the URL www.usatoday.com, and pressing Enter.

In your second browser window, you move to the *USA Today* Web site.

4 On the Windows 95 Taskbar, click the Navigator button representing your first browser window (that is, the button that is *not* currently pushed in). If you're using Windows 3.1, click the window itself.

to open another browser window, choose File→New Web Browser or press Ctrl+N

You switch to your first browser, which still displays your initial Web page, proving that your two Netscape windows are operating independently of each other. Now that you have two browsers open, you can read the information in one while transferring Web data to the other.

5 **Access the home page of MTV (a Web site that typically contains a lot of graphics) by clicking inside Netscape's Location box, typing the URL www.mtv.com, and pressing Enter.**

Your first browser connects to the MTV site and begins transmitting its Web page data. MTV typically crams lots of pictures onto its pages, though, so instead of waiting for the process to complete itself, make good use of your time by switching to your second browser window.

6 **On the Windows 95 Taskbar, click the Navigator button represent-ing your second browser window (that is, the button that is *not* currently pushed in). If you're using Windows 3.1, click the window itself.**

The *USA Today* home page is displayed again. Spend a minute or two scrolling through the page to read today's headlines and see what articles are available.

7 **On the Windows 95 Taskbar, click the Navigator button represent-ing your first browser window (that is, the button that is *not* currently pushed in). If you're using Windows 3.1, click the window itself.**

You should see the complete MTV home page. While you were reading today's news, all the data on this Web page was transmitted in the background. Examine the MTV page until you're ready to exit it.

8 **Press Ctrl+W (or choose File⇨Close) to close your second browser window.**

The window exits, returning you to your first browser window.

9 **If your browser window isn't maximized any longer, click its Maximize button.**

The window fills the screen, providing you with a large Web display.

This exercise demonstrates only one use of multiple browsers. As you become comfortable juggling several browser windows simultaneously, you're likely to find additional uses suited to your particular work habits that help you save time and avoid frustrating waits.

☑ Progress Check

If you can do the following, you've mastered this lesson:

❏ Prevent Web page pictures from being transmitted.

❏ Use the Images button to receive Web page pictures.

❏ Open and use multiple Netscape browser windows.

Lesson 4-2

Adjusting Netscape's Appearance

Netscape is surprisingly flexible in the ways it lets you display both itself and Web data. For example, you can hide and expand parts of its window, adjust how links appear, select different fonts and colors, and even choose to operate in a different language! This lesson shows you how to use such options to tailor Netscape's appearance to your personal tastes.

Eliminating Netscape window elements

Only about two-thirds of your Netscape window is normally available for displaying Web pages. The rest of the window is taken up by such elements as the Toolbar buttons and the Location box (which you used in previous

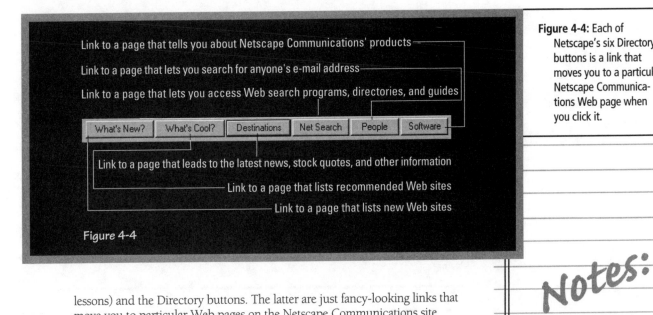

Link to a page that tells you about Netscape Communications' products

Link to a page that lets you search for anyone's e-mail address

Link to a page that lets you access Web search programs, directories, and guides

| What's New? | What's Cool? | Destinations | Net Search | People | Software |

Link to a page that leads to the latest news, stock quotes, and other information

Link to a page that lists recommended Web sites

Link to a page that lists new Web sites

Figure 4-4

Figure 4-4: Each of Netscape's six Directory buttons is a link that moves you to a particular Netscape Communications Web page when you click it.

lessons) and the Directory buttons. The latter are just fancy-looking links that move you to particular Web pages on the Netscape Communications site when you click them (see Figure 4-4).

Although these elements in your Netscape window are convenient, they are *not* necessities. That's because the functions that the Toolbar buttons and Location box provide are all duplicated in Netscape's menu options; you can replicate the Directory button links by creating bookmarks that point to the same Web pages. As a result, you may want to consider eliminating some or all of these items to make more room in the window for your Web page display. Here's how:

1 If you aren't still connected to the Internet, dial in again now.

Your Netscape window should be maximized and displaying a Web page.

2 Click the Options menu.

Notice that three of the options listed are Show Toolbar, Show Location, and Show Directory Buttons, and that they all have check marks next to them to indicate that they're currently turned on.

3 Click Show Toolbar to hide the Toolbar buttons.

The menu closes — and the Toolbar disappears! Also, the Web page display expands to take advantage of the additional space you created in the window.

4 Choose Options⇨Show Location to hide the Location box.

The Location box disappears. Also, the Web page display expands again to take advantage of the extra space.

5 Choose Options⇨Show Directory Buttons to hide this window element.

The Directory buttons disappear, and the Web page expands to take up most of the window (as shown in Figure 4-5).

on the test

Adjusting Netscape to devote an extra-large area for displaying Web pages doesn't require sacrifices in functionality, because you can still access all the usual Netscape commands by using menu options. For example, instead of using a constantly available Location box, you can choose File⇨Open Location or press Ctrl+L to open a temporary Location box that exits after you type a URL and press Enter. As another example, instead of clicking the Back button, you can choose Go⇨Back or press Alt+← (that is, Alt and the left arrow key). A complete list of Toolbar button equivalents appears in Table 4-1.

Notes:

use the Options menu to hide or restore the Toolbar, Location box, and Directory buttons

open a temporary Location box by clicking the Open button, choosing File→Open Location, or pressing Ctrl+L

Figure 4-5: When you eliminate optional elements in Netscape's window, you make more room for Web pages to be displayed.

Figure 4-5

Table 4-1	**Toolbar Button Equivalents**	
Toolbar Button	*Equivalent Menu Option*	*Equivalent Keystroke*
Back	Go⇨Back	Alt+←
Forward	Go⇨Forward	Alt+→
Home	Go⇨Home	None available
Reload	View⇨Reload	Ctrl+R
Images	View⇨Load Images	Ctrl+I
Open	File⇨Open Location	Ctrl+L
Print	File⇨Print	Ctrl+P
Find	Edit⇨Find	Ctrl+F
Stop	Go⇨Stop Loading	Esc

extra credit

The Reload button

The one item in the Toolbar that we haven't discussed yet is the Reload button. As its name implies, this button forces your current Web page's contents to be retransmitted, or *reloaded,* to your Netscape window. This feature is useful because the Web transfers only a "snapshot" of a page at the moment you access it, so what you're viewing doesn't reflect subsequent changes that occur on the Web page. If you're connected to, say, a page of stock quotes that's updated every minute, you need to click Reload periodically to get the latest information from the page.

Another reason you may be viewing old Web data is because Netscape uses a portion of your hard disk to temporarily store pages you've recently traveled to. When you tell Netscape to return to a page you've visited, it checks its storage area and, if the page is there, loads the page from your hard disk immediately instead of making you wait for it to be recopied from the Web. This is a great time-saver when you're accessing Web pages that don't change frequently. If you suspect that a page has changed since your last visit, though, clicking Reload forces Netscape to copy it again from the Web.

Finally, if a Web page you cruise to doesn't transfer properly for some reason, you can click Reload to make Netscape resend the page to your PC.

Although you don't *need* to include the Toolbar, the Location box, and the Directory buttons in your window, you may prefer having their options displayed conveniently in place of having a larger Web page display. Happily, you can always restore these window elements quickly by turning their switches back on. Follow these steps:

1 Click the Options menu.

Notice that the Show Toolbar, Show Location, and Show Directory Buttons options lack check marks next to them, indicating that these switches are currently turned off.

2 Click Show Toolbar to restore the Toolbar buttons.

The Web page display shrinks to provide some extra room in the window, and the Toolbar reappears.

3 Choose Options⇨Show Location to restore the Location box.

The Web page display shrinks some more, and the Location box comes back.

4 Choose Options⇨Show Directory Buttons to restore this window element.

The Web page display returns to its standard size, and the Directory buttons reappear.

Whether you decide to devote a larger area of your window to the Web page display or accept the standard Netscape window is entirely a matter of taste. Therefore, simply choose an arrangement that you're comfortable with and that pleases your eye.

Changing fonts, colors, and other Netscape settings

In addition to rearranging your Netscape window, you can adjust the way the Toolbar is displayed, how links appear, what colors and fonts you see in your Web display — and even which Web page pops up when you run Netscape!

Notes:

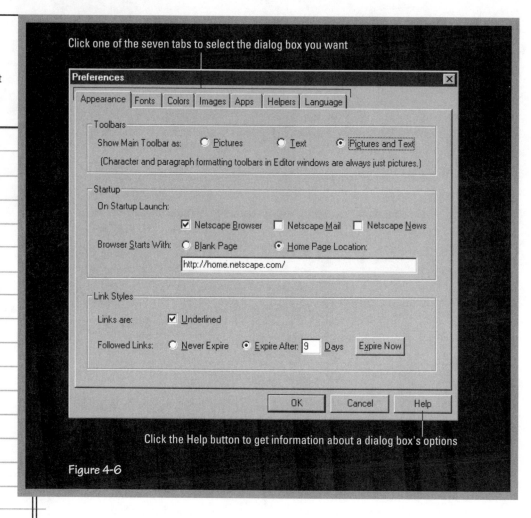

Click one of the seven tabs to select the dialog box you want

Click the Help button to get information about a dialog box's options

Figure 4-6

You can revise any or all of these settings by choosing Options⇨General Preferences and then selecting the appropriate dialog box. To discover the many varied, amusing, and astounding choices that Netscape offers you, follow these steps:

1 Choose Options⇨General Preferences.

A Preferences box like the one in Figure 4-6 appears. As you can see from the tab headings near its top, the settings in Preferences are organized into seven different dialog boxes: Appearance, Fonts, Colors, Images, Apps, Helpers, and Language. You'll explore each of these boxes.

2 If the Appearance dialog box isn't already displayed, click the Appearance tab.

You see an Appearance dialog box divided into three sections. The top section lets you display the Toolbar as all-text or all-pictures, or both (which is the default).

The middle section of the box lets you choose whether Netscape starts up as a Web browser (which is the default), an e-mail window (an option covered in Unit 5), a newsgroup window (an option covered in Unit 7), or some combination of the three.

The middle section also lets you specify the URL you want to go to when Netscape opens! Unless your Internet provider changed it, the default is http://home.netscape.com/, which is the URL for the Netscape Communications home page. To set a different URL (which can point to the home page of a favorite newspaper, a sports scores site, a stock prices site, or any other site that you enjoy visiting frequently), simply double-click inside the

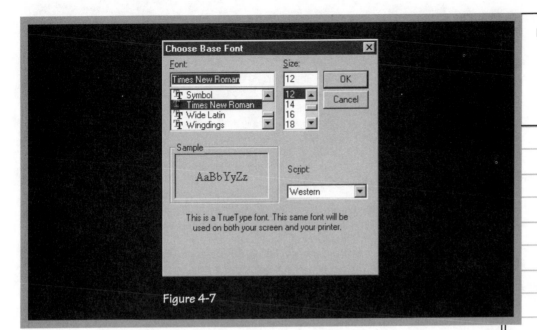

Figure 4-7

Notes:

text box and then type the URL of the Web page you'd most like to see every time Netscape runs.

Finally, the bottom section lets you set text Web links to appear either as normal text or as underlined text (which is the default). It also lets you specify whether links you click turn a different color (which is the default) and for how long the links you've clicked stay a different color (the default is nine days).

3 Click the Help button in the bottom-right corner of the Preferences box.

Detailed information about all the options in the current dialog box appears. You can click Help from each of the seven dialog boxes, so be sure to do so whenever you aren't certain how to use a particular setting.

4 Read the information that currently appears in the Help window, and then click the window's Close button (or choose File⇨Exit from the window's menu) to exit.

The Help window closes, returning you to the Appearance settings. Now that you understand the options in this dialog box, adjust the settings to your tastes or simply leave them as they are.

5 Click the Fonts tab.

Options that let you select which fonts Netscape uses to display Web page text appear. The top option lets you select the language of the font letters and offers such choices as Japanese, Chinese, Korean, and Latin1 (which includes the English alphabet and is the default).

The other two options in the box let you select a proportional font (a font that adjusts the spaces between letters to enhance readability, which is used for most text) and a fixed font (a font that maintains the same space between each letter, which is used for special text such as computer programming code).

6 Click the Choose Font button to the right of the Proportional Font option.

The Choose Base Font box shown in Figure 4-7 appears. First, write down your current font and font size settings so that you can restore them if necessary. Next, scroll through the font list and, if you like, choose a different font and/or font size. When you're done, click the box's OK button to accept your changes, or click its Cancel button to leave the settings unchanged.

Notes:

7 **Click the Colors tab.**

Options appear that let you set the colors Netscape uses to display links you haven't clicked (the default is blue), links you *have* clicked (the default is purple), text (the default is black), and background (the default is gray). The options also let you use a picture file on your hard disk as a background image and specify whether you want your color choices to always override the choices made by the designer of the Web page you're viewing. Make any changes you want, or leave the settings as they are.

8 **Click the Images tab.**

An Images dialog box allows you to set whether colors should be displayed as accurately as possible (Dither), as quickly as possible (Substitute Colors), or as an efficient mix of both that Netscape determines automatically (which is the default). You're also offered the choice of having Web page pictures stay hidden until they're fully transmitted or appear bit by bit as their information is transferred (which is the default). Most people let these settings stand, but if you want to change them, do so.

9 **Click the Apps tab.**

An Apps (short for *applications*) dialog box appears that lets you identify the locations of programs you have on your hard disk that work in conjunction with Netscape. More specifically, program location boxes appear for Telnet (which lets you connect to another computer by using a set of standards named Telnet), TN3270 (which lets you connect to IBM mainframe computers), and View Source (which lets you see a Web page's special formatting codes). In addition, a Temporary Directory option lets you specify which folder should be used to store temporary files created by these programs. Unless you actually have a Telnet, TN3270, or viewer program that works with Netscape, simply skip these options.

10 **Click the Helpers tab.**

A Helpers dialog box appears that lets you match up certain types of files with programs (or *helper applications*) that enable you to view and/or use the files. Windows 95 does the same thing — for example, when you double-click a file ending in txt, the Notepad program automatically runs and loads the file because Windows 95 matches txt files with Notepad. Try out this option with the WinZip program you encountered in Lesson 3-2.

11 **Click inside the list of file types, and then press the End key to jump to the bottom of the list.**

You should land on the *application/zip* entry. (If you don't, locate application/zip yourself and then click it to select it.) This file type refers to files that end with the letters *zip* and have been compressed by a program like WinZip.

Notice that below the list of file types is an Action heading, which determines what action Netscape should take when it encounters the type of file selected. You're offered four options: View in Browser, Save to Disk, Unknown: Prompt User, and Launch Application. The first option is grayed out in this case, because Netscape doesn't have the capability to display zip files. Instead, the Unknown: Prompt User option is selected, which sets Netscape to display an Unknown File Type dialog box whenever you encounter a zip file. To make downloading zip files more efficient, you can click the Save to Disk option, which lets you skip seeing the Unknown File Type box by immediately popping up a Save As dialog box. For greatest efficiency, however, you should choose the Launch Application option, which automatically runs the program you specify to handle the type of file selected.

12 **To set WinZip to automatically handle any zip file Netscape encounters, click Launch Application, click the Browse button below the option, move to the WinZip folder you created in Lesson 3-2, and double-click the name of your WinZip program (for example, Winzip32.exe).**

When Netscape encounters a zip file from now on, it won't even bother popping up a Save As dialog box. Instead, Netscape will simply run WinZip, immediately begin downloading the zip file, and then let WinZip handle the file after the downloading is complete.

For more information about setting up helper applications in Netscape, click the Help button, read the detailed explanation, and then exit Help by clicking the window's Close button.

13 **Click the Language tab.**

Options appear that let you specify which languages Netscape should display (that is, in addition to the one you're using). This feature is useful if you expect to access Web pages written in other languages. If you want to learn more about this feature, click the Help button, read the detailed explanation, and then click the Help box's Close button.

14 **If you're satisfied with all the setting changes you've made, click the Preferences box's OK button. Otherwise, click the box's Cancel button to abandon your changes.**

The box closes and, if you clicked OK, your changes go into effect. If you aren't satisfied with the way everything turned out, simply choose Options⇨General Preferences again, adjust your settings as needed, and click OK.

Wow! We haven't seen so many choices since Ben and Jerry started making ice cream! All these options may be a little overwhelming at first, but as you continue to work with Netscape, you'll probably come to appreciate the flexibility they offer. You can always simply accept the default settings — many people do — but if you find yourself dissatisfied with an aspect of Netscape's appearance or performance, don't hesitate to use the Preferences box to tailor the browser to your personal tastes and needs.

☑ Progress Check

If you can do the following, you've mastered this lesson:

❏ Hide and restore the Toolbar, Location box, and Directory buttons.

❏ Pop up the Preferences dialog box.

❏ Adjust Netscape's dozens of different settings by using the Preferences box's seven dialog boxes: Appearance, Fonts, Colors, Images, Apps, Helpers, and Language.

Unit 4 Quiz

For each of the following questions, circle the letter of the correct answer or answers. Remember, there may be more than one right answer for each question.

1. **To access Web pages more quickly, you can:**

   A. Lure the pages toward you with sweets.

   B. Say the magic words "open sez me" five times fast.

   C. Upgrade your PC system by adding memory, installing a speedier modem, and/or buying a machine with a faster CPU.

   D. Choose Options⇨Auto Load Images to turn off this switch.

Notes:

2. **If Auto Load Images is turned off, you can still view a Web page's pictures by:**

    A. Wearing those 3-D glasses that are now packaged with new PCs.

    B. Clicking the Images button or pressing Ctrl+I.

    C. Choosing View⇨Load Images.

    D. Choosing Images⇨Load Thousand Words.

3. **To open another Netscape browser window:**

    A. Buy another computer, install another copy of Netscape, place your second computer next to your first one, and go wild.

    B. Choose Window⇨New Window.

    C. Choose File⇨New Web Browser or press Ctrl+N.

    D. Trick question; you can't open more than one window at a time.

4. **Clicking Netscape's Open button:**

    A. Makes Netscape communicate with you more frankly and openly.

    B. Leads to treasure, 40 thieves, and a magic lamp.

    C. Reverses the effects of the Close button.

    D. Opens a Location box that lets you type in a URL.

5. **The Preferences dialog box lets you:**

    A. Select the fonts that Netscape uses to display Web page text.

    B. Choose which Web page you move to when you start up Netscape.

    C. Choose which Netscape windows open when you start Netscape.

    D. Set a particular program to activate when Netscape encounters a particular type of file.

Unit 4 Exercise

1. Run Netscape and connect to the Internet.

2. Open a second browser window.

3. In the second window, prevent Web pictures from being transmitted automatically.

4. In the second window, eliminate the Toolbar and Directory buttons.

5. Cruise the Web using your first window, then do the same using your second window, and see which you prefer.

6. If you set WinZip to be a helper application for zip files in Lesson 4-2, test out your setting now by moving to a software distribution site (such as www.tucows.com), locating a file you're interested in that's compressed in the zip format, and then downloading the zip file.

7. When you're done, exit both browser windows and disconnect from the Internet.

Part I Review

Unit 1 Summary

- **Preparing to go online with Netscape:** Make sure that you have the right equipment (primarily a fast PC, a 14,400 or 28,800 bps modem, and a phone line to connect to the modem), sign up for an account with an Internet provider, and get a recent copy of the Netscape program.

- **Starting Netscape:** Double-click the Netscape Navigator icon on your desktop; or click the Windows 95 Start button, choose Programs, click Netscape Navigator from the second menu that appears, and click Netscape Navigator again from the third menu that appears.

- **Moving on a Web page:** Click the arrows, or drag the scroll box, of the vertical scroll bar; or press the PgDn and PgUp keys.

- **Identifying a link:** Move your mouse pointer over an area that's marked in some special way and see whether the pointer's shape changes to a hand.

- **Identifying a link's electronic address:** Point to the link and look at Netscape's message bar, which displays the link's URL.

- **Switching among a few Web pages:** Click Netscape's Back, Forward, and/or Home buttons.

- **Switching among many Web pages:** Click the Go menu and click the page you want, or press Ctrl+H to open the History window and then double-click the page you want.

Unit 2 Summary

- **Using a bookmark to move to a Web page:** Click the Bookmarks menu and click the bookmark you want, or press Ctrl+B to open the Bookmarks window and then double-click the bookmark you want.

- **Creating a bookmark:** Move to the Web page you want to bookmark and then press Ctrl+D or choose Bookmarks⇨Add Bookmark.

- **Deleting a bookmark:** Press Ctrl+B to open the Bookmarks window, click the bookmark you want to delete, and press the Del key.

- **Organizing bookmarks:** From the Bookmarks window, choose Item⇨Insert Folder to create new folders; choose Item⇨Insert Separator to visually separate items; and use Ctrl+C, Ctrl+X, and Ctrl+V to copy, cut, and paste items in the window from one location to another.

- **Typing and activating URLs:** Click anywhere inside the Netscape Location box to highlight the current text, type your URL to replace the text, and press Enter to move to the Web page located at the URL.

- **Searching for information on a Web page:** Click Netscape's Find button to open the Find dialog box, type an appropriate word or phrase in the Find What text box, and click the Find Next button until you locate what you're after.

- **Searching for information across the Web:** Move to a page that lets you access a Web search program, type an appropriate word or phrase in the program's text box, and press Enter to generate a list of topic categories or Web pages.

- **Searching for a broad popular topic:** Use a category-based Web searcher such as Yahoo! or Excite's NetDirectory.

- **Searching for a narrow or obscure topic:** Use an open-ended Web searcher such as AltaVista, InfoSeek, or Lycos.

- **Searching via several different programs:** Use a "meta-search" program such as Savvy Search that plugs your text into several popular Web searchers and then gives you all the initial matches together on the same page and organized by program.

Part I Review

Unit 3 Summary

▶ **Printing the contents of a Web page:** Make sure that your printer is ready to print, click Netscape's Print button to pop up the Print dialog box, adjust any settings you need to change, and click the box's OK button.

▶ **Saving the contents of a Web page as text:** Choose File⇨Save As to open the Save As dialog box; click inside the Save As Type box and click the Plain Text (*.txt) option; double-click inside the File Name box to highlight the current text (if any); type the drive letter, folder name, and filename you want to use (for example, **C:\WebData\HotNews.txt**); and press Enter.

▶ **Saving both the contents and the "look" of a Web page:** Choose File⇨Save As to open the Save As dialog box; click inside the Save As Type box and click the HTML Files option; double-click inside the File Name box to highlight the current text (if any); type the drive letter, folder name, and filename you want to use (for example, **C:\WebData\HotNews.htm**); and press Enter.

▶ **Downloading a file from the Web:** Locate a link to the file and click the link. If an Unknown File Type dialog box appears, click the Save File button to open the Save As dialog box. Otherwise, the Save As dialog box appears immediately. In either case, accept the filename in the Save As dialog box's File Name box; click inside the Save In box and select the drive and folder you want to use to store the file; and press Enter.

▶ **Making zip files useable:** Decompress each file by using the WinZip program that you downloaded in Lesson 3-2 (or that you copied from the CD-ROM included in this book).

Unit 4 Summary

▶ **Preventing Web page pictures from being transmitted:** Choose Options⇨Auto Load Images to turn off the images switch for your current session. To make the change apply to future sessions as well, also choose Options⇨Save Options.

▶ **Receiving Web page pictures when Auto Load Images is turned off:** Click Netscape's Images button, choose View⇨Load Images, or press Ctrl+I.

▶ **Opening another Netscape browser window:** Choose File⇨New Web Browser or press Ctrl+N. You can open as many browser windows as you want (up to the limits of your PC's memory).

▶ **Eliminating the Toolbar:** Choose Options⇨Show Toolbar to turn off the switch. To make the change permanent, also choose Options⇨Save Options.

▶ **Eliminating the Location box:** Choose Options⇨Show Location to turn off the switch. To make the change permanent, also choose Options⇨Save Options.

▶ **Eliminating the Directory buttons:** Choose Options⇨Show Directory Buttons to turn off the switch. To make the change permanent, also choose Options⇨Save Options.

▶ **Forcing the current Web page to be retransmitted:** Click the Reload button, choose View⇨Reload, or press Ctrl+R to update the page.

▶ **Adjusting various Netscape settings:** Choose Options⇨General Preferences to bring up the Preferences box, and then click the tabs of its seven dialog boxes (Appearance, Fonts, Colors, Images, Apps, Helpers, and Language) to display the different settings you want to change. If you aren't sure what a setting does, click the Help button. When you're done adjusting settings, click the Preference box's OK button.

Part I Test

The questions on this test cover all the material presented in Part I, Units 1 through 4.

True   False

T   F   1. Popular national Internet providers include AT&T WebNet, America CruiseLine, and CompuSurf.

T   F   2. The difference between the Standard and Gold editions of Netscape 3.0 is that the latter is stored on an 18-karat gilded CD-ROM and displays its windows in glittering yellow.

T   F   3. The World Wide Web didn't even exist until 1990, but it now provides access to tens of millions of Web pages around the globe.

T   F   4. To find a link on a Web page, you click Netscape's Find button, type **link**, and press Enter.

T   F   5. To use a link, you simply click it. Netscape then uses the link's URL to move you to the appropriate Web page.

T   F   6. If you want to return to your current Web page during future sessions, you should create a bookmark for it by pressing Ctrl+D or choosing Bookmarks⇨Add Bookmark.

T   F   7. You can get information about virtually any subject by using a Web search program to list sites that cover the subject.

T   F   8. If you don't mind skipping the pictures, you can move to Web pages more quickly by choosing Options⇨Auto Load Images to turn off the images switch.

T   F   9. You can run no more than three browser windows at the same time.

T   F   10. A *helper application* is any program you set to activate automatically when Netscape encounters a certain type of file.

Multiple Choice

For each of the following questions, circle the correct answer or answers. Remember, there may be more than one right answer for each question.

11. **The Netscape program allows you to:**

   A. Cruise the colorful and fascinating World Wide Web.

   B. Find information about virtually any topic in minutes.

   C. Send e-mail messages to and receive e-mail from friends and colleagues around the globe.

   D. Participate in any of thousands of ongoing discussion groups covering virtually every topic under the sun.

   E. All of the above.

12. **The World Wide Web:**

   A. Was predicted by HAL 2000 in the film *2001: A Space Odyssey*.

   B. Is run by an international committee headed by the Duke of URL.

   C. Is just another name for the Internet, and the two terms can be used interchangeably.

   D. Is a subset of the Internet, along with other Internet features such as electronic mail and newsgroups.

   E. Is owned by no one and is available to virtually everyone, which is why the Web is so chaotic, enormous, and fascinating.

Part I Test

13. **Links:**

    A. Was the character played by Clarence Williams III on *The Mod Squad.*

    B. Display URLs in the message bar when you point to them.

    C. Was the symbol used in the 1950s to identify Iron Curtain Web sites.

    D. Are a great tool for rambling around the Web and discovering pages you might not have even thought to look for.

    E. Is a wild cat inhabiting the northern U.S. that has thick, soft fur, a short tail, and tufted ears.

14. **The best way to handle the vast amount of information on the Web is to:**

    A. Hide your head under the blankets and hope it all goes away.

    B. Tell endless stories about the good old days when people just watched TV.

    C. Stay on the Web every waking hour so that you miss as little as possible.

    D. Save it all to disk because tomorrow it may be gone.

    E. Take what you can use and let the rest go by.

15. **If you want to preserve a Web page, you can:**

    A. Print it.

    B. Save it to disk as a text file.

    C. Save it to disk as an HTML file.

    D. Print it or save it, but not both.

    E. Rub moisturizer on it daily.

16. **Files you can download from the Web include:**

    A. Business programs such as spreadsheets, database managers, and presentation software.

    B. Fun programs such as games and educational software.

    C. Attractive pictures, including illustrations, paintings, and photographs.

    D. Sound, music, and video clips.

    E. Steel tools with hardened ridged surfaces used for smoothing, grinding down, and boring.

17. **You can't use the Preferences dialog box to specify:**

    A. Whether links are underlined.

    B. Which colors to use for links.

    C. Which fonts to use for text.

    D. Which letter to display above the planet in the Netscape logo.

    E. Which Web page Netscape jumps to when it starts up.

18. **Famous personalities who probably would have used the Web if given the chance include:**

    A. Cleopatra.

    B. Michelangelo.

    C. James Joyce.

    D. Little Miss Muffett.

    E. All of the above; the Web's for everyone (though Little Miss Muffett would probably have been a little put off by its name).

Part I Test

Matching

19. Match the following Netscape Toolbar buttons with the corresponding commands:

A.   1. View⇨Load Images

B.   2. File⇨Print

C.   3. File⇨Open Location

D.   4. Go⇨Back

E.   5. Edit⇨Find

20. Match the descriptions with the buttons on the Toolbar:

A. Displays the Find dialog box   1. [Open]

B. Displays the Print dialog box   2. [Reload]

C. Cuts off data being transferred from a Web page   3. [Find]

D. Displays the Open Location dialog box for typing a new URL   4. [Print]

E. Forces a Web page to be retransmitted   5. [Stop]

21. Match the following keyboard shortcuts with the corresponding feature:

A. Ctrl+D   1. Open the History window

B. Ctrl+S   2. Open the Bookmark window

C. Ctrl+P   3. Create a bookmark for the current Web page

D. Ctrl+B   4. Print the contents of the current Web page

E. Ctrl+H   5. Save the contents of the current Web page

22. Match each navigator/explorer with the land he's best known for reaching:

A. Christopher Columbus   1. Moon

B. Eric the Red   2. Florida

C. Robert Edwin Peary   3. Southwest coast of Greenland

D. Juan Ponce de Léon   4. America

E. Neil A. Armstrong   5. North Pole

Part I Lab Assignment

Create your own list of cool Web sites by following these steps.

Step 1: Run Netscape and connect to the Internet.

Step 2: Peruse Web guides to uncover cool Web pages.

You can start with Yahoo's guide at URL www.yahoo.com/Entertainment/Cool_Links, Excite's NetDirectory at URL www.excite.com/Subject, Netscape Communications's guide at home.netscape.com/home/whats-cool.html (which you can jump to simply by clicking Netscape's What's Cool? button), and this book's own guide at net.dummies.com/internet101/sites.htm. Preserve each list by printing it and/or saving it to disk.

Step 3: Discover more Web guides.

Use some Web search programs, such as Yahoo! or AltaVista, or a "meta-searcher" such as Savvy Search. Again, preserve each list by printing it and/or saving it to disk.

Step 4: Compile a list of promising-looking Web pages.

Study the paper pages and/or files you've generated.

Step 5: Investigate each Web page on your list by moving to it (either by clicking its link or typing its URL).

If you decide that you like the page and want to return to it in the future, create a bookmark for it.

Step 6: When you've worked your way through your list, organize all the bookmarks you've added.

Create a folder with the name of your topic and then move all your new bookmarks into the folder.

Step 7: Visit some interesting sites you've discovered.

And enjoy yourself!

Step 8: After you've finished, disconnect from the Net.

Reading E-mail and Usenet Newsgroups

Part II

In this part . . .

Now that you know how to run Netscape and browse the Web, it's time to learn about the other key use for the Internet: e-mail. E-mail is more widely used than the World Wide Web, with tens of millions of users. In this part of the book, you learn to use the Netscape Mail window to read your e-mail, compose messages, reply to messages, send and receive files by e-mail, and maintain an electronic address book.

Another way to communicate with people on the Internet is by joining some of the thousands of online discussion groups that take place in the Usenet newsgroups. Unit 7 tells you how.

Receiving and Sending E-mail

Objectives for This Unit

✓ Telling Netscape what account you use to send and receive mail

✓ Sending your first e-mail message

✓ Reading e-mail messages

✓ Replying to e-mail messages

✓ Forwarding messages

✓ Printing messages

✓ Deleting messages

✓ Following the rules of e-mail etiquette

Prerequisites
▶ Running Netscape (Lesson 1-1)

N etscape is famous as a Web browser (as you learned in the first part of this book), but the single most-used Internet service is still e-mail. *E-mail* (or *electronic mail*) allows you to type messages on your computer, connect to the Internet, and send the messages to anyone with an Internet e-mail address. While you're connected, you can receive e-mail messages from other people. Netscape comes with an excellent e-mail program, so you've already got everything you need to start sending and receiving e-mail.

In this unit, you use Netscape to send an e-mail message, reply to a message, forward a message, delete a message, and print a message. While you're at it, you find out for sure what your own e-mail address is.

use Netscape to send and receive e-mail

Telling Netscape How to Get Your Mail

Lesson 5-1

Before you can use Netscape's e-mail features, you need to make sure that Netscape is configured to work with your Internet provider to send and receive e-mail. This lesson helps you determine whether your copy of Netscape is already set up to deal with your e-mail and set it up if it's not.

When you installed Netscape, your Internet provider may have configured it automatically to know these computer names already. For example, if you install AT&T WorldNet Service software from the CD-ROM in the back of this book, your copy of Netscape already knows how to get and send your mail, and you can skip right to Lesson 5-2.

To send and receive mail, Netscape needs to know the names of two computers:

POP server =
computer that
stores your e-mail
until you collect it

SMTP server =
computer that
accepts your
outgoing messages
for delivery on the
Internet

   ♦ The computer at your Internet provider that stores incoming mail for you to download (the *POP* or *POP3* server, which stands for Post Office Protocol Version 3). POP servers require you to enter a password so that only you can read your incoming e-mail messages.

   ♦ The computer at your Internet provider that accepts outgoing mail from you and passes it along to the Internet (the *SMTP* server, which stands for Simple Mail Transfer Protocol).

A *server* is a computer that is running a program that provides you with a service, like holding your incoming mail or sending your outgoing mail.

Netscape may not know the names of the computers you need to use if you want to send and receive e-mail. Even if Netscape worked fine in Units 1 through 4 for browsing the Web, it may not be set up for e-mail, in which case you need to *configure* (set up) Netscape to work with your Internet provider's mail servers.

In this lesson, you open the Netscape Mail window, check that Netscape is set up to send and receive mail messages from your Internet provider, and configure Netscape if necessary.

Can Netscape get your mail?

The best way to find out whether your copy of Netscape knows how to get your e-mail is to try it! Follow these steps:

1 Run Netscape and connect to your Internet provider.

See Unit 1 if you aren't sure how. Whatever way you run Netscape, you see the Netscape window, which you are familiar with from Units 1 through 4.

2 In the Netscape window, click the Mail icon, the little envelope in the lower-right corner of the Netscape window.

Alternatively, you can choose the Window⇨Netscape Mail command from the menu bar. (AT&T WorldNet users choose Window⇨AT&T WorldNet Mail from the menu bar.) Either way, Netscape opens the Netscape Mail window and tries to get your mail from your Internet provider.

Mail icon

3 If no error message appears, Netscape knows the name of your Internet provider's mail servers and knows your mail password, so you're ready to send and receive mail. Skip directly to Lesson 5-2, "Sending a Message."

You're in luck! Netscape is already configured to receive and send mail!

4 If you see a message saying that no new messages are on the server, you don't have any e-mail. Click OK and then skip directly to Lesson 5-2, "Sending a Message."

Netscape successfully connected to your POP server, but no messages were waiting for you. Don't worry — we can arrange for you to get some mail!

5 **If you see a message asking for your POP password, skip forward to the section "Telling Netscape your mail password."**

Netscape knows how to get your mail, but it doesn't know your password. If you don't know your mail password, take a look at the information your Internet provider gave you when you signed up for your account. Or call your Internet provider to find out how to get the mail password for your account.

6 **If you see the message** `Netscape is unable to use the POP3 server because you have not provided a username. Please provide one in the preferences and try again`, **Netscape doesn't know the name of your Internet provider's POP server. Click OK to make the error message go away.**

Netscape doesn't know how to contact your POP or SMTP servers — you're going to have to tell Netscape their names.

7 **Disconnect from your Internet provider while you find out the information Netscape needs to know.**

Hang up on your Internet account while you do this — you may need to use the phone line to call your Internet provider's technical support number. You can leave Netscape running — you use it later in this lesson.

Now you know whether Netscape can get and send your mail.

Finding out where your mail is

If you see an error message when you open the Netscape Mail window, Netscape is having trouble checking for mail on your Internet provider's computer. Chances are, Netscape doesn't know the name of your Internet provider's POP (Post Office Protocol) server, the computer that stores your incoming mail until you collect it. Netscape also may not know the name of your provider's SMTP server, the computer that accepts your outgoing mail for posting.

Don't panic. Here's the information you need:

* **Your Internet provider's POP server (to handle incoming mail):** The name is a series of words separated by periods. For example, the AT&T WorldNet POP server is a computer named `postoffice.worldnet.att.net`. Many Internet providers use the word *pop* followed by the provider's domain name, like `pop.sover.net` for SoVerNet (Margy's Internet provider in Vermont). Others use the word *mail*, like `mail.tiac.net` for TIAC (an Internet provider in Boston).

* **Your Internet provider's SMTP server (to send outgoing mail):** The SMTP server may have the same name as the POP server. It's not uncommon for both server programs to run on the same computer.

* **Your Internet provider's NNTP server (to let you read Usenet newsgroups):** You find out what this is in Unit 7. (Hint: It's the computer that provides you with the articles in Usenet newsgroups.)

* **Your user name:** The name you type when you log on to your account. Your user name is usually the part of your e-mail address before the at-sign (@). For example, if your e-mail address is `president@whitehouse.gov` (are you reading this, Mr. President?), your user name is *president*.

Notes:

Notes:

Note to AT&T WorldNet Service users: You see a long number when connecting to AT&T WorldNet Service. Your e-mail user name isn't this number, but the name that you chose when you signed up for your account.

▶ **Your e-mail password:** You need to enter the password for your e-mail, too. Your mail password may be the same as the password you log in with, or it may be different. Many providers won't tell you your password over the phone for security reasons. (Makes sense — how do they know it's really you?) Instead, they mail it to you (using paper mail, of course), and you have to wait until you receive that letter before you can use e-mail.

Get the information you need by reading the information that your Internet provider sent you when you signed up for an account. If you never received this information or you can't find it, call your Internet provider and ask. Write down the information you collect in Table 5-1 and on the Cheat Sheet in the front of this book. Write your e-mail password on a sheet of paper and store the sheet in a safe place.

Table 5-1	Information from Your Internet Provider
What You Need to Know	**Write Your Information Here**
POP server	_____
SMTP server	_____
NNTP server	_____
User name	_____
E-mail password	(write on a separate sheet of paper)

Note: Don't try to use the POP or SMTP server for an Internet provider you don't have an account with. The server will refuse to work and you'll see an error message.

Telling Netscape where your mail is

Great! You've got all the information you need to configure Netscape.

1 Run Netscape (if it's not running already).

You can follow the rest of these steps regardless of whether you see the Netscape browser window or the Netscape Mail window.

2 Choose Options⇨Mail and News Preferences from the menu.

You see the Preferences dialog box.

3 Click the Servers tab along the top of the Preferences dialog box.

The Preferences dialog box shows the settings you see in Figure 5-1.

4 Click in the Outgoing Mail (SMTP) Server box.

This box is the first setting on the dialog box.

5 Type the name of your SMTP server (take a look at your Cheat Sheet if you've forgotten it).

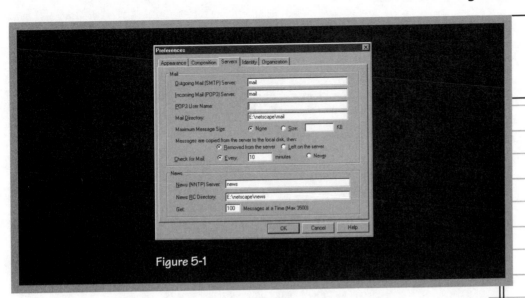

Figure 5-1

If you make a mistake, press Backspace to correct the error and then type the correct text.

6 **Press the Tab key.**

Your cursor moves to the <u>I</u>ncoming Mail (POP3) Server box.

7 **Type the name of your POP server, copying it from your Cheat Sheet, and press Tab again.**

Your cursor is in the <u>P</u>OP3 User Name box, which is where you enter the user name for your Internet account.

8 **Type the user name you wrote in Table 5-1.**

Netscape needs to know your user name when it contacts the POP server to get your mail — Netscape has to know whose mail it is getting!

9 **While you are looking at the Servers tab in the Preferences dialog box, click in the <u>N</u>ews (NNTP) Server box and type the name of your news server.**

You won't use Netscape's news feature until Unit 7, but you may as well get set up for it now!

10 **Click the Identity tab along the top of the Preferences dialog box.**

It's a good idea to tell Netscape your name and e-mail address so that this information appears correctly in your outgoing e-mail messages.

11 **Click in the Your <u>N</u>ame box and type your real name. Then press Tab.**

This name appears in the *From* line of e-mail messages you send.

12 **In the Your <u>E</u>mail box, type your e-mail address. Then press Tab.**

If you're not sure what it is, leave this entry unchanged. You know for sure by the end of Lesson 5-3, and you can come back and enter the information then.

13 **In the Reply-to <u>A</u>ddress box, type the address to which you want people to send replies to your messages.**

Chances are, you want people to reply to the same address you entered in Step 12. Most people use only one e-mail address.

14 **Click the Organization tab along the top of the Preferences dialog box.**

enter set-up information by choosing Options→Mail and News Preferences

Notes:

check mail by
clicking the Mail
icon

☑ Progress Check

If you can do the following,
you've mastered this lesson:

❏ Open the Netscape Mail
window.

❏ Tell Netscape the name of
your provider's mail
server.

❏ Tell Netscape your e-mail
user name and password.

❏ Connect to your Internet
provider and check your
e-mail.

You see some miscellaneous settings (we're not sure why this tab is named
"Organization").

**15 If no check mark appears in the first setting, Remember Mail
Password, click in the box until a check appears.**

This setting tells Netscape to ask you for your e-mail password only once and
to store it (in a safe, encrypted format) on your hard disk. A check in this
setting means that you don't have to type your e-mail password each time you
check your mail.

16 Click OK.

The Preferences dialog box goes away. You're ready to try getting your
mail again.

17 Connect to the Internet.

It's time to try picking up your mail, to test whether Netscape now knows how
to contact your Internet provider's mail servers.

**18 Click the Mail icon, the little envelope in the lower-right corner of
the Netscape window.**

Netscape tries to get your mail from your Internet provider.

If you see a dialog box asking for your password, you're in good shape —
Netscape has contacted your provider's POP server and is trying to get
your mail!

Typing your mail password

When you tell Netscape to get your mail, it connects to your Internet
provider's POP server. To do so, Netscape needs to know your user name and
password. The first time you get your mail, you see a message like the one in
Figure 5-2. You don't have to type this password each time you get your
mail — Netscape remembers it from now on.

1 Type your mail password and click OK.

As you type your password, only asterisks appear so that someone reading
over your shoulder can't find out your password. When you click OK, Netscape
tells the POP server your password. If you gave the right password, Netscape
succeeds in connecting to the POP server and copies all your incoming e-mail
messages to your computer. You see a list of messages in the upper-right part
of the Netscape Mail window (you learn how to read them in Lesson 5-3).
You're all set! Go directly to Lesson 5-2.

**2 If you see a message saying that no messages are on the server,
click OK.**

Netscape succeeded in connecting to your provider's mail computer and
checking your e-mail, but you didn't have any messages waiting. Even though
this message looks like an error message, it's good news, really — Netscape is
ready to do e-mail for you.

**3 If you didn't type the right password, Netscape asks for your
password again.**

Try the password to your Internet account. If that still doesn't work, you
have to call your Internet provider to ask how to find out what your mail
password is.

POP servers allow you to download your messages only if you give the right
password, so other people can't snoop on your e-mail.

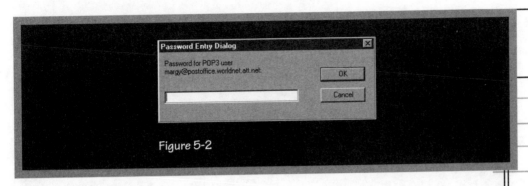

Figure 5-2: To get your mail, you have to give your password.

Figure 5-2

Sending a Message

Lesson 5-2

Now that Netscape is ready to do e-mail, the first thing we'd like you to do is to send us a message. Not surprisingly, when you send e-mail, you must know the *e-mail address* of the person to send it to. E-mail addresses look like this:

    username@computer

The *username* part is the person's user name on the computer system he or she uses. The *computer* part is the name of the computer on which the person's mail is stored. For example, the product information department at Netscape Communications Corp. has this e-mail address:

    info@netscape.com

The user name is *info,* and the computer that stores the mail is named *netscape.com.*

To use Netscape to read and send e-mail, you use the Netscape Mail window, shown in Figure 5-3.

When you compose a mail message, Netscape sends the message to your Internet provider, which sends it out over the Internet to the party you are trying to reach. In the case of your very first e-mail message, you are trying to reach us, the authors of this book!

In this lesson, you open the Netscape Mail window and send a test e-mail message.

Composing a message

To test that your e-mail is working and to make sure that you receive some e-mail that you can read in Lesson 5-3, send a message to *Internet For Dummies Central,* where a tireless mail robot (a program that automatically responds to messages) stands ready to reply to your e-mail message. (Thanks to John Levine, King of the Internet Dummies, for providing this service!) The address to use is

    netscape101@dummies.com

We set up this address especially for readers of this book!

e-mail address
~~format =~~
username@computer

Figure 5-3: When you see this window, Netscape is ready to send and receive e-mail messages.

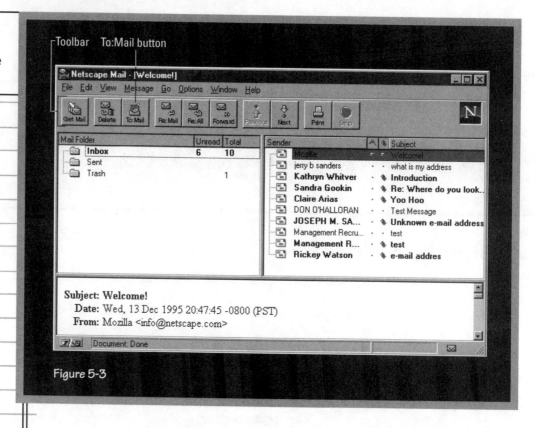

—Toolbar   To:Mail button

Figure 5-3

Mail icon

To: Mail

to create a
message, click the
To:Mail button,
choose File→New Mail
Message, or press
Ctrl+M

to find out your
e-mail address,
send a message to

netscape101@dummies.com

1 **Run Netscape and open the Netscape Mail window by choosing** **Window⇨Netscape Mail from the menu or by clicking the Mail** **icon in the lower-right corner of the Netscape window.**

You see the Mail window shown in Figure 5-3. It has three parts: Your list of folders (which you learn more about in Lesson 6-2) is in the upper-left, the list of messages in the current folder is in the upper-right, and the text of the current message is in the lower half of the window.

2 **If you want as much space as possible for reading your mail on-** **screen, maximize your Netscape Mail window by clicking the box-** **like Maximize button in the upper-right corner of the window.**

The Netscape Main window expands to fill the entire screen.

3 **To start composing a new message, click the To:Mail button on the** **Toolbar.**

The To:Mail button is the third button from the left on the Toolbar. Alternatively, you can press Ctrl+M or choose File⇨New Mail Message from the menu bar.

Netscape creates a new, blank message in the Message Composition window (see Figure 5-4). The top half of the window contains the header lines for the message. The bottom half of the window contains the text of the message (it's blank right now). Your cursor is on the Mail To line.

4 **On the Mail To line, type** netscape101@dummies.com **very carefully.**

Capitalization doesn't matter — you can use all uppercase letters if you prefer. If you type the address incorrectly, use the Backspace key to back up and fix the mistake.

If you want to send your message to several people, you can type one address after another, separated by commas.

5 **Press Tab twice to leave the Cc line blank.**

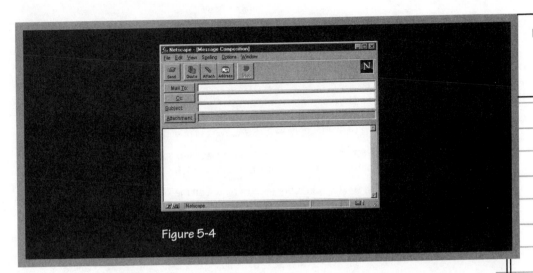

Figure 5-4

Figure 5-4: The Netscape Message Composition window contains a new, blank message.

Don't press Enter, because that key doesn't do a thing right now. Skip the <u>C</u>c line because no one wants to get a copy of your test message.

6 **On the <u>S</u>ubject line, type** Test Message **or whatever you'd like the subject of the message to be. Then press Tab.**

This message is going to a mail robot, but we authors read these messages, too, so be polite. The cursor jumps over the <u>A</u>ttachment line and lands in the message area.

7 **Type a message to the mail robot and the authors of this book.**

How about saying how you like (or don't like) this book? The message can be as long as you want. You don't have to press Enter at the end of each line — Netscape moves to the beginning of the next line as you fill up each line.

When you compose an e-mail message, you use Netscape as a little word processor. Table 5-1 lists some of the keys you can use to edit your message.

press Tab to move from line to line of the Message Composition window

press Enter only at the end of each paragraph

Table 5-2	**Keys for Editing Your E-mail**
Key	*What It Does*
Home	Moves your cursor to the beginning of the line
End	Moves to the end of the line
Ctrl+Home	Moves to the beginning of the message
Ctrl+End	Moves to the end of the message
Backspace	Deletes the character to the left of the cursor; on a blank line, deletes the blank line
Del	Deletes the character to the right of the cursor; on a blank line, deletes the blank line
Ctrl+Del	Deletes from the cursor to the end of the current line
Tab	In header lines when composing a message, moves your cursor to the next header line; in the <u>S</u>ubject line, moves the cursor down to the message area; in the message area, inserts spaces to the next tab stop
Shift+Tab	When composing a message, moves the cursor up to the preceding header line
Ctrl+Z	Undoes the last edit

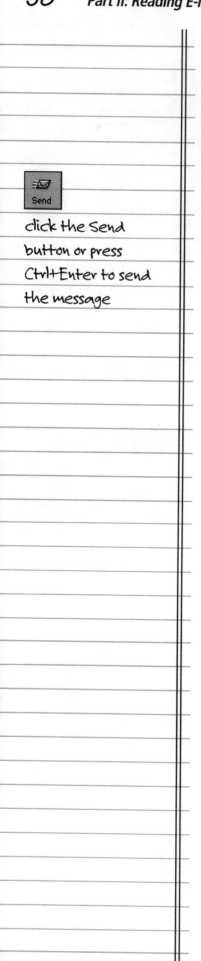

click the Send
button or press
Ctrl+Enter to send
the message

Note: If you begin composing a message and decide not to send it after all, Windows 95 users can click the Close button in the upper-right corner of the Message Composition window. Windows 3.1 users can double-click the Control-menu box (the little gray minus sign) in the upper-left corner of the Message Composition window. Netscape asks whether you're sure that you want to discard your unsent message — click <u>Y</u>es. You can now start over by returning to Step 3.

8 When you are done typing and editing your message, click the Send button, press Ctrl+Enter, or choose <u>F</u>ile⇨<u>S</u>end Now from the menu.

The Send button is the leftmost button on the Toolbar, the button with the flying envelope on it. Netscape sends the message, which takes a few seconds. If you're connected to your Internet provider, messages appear on the bottom line of the Message Composition window, saying Delivering mail and then Connect. If you aren't connected to your Internet provider, you may see the Connect To window or other dialog box to reconnect you — follow whatever procedure you usually use to get connected.

Poof! Netscape sends your message! The Message Composition window disappears.

Congratulations! You just sent your first e-mail. It's pretty exciting, we must admit. But eventually you want to send messages to other people besides us, and when you do, you encounter a variety of e-mail addresses. Taking a quick look at the structure of e-mail addresses is worthwhile so that you know what to expect when you start sending e-mail all over the Internet.

All the major online services as well as Internet providers are connected to the Internet, so you can send e-mail to people with accounts on America Online, AT&T WorldNet Service, CompuServe, Concentric, GNN, The Microsoft Network, Netcom, and Prodigy. See Table 5-3 for how to write to a friend who uses an online service or one of the most popular Internet providers.

Table 5-3	Online Services, Internet Providers, and Their Internet Addresses
Service	**E-mail Address Format**
America Online	Add *@aol.com* to the screen name; if someone has the screen name *SteveCase*, address mail to SteveCase@aol.com.
AT&T WorldNet Service	Add *@worldnet.att.net* to the user name; if someone has the user name *Michaelangelo*, address mail to michaelangelo@worldnet.att.net
CompuServe	Change the comma in the user ID to a period and add *@compuserve.com* to the end; if someone has the user ID *7654,321*, address mail to 7654.321@compuserve.com.
Concentric	Add *@cris.com* to the end; if someone has the user ID *GuruMayi*, address mail to Gurumayi@cris.com.
GNN	Add *@gnn.com* to the user name; if someone has the user name *SantaClaus*, address mail to SantaClaus@gnn.com.
The Microsoft Network	Add *@msn.com* to the user name; if someone has the user name *BillGates*, address mail to BillGates@msn.com.
Netcom	Add *@netcom.com* to the screen name; if someone has the user name *RockNRoll*, address mail to RockNRoll@netcom.com.
Prodigy	Add *@prodigy.com* to the service ID; if someone has the service ID *ABC123*, address mail to ABC123@prodigy.com.

Note: If you want to close the Mail window but continue to use Netscape, you can choose the File⇨Close command. Windows 95 users can click the Close button (the X button in the upper-right corner of the Netscape window). Windows 3.1 users can double-click the Control-menu box, the little gray minus-sign button in the upper-left corner of the window. The Mail window closes, and you return to the Netscape browser window.

extra credit

How to find out someone's e-mail address

You hear that your aunt has an e-mail address, and you want to send her a message. Here's the best way to find out your aunt's address:

Call and ask.

True, this method is neither zoomy nor high-tech, but it is by far the quickest and easiest way.

But what if you don't know your aunt's phone number or address? A few e-mail directories have sprung up on the World Wide Web. Using the Netscape browser window, try searching for an e-mail address at the Four11 Directory Services Web page at www.four11.com, the WhoWhere? Web page at www.whowhere.com, or the Internet Address Finder Web page at www.iaf.net.

Exiting the Netscape Mail window

When you are done sending messages, here's how to leave Netscape:

1 Choose File⇨Exit from the menu.

Netscape asks whether you want to close all Netscape windows.

2 Click Yes.

Netscape disappears.

3 You may still be connected to your Internet provider. Follow your usual procedure to disconnect from your provider.

Now you know how to get in and out of the Netscape Mail window — mission control for e-mail. And you've sent an e-mail message to *Internet For Dummies Central* (you receive a reply in the next lesson). Good work!

Note: If you're done reading your mail but want to return to the Netscape browser window, choose File⇨Close from the menu instead of File⇨Exit. Netscape closes the Netscape Mail window but any other open Netscape windows remain open.

extra credit

Checking your spelling

Netscape doesn't come with a built-in spelling checker, but you can add one. Using the CyberSpell plug-in, you can add a Spelling command to the menu of the Message Composition window. See Lesson 8-7 for how to install and use the CyberSpell plug-in.

☑ Progress Check

If you can do the following, you've mastered this lesson:

❑ Open the Netscape Composition window.

❑ Enter the e-mail address of a person to whom you want to send a message.

❑ Compose and edit the text for your e-mail message.

❑ Send your e-mail message.

❑ Exit the Netscape Mail window.

Recess

You've sent your first e-mail out onto the Internet. Take a walk around the block while your e-mail message wends its way back to you. If you want to exit Netscape and hang up on the Internet, go ahead (hanging up on your Internet provider is a good idea whenever you'll be away from your desk for more than a few minutes, especially if you pay by the hour). When you return, just reconnect to your Internet account, fire up Netscape, and open the Netscape Mail window.

Lesson 5-3   # Reading E-mail Messages

Reading messages is a lot easier than sending them because you don't have to do any typing. When you receive an e-mail message from the Internet, your Internet provider holds the message for you until the next time you connect. To retrieve your messages, you click the Get Mail button on the Netscape Mail window. Netscape requests your messages from your Internet provider, which copies, or *downloads,* your mail to your computer, where you can read the messages, compose replies, and file messages that you want to keep.

When Netscape receives messages for you, it stores them in a *folder,* or a group of messages. Netscape comes with a folder named *Inbox,* where incoming messages wait for you to read them. Netscape creates other folders for you later, like a Trash folder for messages you delete and a Sent folder for messages you have sent.

click the Get Mail
button to download
your incoming
messages

mail folders contain
groups of messages

Your folders are listed in the upper-left corner of the Netscape Mail window under the title *Mail Folder.* When you click the Inbox folder, a list of the messages in the Inbox folder appears in the upper-right part of the Netscape Mail window. To read a message, you click it, and the text of the message appears in the lower part of the Netscape Mail window.

In this lesson, you retrieve your incoming e-mail messages and take a look at them in the Netscape Mail window.

Going to the mailbox for your mail

Here's how to get your e-mail and read it.

1   **Run Netscape. If you aren't connected to your Internet provider, follow your usual procedure to get connected.**

2   **Open the Netscape Mail window by clicking the Mail icon in the lower-right corner of the Netscape window or by choosing the Window⇨Netscape Mail command from the menu.**

When you open the Netscape Mail window, Netscape automatically checks your mail. Convenient! You should receive a reply to the message that you mailed in Lesson 5-2. You may also receive messages from anyone to whom you've revealed your e-mail address.

If Netscape asks for your e-mail password, type the password you typed in Lesson 5-1.

While Netscape is retrieving your messages, the bottom line of the Netscape Mail window shows what Netscape is doing: You see messages saying when Netscape connects to your provider, how many messages it is downloading, and when it is done. Sometimes it's impossible to figure out what the information on the bottom line of the Netscape Mail means — but you know that Netscape is still retrieving mail if the Netscape logo in the upper-right corner of the window continues to move. (Depending on your version of Netscape, the motion may consist of the logo twirling or of shooting stars dropping in the background.)

After you're done getting your messages, the Netscape Mail window looks like Figure 5-5. Netscape displays the first message in the lower half of the window.

Note: If you don't have mail waiting, you may want to wait an hour and try again. If you wait a day and still don't get the reply to the message that you sent, try sending a message to yourself.

3 **Click the Inbox folder in the Netscape Mail window if it's not already selected.**

To the right of the folder name (Inbox, in this case), Netscape tells you the number of messages in the folder and the number you haven't read yet.

incoming mail appears in your Inbox

When you select the Inbox folder, a list of the messages in your Inbox appears in the upper-right part of the Netscape Mail window. Each message appears on one line, showing who it's from and the subject. The messages you haven't read yet appear in boldface, with a green gemlike thingy between the Sender and Subject columns.

4 **To read a message, click its header on the list of messages.**

The text of the message appears in the lower half of the Netscape Mail window. The message starts with header lines that tell you who the message is from, the subject of the message, and when your Internet provider received the message. You can read any message you like by simply clicking its line on the list of messages.

Note: You can make your Netscape Mail window larger by dragging the lower edge of the window downward with your mouse or by maximizing the window (by clicking its Maximize button). You can also adjust the sizes of the list of folders, list of messages, and text of the current message by dragging the dividers between these parts of the window.

If the message is too long to fit in the window, click in the text of the message. Then you can use the down arrow key to move down one line or the PgDn keys to move down by one screenful, or you can click on the downward-pointing triangle button in the lower-right corner of the window. This button is the bottom end of the vertical scroll bar that runs down the right side of messages that are too long to fit in the window.

to read long messages, scroll the message window down

5 **After you're done reading this message, click the next message in your Inbox, if there is one.**

6 **Take a look at the message you received from *Internet For Dummies Central* — it tells you your official Internet e-mail address, in case you weren't sure.**

And you know the address works because this message arrived!

Figure 5-5: Your incoming messages are stored in the Inbox folder.

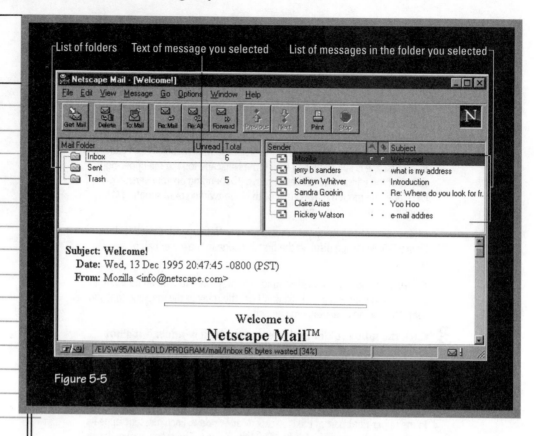

List of folders   Text of message you selected   List of messages in the folder you selected

Figure 5-5

Checking your e-mail again

If you are expecting an important e-mail message from someone, you don't have to sit and stare at the Netscape Mail window waiting for it to come through. You can exit the Mail window, do some cruising, and then come back to check your e-mail later.

To check your mail anytime, just follow these easy steps:

1 **Click the Get Mail button on the Toolbar (the first button), click the Mail icon in the lower-right corner of the window (the little envelope icon), press Ctrl+T, or choose File⇨Get New Mail from the menu.**

If you don't have any new messages, Netscape displays the message *No new messages on server,* which means that you don't have any new mail.

2 **If you receive a message saying that you have no new mail, click OK to make the message go away. If you have a new message (or several), go ahead and read it (or them)!**

☑ Progress Check

If you can do the following, you've mastered this lesson:

❑ Pick up your new e-mail messages.

❑ Read your e-mail messages.

Replying to, Forwarding, Printing, and Deleting Messages

Some messages are destined for oblivion, while others need a reply or should be passed along to someone else. In this lesson, you learn how to reply to messages, forward messages to other people, print messages, and delete unwanted messages.

Replying to a message

Other messages deserve a reply, and composing one is easy. By clicking the Re:Mail button on the Toolbar, pressing Ctrl+R, or choosing the Message⇨Reply command from the menu bar, you can ask Netscape to create a new message that is already preaddressed to the person who sent you the message. In addition, the text of the original message to you is *quoted* in the new message. That is, the text appears with each line preceded by a > character. Quoting the interesting parts of the original text is a good way to help you and the person you are writing to remember what the heck you were both talking about. Deleting the boring parts or the parts you aren't replying to is polite.

To learn how to reply to an e-mail message, send a reply to the *Internet For Dummies Central* message.

1 **Run Netscape and open the Netscape Mail window by clicking the Mail icon in the lower-right corner of the Netscape window.**

You see the Netscape Mail window.

2 **Click the Inbox folder in the Netscape Mail window.**

You see the messages you've received, including the message from *Internet For Dummies Central.*

3 **Click the header for the message from us, which says "Automated response."**

The text of the message appears. If you'd rather reply to a different message you've received, feel free.

4 **Click the Re:Mail button on the Toolbar, press Ctrl+R, or choose Message⇨Reply from the menu bar.**

You see the Message Composition window again, shown in Figure 5-6. Netscape has created a new message addressed to us because you are replying to a message from us (the address is `Automated response <netscape101@dummies.com>`). The subject of the message is the same as the subject of the original message, with *Re:* added to the front. (*Re* is short for the Latin *in re,* in case you were wondering, which means *about the thing.*) You can edit this subject, if you like, by clicking in the Subject box and typing a different subject.

If you scroll up to the top of the message area of the new message, you see a line like this:

`Automated response wrote:`

---

quoted text appears with a > at the beginning of each line

reply to a message by clicking the Re:Mail button, pressing Ctrl+R, or choosing Message→Reply

Figure 5-6: Replying to a message is easy because you don't have to type any e-mail addresses.

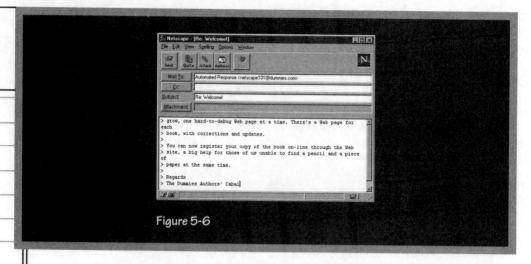

Figure 5-6

Notes:

Netscape thinks that you're replying to a message from someone named Automated Response, which is how our mail robot signs messages. Then you see the quoted text of the original message. Each line of the quoted text begins with a >, so you can tell the lines of the original message from the lines you are about to type.

Note: If the quoted text of the message doesn't appear, choose Options⊅Mail and News Preferences from the menu, click the Composition tab at the top of the dialog box that appears, click the Automatically quote original message when replying box until it contains a check, and click OK. This setting tells Netscape to include the original message when you compose a reply.

5 **With your cursor at the top of the message area, press Enter once to leave a blank line and then type a message to us, like** Thanks for the nice message.

While you're at it, tell us how long it took for our first message to get to you. (Days? Hours? Minutes? Just a rough idea is fine.)

When you reply to a message, deleting all but the interesting parts is considered polite. If the quoted text includes salutations, lots of blank lines, or other unnecessary text, delete each excess line by moving your cursor to the beginning of the line, pressing Ctrl+Del to delete its text, and then pressing Del to eliminate the now-blank line. Repeat as needed.

6 **Delete more or all of the original message.**

If you're replying to the message from *Internet For Dummies Central,* you can delete the whole message, because we are already familiar with what it says.

7 **Connect to your Internet provider.**

Now that you're ready to send your message, you'd better be online!

8 **Click the Send button to send your reply.**

Netscape sends your message. The next time you get your messages, you receive a reply from *Internet For Dummies Central* — our mail robot just can't leave a message unanswered!

Netscape files a copy of the message you just composed in your Sent folder.

Nice work! If you're like most people, you'll spend as much time replying to messages as you do writing new ones.

heads up

If you want to reply to a message and also address it to people who received copies (cc's), click the Re:All button, press Ctrl+Shift+R, or choose Message⊅ Reply to All from the menu.

include only the relevant parts of the original message in your reply

click the Send button to send messages

Forwarding a message

If you get an interesting message, or one that should really have been sent to someone else, you can easily forward it along. Just select the message you want to forward and click the Forward button, press Ctrl+L, or choose Message⇨Forward. Netscape opens the Message Composition window. The message area appears blank, but the complete text of the message you selected will appear when you send the message. The subject box contains *Fwd:* followed by the subject line from the original message. All you have to do is address the message and send it off.

Another way to forward a message is to choose Message⇨Forward Quoted from the menu. The Message Composition window appears, with the original message in the text area. Every line of the original message appears preceded by a >, to show that you are quoting the original message. The first line in the text box says something like *Madonna says:* (with the name of the person who wrote the original message). By using this command, you can edit the message you are forwarding, deleting the boring part and inserting your own comments.

Try forwarding the message you received from *Internet For Dummies Central* or any other message you've received. You can forward the message to yourself (which doesn't make a lot of sense in real life, but it's a good way to practice).

1 Click the message that you want to forward.

Unless you have a better candidate, click the message you received from us.

2 Click the Forward button, the sixth button from the left on the Toolbar.

If you'd rather, you can choose Message⇨Forward from the menu bar — your choice. Netscape displays the Message Composition window. The Subject box contains something like [Fwd: Welcome to Internet For Dummies]. The text box is totally empty, even though when Netscape sends the message, the message you are forwarding will appear.

3 Address the message by typing your e-mail address in the Mail To box.

If you aren't sure what your e-mail address is, look in the message that you received from us — it tells you exactly what your e-mail address looks like.

4 Press Tab three times or click in the text area (the big white box).

You can type your own message to go along with the message you are forwarding.

5 Type something like Get a load of this!

What you type appears at the top of the e-mail message, followed by the text of the message you're forwarding.

6 Click the Send button, the leftmost button on the Toolbar.

Netscape mails the message.

The original message is still sitting in your Inbox, in case you want to reply to it, forward it to someone else, or file it. (You learn how to file a message in other folders in Lesson 6-2.)

forward the current message by clicking the Forward button, pressing Ctrl+L, or choosing Message→Forward

Forward button

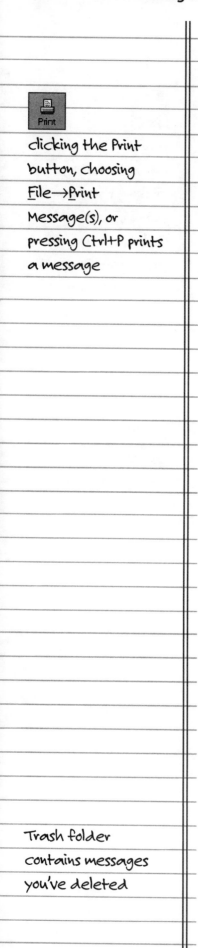

clicking the Print
button, choosing
File→Print
Message(s), or
pressing Ctrl+P prints
a message

Printing a message

Sometimes you need to print a message to file it in a manila folder, to give to someone, or to carry around in your pocket. (Perhaps you just received a love letter by e-mail.) Printing your e-mail is easy — you just click the Print button on the Netscape Mail Toolbar, choose File⇨Print from the menu, or press Ctrl+P.

Before you can print a message, your printer must be connected to your computer, turned on, and loaded with paper. Then you can begin.

1 Click the header of the message you want to print.

When Netscape displays the text of the message in the lower half of the Mail window, make sure that the message is the one you want to print.

2 Click the Print button on the Toolbar, choose File⇨Print from the menu, or press Ctrl+P.

You see the Print dialog box, shown in Figure 5-7. It looks like the Print dialog box in most other Windows programs, and it lets you choose which pages to print and how many copies.

3 Click OK to print the message.

Netscape displays a box telling you that the message is printing, and then voilà! Your message is on paper.

Netscape automatically prints a title at the beginning of the message, containing incomprehensible gobbledygook about where the message is stored (as far as we can guess). At the bottom of each page it prints the page number and the date.

If you want to print only part of a long message, click the Pages button on the Print dialog box and fill in the range of pages you want. But because you can't see on-screen where pages start and end, this option is useful mainly for printing only the beginning of a long message — print only pages 1 through 1.

extra credit

Avoiding gobbledygook when printing messages

You can tell Netscape not to print incomprehensible junk at the top of each e-mail message you print. Choose File⇨Page Setup from the menu bar, click the Document Title and Document Location (URL) boxes to turn *off* those switches, and then click OK.

Deleting a message

Having read a message, you may want to place it carefully in the circular file or in the Great Bit Bucket in the Sky. In Netscape, you place such important messages in the aptly named Trash folder by selecting the message from your Inbox (or from any folder in Netscape) and clicking the Delete button (or by choosing Edit⇨Delete Message from the menu bar or pressing the Del key). Netscape creates a folder named Trash the first time you delete a message.

Trash folder
contains messages
you've deleted

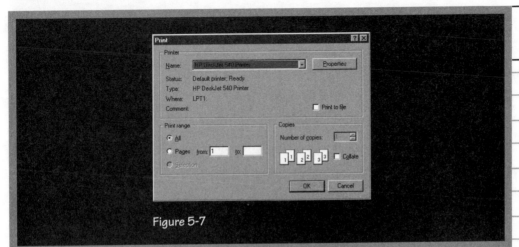

Figure 5-7

Figure 5-7: The Print dialog box.

Notes:

1 **Click the message you want to delete.**

You can delete the message from us or any other message that is sitting in your Inbox folder. When you select the message, the text of the message appears in the lower part of the window.

2 **Click the Delete button on the Toolbar, press the Del key, or choose Edit⇨Delete Message from the menu bar.**

Or you can drag the message to the Trash folder. The message disappears from the Inbox folder. Actually, Netscape didn't delete the message. It's in your Trash folder. If you suddenly decide that you want the deleted message back, you can undelete it.

3 **Open the Trash folder by clicking it on the list of folders in the upper-left part of the Netscape window.**

Wonder of wonders! Your deleted message is in the Trash folder, and it's not covered with old coffee grounds like when you throw something away in your off-screen trash.

heads up

You can read messages in your Trash folder by clicking them. You can move a message from the Trash folder back into your Inbox folder by clicking the message and then choosing Message⇨Move⇨0 Inbox from the menu.

Deleted messages lie around in your Trash folder until you take out the garbage by choosing File⇨Empty Trash Folder from the menu bar.

Recess

You know all the basics of e-mail now — good work! Take a quick breather and come back to learn some basic rules of e-mail etiquette. After the next lesson, your messages will look like they are from an experienced e-mail user.

delete the current message by clicking the Delete button, pressing Del, or choosing Edit→Delete Message

☑ **Progress Check**

If you can do the following, you've mastered this lesson:

❑ Reply to a message.

❑ Forward a message.

❑ Print a message.

❑ Delete a message.

E-mail E-tiquette

Lesson 5-5

heads up

Something about e-mail makes people take offense easily and forget that they are corresponding with a living, breathing human being with feelings. Perhaps it's because you can't see the other person's face or hear a live voice, or perhaps it's a side effect of our pent-up hostility toward computers. Whatever the cause, ticking people off by e-mail is remarkably easy.

don't write flippant, rude, or angry e-mail messages

☑ Progress Check

If you can do the following, you've mastered this lesson:

❑ Respond to angry, unreasonable, and downright stupid messages by deleting them, or at least by waiting a day before replying.

❑ Respond to chain letters by pressing the Del key.

❑ Use good e-mail etiquette when sending messages.

This lesson doesn't have any steps, but don't skip over it; this stuff is really important. Here are some words of advice about e-mail etiquette:

♦ **Use specific subjects.** Your subject appears in the listing of messages in the recipient's Inbox. Make it easy for your correspondent to decide what to read first by typing a very short summary of your message.

♦ **Don't use all capital letters in e-mail.** It looks like SHOUTING.

♦ **Avoid sarcasm.** In e-mail, it just sounds obnoxious. In an e-mail message, it can be hard to tell when someone is joking.

♦ **Check your spelling and punctuation before sending messages.** People who don't know you can only judge you on the content of your messages, so make them impressive! In Unit 8, you find out how to install CyberSpell, a spelling-checker plug-in for Netscape.

♦ **Avoid writing anything in e-mail that would embarrass you if distributed widely.** You never know who may decide to forward your message to others.

♦ **If you get a truly offensive message and you are tempted to shoot off a truly offensive response, don't.** Take a walk instead and calm down. The person is probably just having a bad day. As Margy's mother used to say, "His feet probably hurt." If you feel that you need to respond, write the message and then delete it. Or send it to nobody@dummies.com, which gives your message the attention it deserves by automatically throwing your message away.

♦ **Don't flame.** An angry message is called a *flame*. Sending angry messages is called *flaming*, and an exchange of flames is called a *flame war*. Try to stay out of them — flame wars are bad for your blood pressure and for your reputation on the Net.

♦ **Don't get ticked off at someone for not responding to your e-mail.** The Internet eats e-mail from time to time, so you may want to send a follow-up message asking whether your correspondent got the first message.

♦ **Don't believe everything you read.** Just because you get e-mail from someone claiming to be a female 20-something aerobics instructor doesn't mean that you didn't actually hear from a lonely 14-year-old boy looking for friends.

Here's another piece of advice: Never pass along chain letters by e-mail. A few well-known chain letters (that is, messages that tell you to pass the message along to lots of friends and coworkers) to avoid include messages announcing the Good News virus (the virus doesn't exist), get-rich-quick schemes (the most famous of which has the subject line *MAKE MONEY FAST*), messages about a nonexistent modem tax, and messages claiming that a dying boy in England wants to receive greeting cards (he got well a decade ago).

Just read chain letters and delete them. Optional: Skip reading them.

Unit 5 Quiz

For each of the following questions, circle the letter of the correct answer or answers. Remember, each question may have more than one right answer.

1. **An Internet e-mail address looks like this:**

    A. username@computer

    B. username@hostname

    C. yourname@myname

    D. vegetable@mineral

    E. netscape101@dummies.com

2. **You can use Netscape's Mail window to:**

    A. Read e-mail messages addressed to you.

    B. Send e-mail messages to anyone with an Internet account.

    C. Send e-mail messages to anyone with an account on America Online, CompuServe, or an Internet provider, among others.

    D. Reply to e-mail messages you receive.

    E. Impress your friends.

3. **Clicking the To:Mail button on the Toolbar:**

    A. Opens the Message Composition window.

    B. Sends the current message to the President of the Internet.

    C. Lets you write an e-mail message.

    D. Prints the current message so you can put it in an envelope, put a stamp on it, and send it via U.S. Mail.

    E. Creates a new, blank e-mail message.

4. **To send the same message to several people:**

    A. Type the message over and over again, sending it to one person at a time.

    B. On the Mail To line of the message, type a list of the e-mail addresses to which you want to send the message, separated by commas.

    C. Send it to one person and ask that person to pass it along to the other people.

    D. Type one person's address on the Mail To line and another person's address on the Cc: line.

    E. Type the message once, print it out, photocopy the printout, and mail the message to each person by using postal mail.

5. **In the movie *Harriet the Spy*, Harriet's best friends are named:**

    A. Marion, Rachel, and Pinky.

    B. Meg, Zac, and Emily.

    C. Huey, Dewey, and Louie.

    D. Tic, Tac, and Toe.

    E. Sport, Janie, and Ole Golly.

Notes:

Unit 5 Exercise

1. Call a friend who has an Internet or online account. Ask for your friend's e-mail address. Write it down very carefully, including the @ and all the dots (or type it right into a new message in Netscape). Don't worry about capitalization, because it rarely matters in e-mail addresses.

2. Fire up Netscape and create a new e-mail message. Address the message to your friend.

3. In the text of the message, ask your friend to send back a reply.

4. Send the message.

5. Wait a day, or at least an hour or two, and check your incoming e-mail.

6. When you receive it, read your friend's message.

7. Send your friend a reply.

More Mail Moves

Objectives for This Unit

✓ Keeping an address book

✓ Filing messages in your own folders

✓ Sending files by e-mail

✓ Receiving attached files

Prerequisites

▶ Opening the Netscape Mail window (Lesson 5-1)

▶ Sending and receiving e-mail messages (Lessons 5-2 and 5-3)

on the CD   ▶ Meg.gif

Y ou've joined the world of online communications — you can send and receive e-mail. Now when your friends and colleagues exchange e-mail addresses, you can toss yours into the conversation. Why not put your e-mail address on your business cards and stationery?

Now it's time to learn how to save messages that you want to keep, create an address book so that you don't have to type those yucky e-mail addresses over and over, and send files along with your e-mail messages.

Using Your Address Book   Lesson 6-1

Typing e-mail addresses is painstaking and annoying work. One period or at-sign (@) out of place and you're sunk. Luckily, you don't have to type any e-mail address more than once — just type it right into your own personal Netscape Address Book. For each person you correspond with, you can store the following information in your address book:

▶ **Nick Name:** The preferred name of the person who will receive your e-mail. If you are writing a message to your mom, the nickname may be *Mom.*

The nickname can be only one word, with no punctuation. You can enter the person's first name, nickname, or initials. Nicknames can be really long, but keep them short so they're easy to type. Netscape stores all nicknames using small letters, so capitalization doesn't matter.

Notes:

You can leave the Nick Name box blank, if you prefer, and just use the person's real name.

▶ **Name:** The person's real name, which can contain spaces and punctuation.

▶ **E-Mail Address:** The address you want to avoid typing.

▶ **Description:** Notes, such as alternative addresses, company names and titles, or whatever. We like to make a note of the context in which we know the person (work, personal, or some online discussion group).

choosing
Window→Address
Book displays your
address book

In Netscape, your address book appears in a different window, the Address Book window (see Figure 6-1), which you can leave open all the time when you're using Netscape. Leaving the window open makes it easy to address a message with just a few keystrokes or mouse clicks. To see your address book, choose Window⇨Address Book from the Netscape Mail window menu bar.

on the test

In this lesson, you create an entry or two in your address book and use the Address Book to address a message. After you create an address book entry, you can use it to address a message in a number of ways:

▶ When you start a new message, type the person's nickname (instead of his or her e-mail address) in the Mail To or Cc box. When Netscape mails the message, it replaces the nickname you typed with the person's name and e-mail address. Typing a nickname gives you a quick way to address an e-mail message without having to type an e-mail address or switch to the Address Book window.

▶ When you start a new message, click the Address, Mail To, or Cc button to see a list of your address book entries.

▶ Double-click the person's name in the Address Book window. Netscape adds the name to the new message if you are already creating one. If you haven't already created a new message, Netscape makes a new message and addresses it to the person.

Adding names to your address book

We want to hear your comments about this book, so you're going to create an address book entry that makes it easy for you to write to us authors, Margy and Hy, and tell us what you think about this book.

1 **If Netscape isn't already running, run it and display the Netscape Mail window.**

You don't have to be connected to your Internet provider while you're editing your address book. Your address book is stored on your own computer system.

2 **Choose Window⇨Address Book from the menu.**

You see the Address Book window shown in Figure 6-1. The address book is completely empty to begin with, so you don't see much.

Item→Add user
creates an Address
Book entry

3 **Choose Item⇨Add User from the Address Book menu bar.**

You see an Address Book window for adding or editing entries, shown in Figure 6-2.

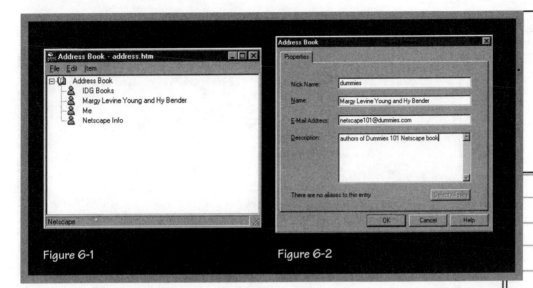

Figure 6-1

Figure 6-2

Figure 6-1: The Netscape
Address Book can store
the e-mail addresses of
your friends and
coworkers.

Figure 6-2: Use this window
to create an address
book entry.

4 **In the Nick Name box, type** dummies.

5 **Click in the Name box or press Tab once to move there. Then type**
Margy Levine Young and Hy Bender.

That's Margy with a hard *G*, please! The Name entry is what appears in your
address book and in your outgoing messages to the person you're addressing,
so you should type carefully.

6 **In the E-Mail Address box, type** netscape101@dummies.com.

Don't type the period at the end (you already knew that). Be sure to get all
those pesky at-signs (@) and periods right!

7 **In the Description box, type** Authors of Dummies 101: Netscape
Navigator book.

This information doesn't appear anywhere except in this very window, so type
whatever you like.

8 **Click the OK button.**

Netscape saves the new address book entry. The entry appears in the Address
Book window with a peculiar-looking icon that we think is supposed to look
like a little person. If you typed spaces or punctuation in the Nick Name box,
Netscape displays a box chiding you about this error, and then Netscape saves
the address book entry with a blank nickname. Not to worry — it's fine for
address book entries not to have nicknames. You can still use this address by
picking it from the list of entries in your address book.

Now you can address messages to us authors by typing **dummies** instead of
netscape101@dummies.com in your message.

9 **Repeat Steps 3 through 8 to create an entry for yourself, typing**
me **for the Nick Name and your own name and e-mail address in
the Name and E-Mail Address boxes.**

You can use this entry to send yourself a test message — in fact, you do so in
a minute!

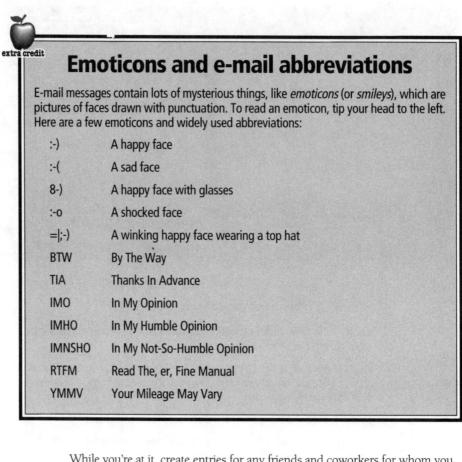

Emoticons and e-mail abbreviations

E-mail messages contain lots of mysterious things, like *emoticons* (or *smileys*), which are pictures of faces drawn with punctuation. To read an emoticon, tip your head to the left. Here are a few emoticons and widely used abbreviations:

:-)	A happy face
:-(	A sad face
8-)	A happy face with glasses
:-o	A shocked face
=|;-)	A winking happy face wearing a top hat
BTW	By The Way
TIA	Thanks In Advance
IMO	In My Opinion
IMHO	In My Humble Opinion
IMNSHO	In My Not-So-Humble Opinion
RTFM	Read The, er, Fine Manual
YMMV	Your Mileage May Vary

While you're at it, create entries for any friends and coworkers for whom you have e-mail addresses.

heads up

You may want to leave your address book open most of the time. If it takes up too much of your screen, you can minimize it (shrink it to icon size) by clicking the Minimize button in the upper-right corner of the Address Book window. You can then reopen it at any time by double-clicking it in Windows 3.1 or clicking its button on the Windows 95 Taskbar.

If you keep the address book open, you can create and address a message quickly. Just switch to the address book and double-click the entry of the person you want to write to. Netscape creates a new message addressed to that person, or adds the address if you are already composing a message.

If you want to edit an address book entry later, open the address book by choosing Window⇨Address Book from the Netscape Mail menu, select the entry that you want to change, and choose Item⇨Properties from the Address Book menu. You see the same window you saw when you created the entry in the first place. Make the necessary changes and click OK.

You can delete address book entries that you no longer use by selecting the entry in the Address Book window and pressing the Del key. If you change your mind after you delete, you can get your entry back by choosing Edit⇨Undo or pressing Ctrl+Z. This trick works only immediately after you delete an entry.

Minimize button

extra credit

Don't retype e-mail addresses!

If you receive an e-mail message from someone whom you want to add to your address book, display the message and then choose Message⇨Add to Address Book from the menu. Netscape pops up an Address Book window ready for you to create an address book entry for the person. Best of all, the person's name and e-mail address are already filled in — Netscape copies the information from the message you were reading. All you have to do is fill in a nickname, if you want the entry to have one, and a description (also optional).

If a message contains an e-mail address in the text, you still don't have to retype it. Instead, you can use the Windows cut-and-paste commands to copy the address into your address book. Here's how:

1. **Display the message.**

2. **Highlight the e-mail address by using the mouse.**

3. **Press Ctrl+C (or choose Edit⇨Copy from the menu) to copy the e-mail address to the Windows Clipboard, an invisible holding area that you can use for storing information.**

4. **Open the Address Book window by choosing Window⇨Address Book.**

5. **Create a new entry by choosing Item⇨Add User.**

6. **With your cursor in the E-Mail Address box, press Ctrl+V to paste the contents of the Windows Clipboard into Netscape. The e-mail address appears!**

7. **Click OK to save the address book entry.**

Use the cut-and-paste commands whenever possible so that you don't have typos in those pesky e-mail addresses.

Addressing messages by using the address book

Try sending a message to yourself by using the address book entry you just created:

1 Click the To:Mail button on the Toolbar.

The Message Composition window pops up.

2 Click the Address button or the Mail To button.

Both buttons display the Select Addresses window, which shows a list of entries in your address book, as shown in Figure 6-3.

3 Click the entry for yourself and then click the To button.

Netscape enters your e-mail address in the message you're composing. Alternately, you can double-click the address you want.

If you want to send a message to several other people on your address list, you can select each name and click the To button after each, or double-click each name. Or you can address your message to a group of people at the same time by clicking the first person's name, holding down the Ctrl key while clicking the other names, and then clicking the To button.

Notes:

Address

the Address button
in the Message
Composition window
displays your
address book
entries

Figure 6-3: Choose an address book entry and then click a button to tell Netscape what to do with it.

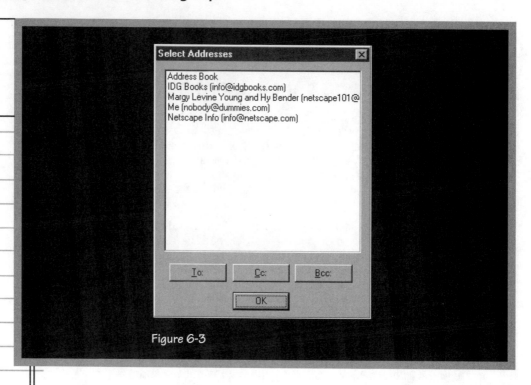

Figure 6-3

 Click OK.

The Select Addresses window goes away, leaving you looking at the Message Composition window.

 Click in the Subject box and type a subject.

Something like **You're terrific!** is always appropriate.

 In the message area, type a short message telling yourself something that you've been meaning to think about and then click the Send button.

The Message Composition window closes after Netscape sends the message.

The next time you get your e-mail (or soon, anyway), you get the message you sent.

heads up

Because you entered *dummies* as a nickname for our address book entry, you can also address messages to us authors by typing **dummies** in the Mail To box. You can also address messages to yourself using the nickname *me*. When you send the message (or while you edit the message), Netscape replaces the nickname with the full name and e-mail address.

Note: The Cc button also displays the Select Addresses window, but when you double-click a name it appears in the Cc box in the Message Composition window — perfect for sending copies of a message.

Recess

Now that you've sent a message to yourself, take a little walk or go wash the dishes for a few minutes to give the Internet time to deliver your message to you.

☑ Progress Check

If you can do the following, you've mastered this lesson:

❑ Create address book entries for your friends and coworkers.

❑ Address e-mail messages by using the address book.

❑ Look at your list of entries in the Address Book window.

Filing Messages in Folders　　Lesson 6-2

When you receive important correspondence on paper, you file it in folders for safekeeping. (Yeah, right — who are we kidding? You probably just stack it on top of all those other important papers, like we do.) The same is true when you receive an important e-mail message — except that the folders are on your hard disk instead of in a filing cabinet. When you run Netscape Navigator for the first time, you have one folder named Inbox. The first time you delete a message, Netscape makes a folder named Trash to put the deleted message in. When you send your first message, Netscape creates the Sent folder to put a copy of the sent message in. But Netscape isn't the only one who can create folders; you can create as many folders as you want for storing messages according to topic or according to the sender.

To create a new folder, choose File⇨New Folder from the Netscape Mail menu. Netscape asks for the name of the folder — type an appropriate name and click OK. The folder appears in the list of folders, along with your existing folders.

To see the messages in a folder, click the folder name on the list of folders in the upper-left corner of your Netscape Mail window. Of course, right after you create a folder, it is completely empty. Not a problem — you can move or copy messages into a folder by using the Message⇨Move and Message⇨Copy commands.

You may want to make a folder for each project you're working on, like *Budget, Big Report,* and *Dummies 101 Book.* Or you can make a folder for each person you correspond with. You may also want a *To Do* folder for messages that you have to do something about.

If you get tired of a folder and all the messages in it, delete the folder by choosing Edit⇨Delete Folder from the menu.

In this lesson, you create a new folder and move a message into it.

extra credit

Displaying the Netscape Mail window automatically

You can tell Netscape that when you start it up, you'd like to see the Netscape Mail window first thing. Choose Options⇨General Preferences from the menu to display the Preferences dialog box. Click the Appearance tab in the upper-left corner of the window (if it isn't already selected). In the Startup section of the window are the On Startup Launch settings. Ordinarily, only the Netscape Browser setting is selected (that is, a check mark appears in its box). This window is used for browsing the World Wide Web, as you learned in Unit 1.

To tell Netscape to display the Mail window in addition to the browser window, click the Netscape Mail box so that it contains a check. Then click OK to make the Preferences dialog box go away.

From now on, when you double-click the Netscape icon, both the browser window and the Mail window appear automatically.

---

create folders by project or for each person you correspond with

Notes:

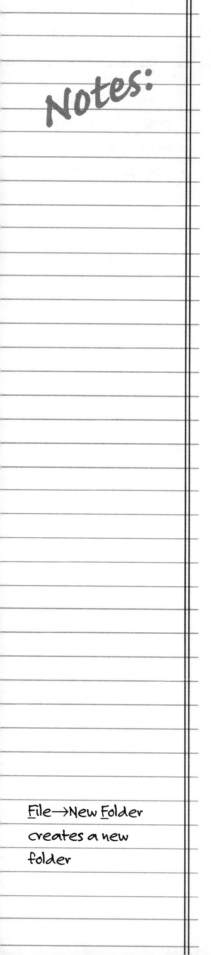

Notes:

extra credit

Creating a signature

Many e-mail users like to create a *signature,* or a few lines of text that Netscape automatically adds to the end of every message you send. Instead of typing your name and e-mail address at the end of every message, you can have Netscape do it for you.

Your signature should include your whole name, your e-mail address, and (optionally) a pithy saying or message that tells your correspondents something interesting about you (or your organization) and piques their interest. Don't include long sayings, quotes, or cute pictures created from characters (also known as *ASCII art*). They can be interesting the first time someone gets mail from you, but they get old fast after the second or third message. The entire signature should be no more than four lines long.

To create a signature for yourself, follow these steps:

1. **Create a *signature file,* or a text file that contains the lines you want in your signature.**

   You can use Notepad (the Windows built-in text editor) to create your signature file, or use any word processor that can save the signature file as an ASCII text file (a file that contains only characters, with no formatting).

2. **Save the file in your Netscape program folder using the name** Signature.txt.

   Now you can set the Netscape option that adds the text in your signature file to each e-mail message you send.

3. **Choose Options⇨Mail and News Preferences from the Netscape menu.**

   You see the Preferences dialog box.

4. **Click the Identity tab and then click the Browse button to the right of the Signature File box. Find the signature file you just created and click Open.**

   Now the name of your signature file appears in the Signature File box.

5. **Click OK.**

   Netscape saves your settings, including the name of your signature file.

Creating a new folder

You probably need a Personal folder, unless you never get e-mail from friends. Here's how to create a Personal folder. (If you've already created a Personal folder, create a folder with another name.)

1   Run Netscape if it's not already running, and open the Netscape Mail window.

You see the usual list of folders, including Inbox and Trash. You don't need to be connected to your Internet provider to create folders and move messages around from folder to folder.

File→New Folder
creates a new
folder

2   Choose File⇨New Folder from the menu.

Netscape asks for the name of the new folder.

3   Type Personal **and press Enter or click OK.**

The new folder name appears on the list of folders. The list of the messages in the Personal folder is blank, because the folder is empty.

After you create a folder, you can transfer messages into it by using the Message⇨Move or Message⇨Copy command. You can read, reply to, delete, and print messages in folders that you create by using the same techniques you learned in this unit and Unit 5.

Sorting your mail

Move a message into your Personal folder like this:

1 **Click the Inbox folder on your list of folders.**

2 **Click the message you received from *Internet For Dummies Central*.**

The entry in the Sender column says `Automated response`. This message definitely deserves to get filed.

3 **Choose Message⇨Move from the menu.**

You see a little numbered list of your folders, including your new Personal folder.

4 **Choose Personal from the list.**

The message disappears from the list of messages in your Inbox folder. And the number to the right of the Personal folder is now 1, indicating that the folder contains one message. Guess which one it is?

5 **Click Personal in the list of folders in the upper-left corner of the Netscape Mail window.**

See? Your message from us is now in your Personal folder.

An easier way to move messages from one folder to another is to drag them there with your mouse. You can *copy* a message to another folder by holding down the Ctrl key while you drag a message.

You can move more than one message at a time. If you want to select a bunch of messages that appear together in a list of messages, click the top message and then hold down the Shift key as you click the bottom message. Netscape selects the entire set of messages. If you want to select messages that don't appear together, click the first message you want to select and then hold down the Ctrl key as you click each of the other messages that you want to select. After you select the messages that you want to move, choose Message⇨Move from the menu.

You can also copy a message to another folder by using the Message⇨Copy command. Netscape leaves a copy of the message in the original folder and puts a copy in the folder you specify.

Try filing your important messages in Netscape folders rather than printing each message and filing it in a manila folder. Save a tree!

move messages by using Message→Move; copy them by using Message→Copy

☑ **Progress Check**

If you can do the following, you've mastered this lesson:

❑ Create a new folder.

❑ Move a message into a folder.

Lesson 6-3

Sending Files Along with Your Messages

We love e-mail, and we use it for just about everything, including submitting the units in this book to our editors at IDG Books Worldwide. But e-mail messages are limited to just plain text — you can't use boldface, italics, underlining, or large flashy fonts in e-mail messages. To submit units with all the formatting that our editors need, we *attach* word processing documents to our e-mail messages. In fact, you can attach almost any file to a message — word processing documents, spreadsheets, data files, graphics files, you name it! The only limit is the size of the file; many e-mail systems choke on files larger than about 50K (50,000 characters).

Why send a file by e-mail? Here are some common reasons:

- You want someone to know what you look like, so you want to send a graphics file containing a scanned picture of yourself.

- You want to send your company's sales figures to your business partner in an Excel spreadsheet file.

- You ran across a great public domain program for creating genealogy charts that you'd like to share with your sister.

- You've created an inventory of your jazz collection with a database program and now want to get it to a dealer who's interested in buying rare music albums.

To send a file by e-mail, you *attach* the file to an e-mail message. The file you send is called an *attachment*.

In this lesson, you learn how to send a message with a file attached to it. Lesson 6-4 tells you what to do when you receive an attached file.

You have three ways to attach a file to a message (think of these methods as tape, staples, and glue): MIME, uuencoding, and BinHex. These methods all result in the same thing — a file arrives along with an e-mail message. All three methods work by converting your file into specially encoded text so that it can be sent by e-mail. The problem is that not all e-mail programs and online services can handle all three methods. For a file to arrive safely, both the sender and the receiver have to be able to handle the same method. If the recipient's e-mail program can't convert the specially encoded text back into the original file, the file transfer doesn't work.

Netscape uses MIME (the most modern, up-to-date method) when sending attached files. Netscape can handle incoming e-mail messages that use any of the three attachment methods.

Most e-mail programs, including the following, can receive and read MIME attachments:

- Eudora Light and Eudora Pro (excellent Windows and Macintosh e-mail programs)

- Microsoft Internet Explorer (a Web browser that does e-mail, too)

- PINE (a UNIX e-mail program)

- Pegasus (a free Windows and Macintosh e-mail program)

attachment = file that is sent as part of an e-mail message

Netscape sends files by using MIME

extra credit

What happens to dead letters?

If you type an e-mail address incorrectly, Netscape usually can't deliver the message. Undeliverable messages usually return to you with an error message. If you get a large, scary-looking message from a Mail Delivery Subsystem, or some other official-sounding program, read through the message until you find the part where it tells you what address the original message contained.

If you kept a copy of the original message in your Sent folder, you can create a new message, copy the text from the old message to the new message, type the correct e-mail address, and click the Send button. (To copy text from one message to another, highlight the text to copy with your mouse and press Ctrl+C. Click in the message area of the new message and then press Ctrl+V.)

▶ America Online access program (software that comes with America Online, the largest commercial online service)

▶ GNNconnect (software that comes with Global Network Navigator, or GNN, a national Internet provider)

▶ NetCruiser (software that comes with Netcom, a national Internet provider)

Sending files to people who use these online services and e-mail programs should work fine.

However, the following e-mail programs and online services *can't* handle files attached using MIME (at least at the time we wrote this book):

▶ Microsoft Mail (a mail system used on local area networks, which connect computers that are in the same building)

▶ Some UNIX e-mail programs (such as elm)

▶ WinCIM and MacCIM (programs used to access CompuServe, another big online service)

▶ Microsoft Exchange (the e-mail program that comes with Windows 95 and is used by many Microsoft network users)

Which e-mail program you use controls whether you can send and receive attached files. Because you use Netscape Mail, you can send MIME attachments and receive any type of attachment, regardless of the type of account you use Netscape with.

If you send a message with an attached file to someone whose e-mail program can't deal with attachments, the message appears as a long series of incomprehensible gibberish when they open it, and you may get some complaints. We tell you what to do about sending messages to these people in just a minute.

heads up

▶ Before you send a message with an attached file to, say, your mother, take a look at her e-mail address. If the part after the at-sign (@) is `worldnet.att.net` (AT&T WorldNet Service, which uses Netscape and Eudora for mail), `aol.com` (America Online), `gnn.com` (GNN), or `ix.netcom.com` (Netcom), you know that sending an attachment to Mom will work fine.

(margin note:) Notes:

some e-mail programs can't handle MIME attachments

ask before sending
files via e-mail

Notes:

Otherwise, write a note first asking what types of attachments her e-mail program can deal with. (Most e-mail users don't know the answer to this question, but asking it is a great way to impress people.) If the intended recipient can't handle an attached file, there's no point sending one! If your recipient isn't sure what kind of attachments work, refer to the preceding list or try MIME first.

▸ Regardless of the type of online account or e-mail program your correspondent uses, make sure that he or she can deal with the file that you want to send.

For example, if you plan to send a WordPerfect document or an Excel spreadsheet, write to ask whether the recipient can read WordPerfect documents or Excel spreadsheets. You may need to save your file in a special format that the recipient can handle. Most word processors, spreadsheet programs, and database programs can save files in a wide variety of formats.

▸ Before sending a file, make sure that the addressee wants to receive it!

We receive a lot of e-mail from people we don't know, and we find it annoying when people send us files, especially large ones. Ask before you send! Receiving a large file can take several minutes to download, typing up the phone and making the recipient wait around to read the incoming mail. For people who pay by the hour to connect to the Internet, this costs the recipient money.

▸ Consider compressing the file before sending it. Appendix B describes how to install and use WinZip, a widely used file-compressor that is on your *Dummies 101* CD-ROM. Make sure that the recipient knows how to decompress the file!

When you're sure that the person to whom you want to send a file can deal with a MIME attachment, attaching the file to a message is easy.

on the CD

Follow these steps to send a file to yourself, just for practice:

1 **Run Netscape and display the Netscape Mail window.**

2 **Start composing a new message by clicking the To:Mail button on the Netscape Mail window Toolbar.**

You see the Message Composition window. (By the way, you can also attach a file when you are replying to a message — you can click the Attach button whenever you use the Message Composition window. But this is a test, and sending your first attachment to yourself is safer.)

3 **In the Mail To box, type your own e-mail address. If you created a nickname for yourself in Lesson 6-1, type the nickname instead.**

You are mailing a file to yourself so that, in the next lesson, you can see what receiving a file is like.

4 **In the Subject box, type something like** Picture by five-year-old Meg.

Margy's daughter Meg drew a self-portrait while wearing a blue dress with black dots. We scanned it in and stored it in a graphics file.

5 **In the text of the message (above your signature), type something like** Here's a graphics file in GIF format with a child's picture.

Always include information about the file that you're attaching, including what the file is about and what format the file is in. Otherwise, the recipient may not know what to do with it! (If you're wondering, *GIF* format is a standard format for graphics files. Pictures are stored in files in a variety of formats with various unpronounceable names.)

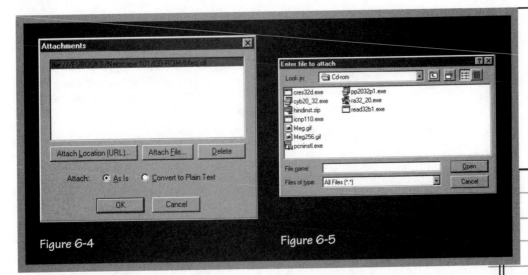

Figure 6-4

Figure 6-5

Figure 6-4: The Attachments window lists the files that are attached to a message.

Figure 6-5: The Enter file to attach dialog box tells Netscape which file (or files) you want to send with your message.

6 **Click the Attach button on the Message Composition Toolbar or click the Attachment button in the top part of the window.**

If you prefer, you can choose File⇨Attach File from the menu bar of the message composition window. You see the Attachments window, shown in Figure 6-4. The big white box contains a list of attachments to the current message. (It starts out empty and ends up containing a list of the names of the files attached to the message.) You can attach more than one file to a message.

The As is button is selected in the Attachments dialog box, indicating that Netscape doesn't plan to fool around with the contents of the graphics file you just selected. And a good thing, too!

7 **Click the Attach File button.**

You see the Enter file to attach dialog box (shown in Figure 6-5). In Windows 95, the Look in box shows the current folder. In Windows 3.1, look at the Directories box for the current folder.

on the CD

8 **Stick the *Dummies 101* CD-ROM in your CD-ROM drive.**

Be sure to touch only the edges of the disc and to insert the disc with its label side up. The file you're going to attach is on the CD-ROM that came with this book.

9 **Windows 95 users only: If the *Dummies 101* installation program appears, click its Exit button.**

You don't need to install the little graphics file that you're about to attach to your e-mail message. You can attach it directly from the CD-ROM to avoid cluttering up your hard disk.

10 **For Windows 95 users, click in the Look in box in the Enter file to attach dialog box and choose your CD-ROM drive from the list that appears. For Windows 3.1 users, click in the Drives box and choose your CD drive.**

You see a list of the files and folders on the *Dummies 101* CD-ROM. A bunch of stuff is there — some Netscape plug-in programs that you find out about in Unit 8, the software for AT&T WorldNet Service (in case you don't already have an Internet account), other programs, and a little graphics file named Meg.gif.

11 **Click Meg.gif so that the filename appears in the File name box, and click the Open button.**

Attach button

No, Netscape doesn't actually open the file and display it — the Open button is misnamed. Instead, Netscape adds the filename to the list of items to attach to your e-mail message. The Enter file to attach dialog box disappears, and you see the Attachments dialog box with a strange-looking item listed. The listed item looks something like this:

```
file:///D|/Meg.gif
```

This is Netscape's way of saying that Meg.gif is a file and that it is stored (in this case) in D:\Meg.gif. (This strange-looking thing is a URL, which you learned about in Unit 1.) In this example, the CD-ROM drive is drive D.

If you wanted to attach another file to this message, you would repeat Steps 7 through 11 and choose the name of the additional file to attach.

12 **Click OK at the bottom of the Attachments dialog box.**

The Attachments dialog box evaporates, and you return to the message composition window. The filename Meg.gif appears faintly in the box to the right of the Attachment button.

Your message is ready to send, complete with attached file.

13 **Make sure that you're connected to your Internet provider and then click the Send button.**

Netscape sends the message. Because this file is not very large (16K), sending it and receiving it should not take too long (under a minute). If, in the future, you decide to send larger files (50K or more), sending the message may take a minute or two.

Messages appear in the bottom line of the Netscape Mail window, telling you what is going on. You see messages like `Contacting host` and `Sending file`.

As you can see, sending a file by e-mail is easy — just compose a message, attach the file to the message, and send the e-mail as usual by clicking the Send button. You'll be happy to know that receiving and reading an attached file is just as easy.

extra credit

Copying is sometimes better than attaching

Sometimes you want to send files that contain text, the format of which isn't very important. In cases such as these, you can eliminate the risk that the recipient of your message doesn't have the word processor that created your file (that is, won't be able to read your file). Instead, you can copy the text from your file directly into your message and leave it at that.

Run the word processor or other program that you used to create the text file and then open the file that contains the text you want to send. Use your mouse to select all the text you want to include in your e-mail message. Then press Ctrl+C or choose Edit⇨Copy from the menu to copy the text into your Windows Clipboard.

Next, switch to Netscape Navigator. Start a new message by clicking the To:Mail button and then click in the message area of the Message Composition window. Press Ctrl+V to paste the text from the Windows Clipboard into your message; the text is inserted at your cursor position.

You may need to edit the text after copying it into your message. For example, carriage returns may appear in the wrong places in the message. You may also need to add blank lines between paragraphs. But that's okay — you can take this opportunity to review the text one last time.

☑ **Progress Check**

If you can do the following, you've mastered this lesson:

❑ Attach a file to a message.

❑ Send the message.

Receiving an Attached File   Lesson 6-4

Netscape can handle incoming messages with files attached using MIME, uuencoding, or BinHex — all three methods of attaching files. Most people send MIME attachments because MIME is the most widely used attachment method, but people with older software may send uuencoded attachments. Mac mail programs sometimes use BinHex attachments. When you receive the message, Netscape shows you the filename. You can tell Netscape whether you want to download the file:

1 **Run Netscape and display the Netscape Mail window if it's not already on your screen.**

2 **Click the Inbox folder on your list of folders.**

Display your Inbox before you get your mail so that you can see when new messages arrive.

3 **Click the Get Mail button on the Toolbar or press Ctrl+T.**

Netscape collects the e-mail message that you just sent to yourself and downloads it to your computer. This process may take a minute or two, because messages with attached graphics files are much larger than text-only messages. You see the message `Connect: Host contacted, sending login information` or `Connect: Contacting host` on the bottom line of the Netscape Mail window for what may seem an interminable amount of time. Don't worry — these messages just mean that Netscape is getting your mail.

You may need to wait a few minutes and click the Get Mail button again. Your Internet provider may need several minutes to process the message you sent in Lesson 6-3 and put it in your mailbox, ready to download.

When the message you sent in Lesson 6-3 arrives, it is listed along with the messages in your Inbox.

4 **Click the message.**

The text of the message appears in the lower part of the Netscape Mail window, along with . . . look at that! A picture that looks as though it was drawn by a five-year-old! (In fact, it *was* drawn by a five-year-old, but the authors of this book couldn't have done much better.) Take a look at Figure 6-6.

Netscape knows how to display some types of graphics files, including GIF files, which is what this picture is. If you receive another type of file, like a word processing document, you see an attachment box in your message with information about the file. See the end of this lesson for what to do when you see an attachment box.

extra credit

URLs in e-mail messages

When Netscape spots a URL (which you learned about in Unit 1) in an e-mail message, Netscape highlights the address by displaying it in blue or purple and underlining it. If you click the URL in the message, and you're connected to the Internet at the time, Netscape displays the appropriate Web page or other information in its browser window.

Notes:

some attached pictures appear right in the message

Figure 6-6: Netscape
displays an attached
picture as part of the
e-mail message — cool!

Figure 6-7: What do you
want to do with this
attached picture?

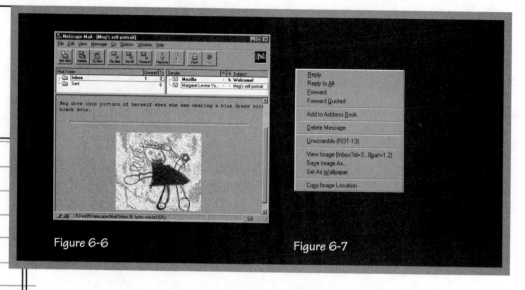

Figure 6-6   Figure 6-7

to save a picture
file, right-click the
picture and choose
Sa<u>v</u>e Image As

Up One Level button

to save other
attachments, click
the attachment
link and click Save
File

5 **Using your *right* mouse button, click the picture.**

A menu pops up, as shown in Figure 6-7. You can save the picture in a
separate file for use with other programs.

6 **Choose the Sa<u>v</u>e Image As option.**

You see the Save As dialog box, shown in Figure 6-8.

7 **Choose a folder in which to save the graphics file.**

C:\My Documents or C:\DOCS may be a good choice. In Windows 95, click the
Up One Level button to move up one folder. Keep clicking it until you get to
the root folder (C:\) of your hard disk. (If you use a hard disk with a letter other
than C, select that drive instead.) Then move down into the folder you want to
use by double-clicking the folder name. In Windows 3.1, change folders by
clicking in the <u>D</u>irectories box.

8 **Click in the File <u>n</u>ame box and type Meg.gif.**

You can use a different filename, but use *gif* as the extension, because this file
contains a picture in GIF format. With luck, the text of the message tells you
the filename of the picture, so you know what to call it. Windows knows how
to handle files by looking at their extensions.

9 **Click the <u>S</u>ave or OK button.**

You see the Saving Location window as Netscape saves the file.

Netscape doesn't know what to do with lots of file types — programs, word
processing documents, sound files, video clips, and the like. These files appear
as boxes in your message. If your attached file appears as a box, click the left
part of the box, which says something like *Attachment 1* or *Attachment 2* in
blue underlined text. You see the Unknown File Type dialog box.

extra credit

Practice safe computing

If someone sends you a program by e-mail, should you go ahead and run it? Depends on
who sends it to you! If you don't know the sender, don't run the program unless you run
a virus-checker first. See Lesson 3-2 for information about checking programs for viruses.

Figure 6-8: Where do you want to save the file?

Figure 6-8

If you see the Unknown File Type dialog box, you may be tempted to click the More Info button, but we haven't found that it displays any useful information. Instead, take a look at the filename extension (the part of the filename after the last period) to figure out what type of file it is. Then click the Save File button and tell Netscape where to save the file.

After you save the file, run Windows Explorer, My Computer, or File Manager and display the folder you put the file in. Double-click the filename. If the file is a program, Windows runs it. If Windows recognizes the filename extension, it runs the appropriate program for viewing or reading that type of file, assuming that you have the program. If Windows doesn't recognize the filename extension, you need to manually run a program that works with that type of file.

☑ **Progress Check**

If you can do the following, you've mastered this lesson:

❑ Receive a file with an attachment.

❑ Save an attached picture in a separate file.

❑ Save other types of attachments in separate files.

Unit 6 Quiz

For each of the following questions, circle the letter of the correct answer or answers. Remember, some questions may have more than one right answer.

1. **A nickname is:**

   A. A cute name that only your childhood friends can get away with calling you.

   B. An entry in the Nick Name box.

   C. From the Middle English *eekname,* meaning "also name."

   D. A name you can use when addressing e-mail messages so that you don't have to type the person's actual e-mail address.

2. **To make a new mail folder:**

   A. Get the materials at a hardware store.

   B. Select a message to put in the new folder and choose Message⇨Move from the menu.

   C. Open the Netscape Mail window and click the New button.

   D. Open the Message Composition window and click the New button.

Notes:

3. **To attach a file to an e-mail message, you:**

    A. Choose the Edit⇨Paste command to glue the file to the message.

    B. Click the Attach button on the Message Composition window.

    C. Send a message to the intended recipient of the file asking for his or her mailing address, copy the file to a diskette, put the diskette into a mailer, and mail the diskette.

    D. Choose File⇨Attach File from the menu bar of the Message Composition window.

4. **Reasons to attach a file to an e-mail message include:**

    A. Sending word processing documents to colleagues who are collaborating on a writing project.

    B. Sending pictures of your kids to your parents.

    C. Wanting to show off how much you know about the Internet.

    D. Sending a file full of vital top-secret information to yourself just before enemy agents break down your door so that you can delete the original file from your hard disk and claim that you don't know what file they are talking about.

5. **Before sending a file to someone, you should be sure that:**

    A. The person's e-mail program can handle MIME attachments, because Netscape attaches files by using MIME.

    B. The person has software that can read the type of file that you are sending; for example, the appropriate word processor, spreadsheet, or database program.

    C. The person feels like dealing with the whole subject of attached files.

    D. The person wants to receive the file.

Unit 6 Exercise

1. Remember that friend you exchanged messages with in the Unit 5 Exercise? Get hold of that person's e-mail address. You can find it by opening the message you sent, if the message is still in your Sent folder.

    Note: If you skipped the Unit 5 Exercise, find a friend with an e-mail address. Write down the address very carefully.

2. In the Address Book, create an entry for your friend. Type your friend's first name or initials as the nickname.

    Extra credit: Use the cut-and-paste commands to copy your friend's address from a message in your Sent folder to the address book.

4. Create a new message and address it to your friend by using the address book.

5. Type a message to your friend. Be sure to mention that you're reading this wonderful book about learning how to use Netscape Navigator.

    Extra credit: Find out whether your friend's mail program can handle MIME attachments and attach an appropriate file to your message.

6. Send the message.

Joining Usenet Newsgroups

Objectives for This Unit

✓ Understanding what Usenet newsgroups are all about

✓ Opening and using the Netscape News window

✓ Subscribing to and reading newsgroups

✓ Posting articles to newsgroups

✓ Finding articles on specific topics

Prerequisites

▶ Browsing the Web
(Lessons 1-2, 1-3, and 2-1)

▶ Entering a URL
(Lesson 2-3)

▶ Searching the Web
(Lesson 2-5)

▶ E-mail etiquette
(Lesson 5-5)

A mong the best resources of the Internet are its tens of thousands of ongoing discussion groups, which conduct lively conversations devoted to virtually every subject under the sun (and even a few beyond it).

on the CD

Some of the most useful and interesting discussions take place via e-mail mailing lists. More information about this form of discussion group appears in Unit ML, "Joining Discussions by E-mail," which is stored on the CD-ROM that came with this book in a file named maillist.pdf. You can read this file by using the Acrobat Reader program, which is also stored on the CD-ROM. (For more information, see Appendix B.)

on the test

Another way to participate in online discussions is to join newsgroups. A *newsgroup* is an ongoing discussion of a particular topic that takes place via an area of the Internet called *Usenet*. Thousands of newsgroups exist, so you can find discussions on virtually any subject you can think of, ranging from baseball (`rec.sports.baseball`) to orthopedic surgery (`sci.medicine.orthopedic`), and from pantyhose (`alt.pantyhose`) to the afterlife (`alt.life.afterlife`). Over 50,000 new messages — or, as they're referred to on Usenet, *articles* — pour into newsgroups every day, making these collective talkfests a rich resource for both learning and fun.

Each newsgroup has a name consisting of a bunch of words (or parts of words) strung together by dots.

newsgroup = ongoing discussion or series of announcements

Usenet = system of thousands of newsgroups

article = message distributed via a Usenet newsgroup

newsgroups are
organized into
hierarchies

The first word in a newsgroup name tells you the general category the newsgroup falls under (for example, `rec` for recreational or `sci` for scientific). The following word or words in the name further define the newsgroup's topic. Depending on how specific the newsgroup is and how many similar newsgroups exist, the name may have several words, or only two. For example, precisely one U.S. newsgroup discusses the joy of flying kites, so the name of the newsgroup is `rec.kites`. However, lots of newsgroups talk about pets, so the name of the cats newsgroup is `rec.pets.cats`.

on the test

All the newsgroups that start with the same initial word or words are called a *hierarchy*. The following are the seven major hierarchies; that is, the seven types of newsgroups that are the most widely distributed:

- ▶ `rec:` Recreational topics, such as sports, games, collecting, music, and art

- ▶ `soc:` Both social issues (such as politics, religion, and human rights) and socializing (such as singles and pen-pal newsgroups)

- ▶ `talk:` Impassioned debate about topical and controversial issues (though often more heat than light is shed here)

- ▶ `sci:` Scientific topics, such as physics, chemistry, biology, and medicine

- ▶ `comp:` Computer-related topics, including discussions of PC software and hardware

- ▶ `news:` Topics concerning Usenet and newsgroups themselves

- ▶ `misc:` Miscellaneous topics that don't fit neatly under the other six hierarchies, such as health and fitness, screenwriting, job hunting, and for-sale notices

extra credit

What's the difference between newsgroups and mailing lists?

If you've read Unit ML, "Joining Discussions by E-mail," you may wonder how getting involved in newsgroups differs from joining mailing lists.

Newsgroups are similar to mailing lists in that they let you read and participate in focused discussions along with other nice people on the Internet. Also, like mailing lists, newsgroups can be announcement only (just one person posts articles to the newsgroup), moderated (one person acts as a censor, approving articles before making them public), or open discussion (anyone can post articles).

However, a mailing list is managed at one computer, by one person or program, and sends each of its messages directly from the list manager to the subscriber. In contrast, newsgroup articles aren't sent directly to subscribers, but are passed along all over the Internet by various computers (called *news servers*) that are especially assigned to receive them, with no central management. This means that you can reach out and grab articles from any newsgroup at any time, whether you're subscribed to the newsgroup or not. In fact, when you subscribe to a newsgroup, that action affects only the behavior of Netscape Navigator, not other computers. (Specifically, your subscribing to a newsgroup makes Netscape put your selection in a special *subscribed* list so that you can display the newsgroup quickly and tells Netscape to keep track of your unread messages in the newsgroup.)

The bottom line, however, is that both mailing lists and newsgroups let you share information with millions of other knowledgeable people around the world. What you should concentrate on isn't picking which message distribution system you prefer (there's no reason not to use both), but discovering which discussions taking place on the Internet are the most likely to help you out or make you happy.

Many newer or more narrow hierarchies aren't as "official" but are of great interest anyway. The most notable of these by far is `alt` (short for *alternative*), which contains over 2,500 wildly diverse newsgroups. These range from the benign (`alt.sewing`, `alt.algebra.help`, `alt.comedy.slapstick.3-stooges`) to the serious (`alt.adoption`, `alt.alcohol`, `alt.censorship`, `alt.save.the.earth`) to the off-the-wall (`alt.alien.visitors`, `alt.fan.lemur`, `alt.barney.dinosaur.die.die.die`).

Other newsgroup hierarchies include those devoted to a particular company (for example, `microsoft` for Microsoft or `netscape` for Netscape Communications) or region (for example, `ny` for topics related to New York or `fr` for topics that are related to France *and* are discussed in French).

Because keeping up-to-date on all these newsgroups consumes a huge amount of an Internet provider's computer resources, some providers choose to not carry hierarchies outside the seven long-established ones listed earlier.

In this unit, you first open the Netscape News window and use it to read a few newsgroup articles. You then learn how to find newsgroups devoted to topics that interest you, join newsgroups, and post your own newsgroup articles.

Notes:

Reading Newsgroup Articles

Lesson 7-1

To get the articles that make up newsgroups, Netscape has to connect to a *news server* (or *news host*), a computer that provides newsgroup articles. Your Internet provider or online service has a news server you can use. Your copy of Netscape Navigator may already know the name of your provider's news server, or you may have to tell it. You can use more than one news server — in fact, the company that makes Netscape has its own news server that you can use to read special newsgroups for Netscape users.

Start out by opening the Netscape News window, making sure that you're connected to your Internet provider's news server, and reading the articles in a newsgroup for beginners.

Opening the Netscape News window

To examine the Netscape News window, follow these steps:

1 Connect to your Internet provider and run Netscape.

You see the Netscape browser window (unless you've told Netscape to open another window upon startup).

2 Choose Window⇨Netscape News from the menu bar.

You see the Netscape News window shown in Figure 7-1. The window looks a lot like the Netscape Mail window that you got friendly with in Unit 5. However, instead of listing folders on your hard disk, the upper-left section of the window lists news servers and newsgroups (under the heading *News Server*). After you select a newsgroup, the upper-right section of the window lists the articles in the newsgroup, and the lower part of the window displays the text of each selected article.

to read newsgroups, choose Window→ Netscape News

Figure 7-1: The Netscape News window lists newsgroup names in the upper-left part of the window.

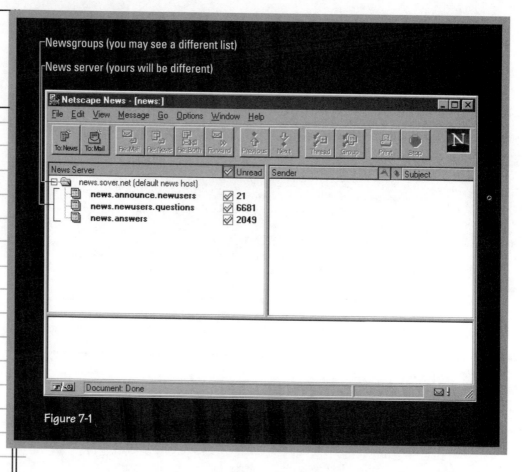

Figure 7-1

3 **If you didn't see an error message, skip the next section and go directly to the following section, "Seeing a list of newsgroups."**

You are ready to read some newsgroup articles!

If you see an error message that says that Netscape is unable to locate your news server, or if no news servers appear in the news server list, click OK and continue with the next section, "Telling Netscape about your news server."

You can't read newsgroup articles until Netscape can contact a news server.

Telling Netscape about your news server

If you don't see any news servers in the upper-left part of the Netscape News window, or if you see error messages when you try to read articles, follow these steps:

1 **Call your Internet provider to find out the name of its news server.**

Write the name on the Cheat Sheet at the front of this book. The name of the news server is usually the word *news* followed by a dot and the name of your provider. For example, the AT&T WorldNet news server is named netnews.worldnet.att.net.

2 **Choose Options⇨Mail and News Preferences from the Netscape News window.**

You see the Preferences dialog box.

3 **Click the Servers tab along the top of the Preferences dialog box.**

4 **Click in the News (NNTP) Server box and type the name of the news server.**

5 **Click OK.**

Now your provider's news server appears in the list of news servers, with the notation `(default news host)`.

If other news servers appear in your news server list, just ignore them. For example, before you told Netscape about your provider's news server, it may have tried to use a nonexistent news server named just *news,* and this news server may still be hanging around on your list of news servers.

Note: You can delete a news server that you're sure you can't or won't use by clicking the news server and choosing File⇨Remove News Host from the menu bar. When Netscape asks whether you really want to delete the news server and all the newsgroups that it carries, click OK. Don't worry — you aren't really deleting newsgroups; you're just deleting them from your Netscape window.

Seeing a list of newsgroups

A little yellow folder icon appears to the left of each news server on your list, along with a box that contains either a plus sign or a minus sign. When the little folder icon is open, a list of newsgroups appears under the name of the news server, and you can click the minus sign box to close the folder icon and make the list of newsgroups go away. If the yellow folder icon to the left of the news server name is closed, no newsgroups appear, and you can click the plus sign box to make the list of newsgroups appear. In Figure 7-1, the folder to the left of the news server is open, a minus sign appears to the left of the news server, and a list of newsgroups appears.

If you plan to read a newsgroup regularly, you *subscribe* to it. Then the newsgroup appears on your list of subscribed groups, so it is easier to find among the thousands of newsgroups that your news server carries. Netscape also keeps track of which articles you've read in each newsgroup you subscribe to. You can tell whether you are subscribed to a group by looking for a yellow check mark to the right of the newsgroup name. You can tell how many articles remain to be read in each newsgroup by the number that appears to the right of the check mark (under the heading *Unread*).

The newsgroup list can include all the newsgroups available from the news server, only those that you subscribe to, or other options (as you'll see).

1 **To make the Netscape News window bigger, click its Maximize button, which is the middle button in its upper-right corner.**

The News window expands, making it easier to read.

Maximize button

2 **If your news server has a plus sign to its left, click the plus sign.**

The plus sign displays a list of newsgroups.

If a minus sign appears to the left of your news server, its newsgroups are already listed.

3 **List only the groups to which you are subscribed by choosing Options⇨Show Subscribed Newsgroups from the menu.**

You see a list of the newsgroups to which you're subscribed. You may be subscribed to some newsgroups, such as the newsgroups designed for new users, or you may not see any newsgroups.

Figure 7-2: The Netscape News window lists newsgroups in the upper-left, articles in the selected newsgroup in the upper-right, and the text of a selected article in the lower half of the window.

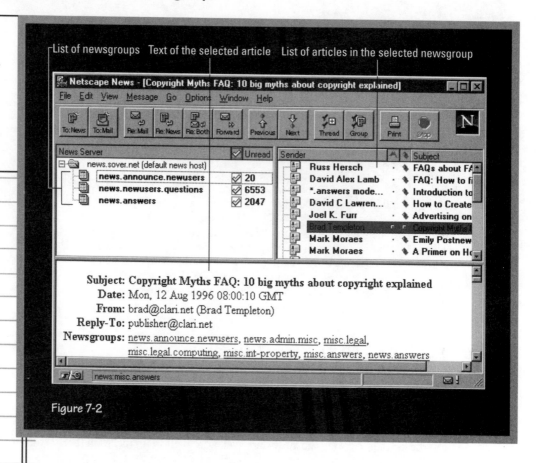

List of newsgroups   Text of the selected article   List of articles in the selected newsgroup

Figure 7-2

Reading an article

Get ready to look at articles in the news.announce.newusers newsgroup, a newsgroup with (not surprisingly) announcements for new users.

1 **If the** news.announce.newusers **newsgroup doesn't appear on your list of subscribed newsgroups, choose File⇨Add Newsgroup from the menu, type** news.announce.newusers **in the box that appears, and press Enter.**

The newsgroup appears on your list. Every Internet provider we know carries this newsgroup.

2 **Click the** news.announce.newusers **newsgroup to select it (if it isn't already highlighted).**

The upper-right portion of your window lists the articles in the newsgroup you selected, as shown in Figure 7-2. As the headings above the list indicate, each article is represented by the name of its *Sender* (the message's author), *Subject* (a brief phrase describing what the article is about), and *Date* (when the article was posted). Also, each article is currently boldfaced and has a green gem-like symbol in front of its Subject, which indicates that the article hasn't been read yet.

3 **Click any article listed in the upper-right portion of the window.**

The text of the article appears in the lower half of your window. (If you get an error message instead, simply select a different article.) Also, the boldfacing and green gem-like symbol by the article's title disappear to indicate that the article is no longer unread.

4 **Click anywhere in the lower portion of the window to activate the message area and then press the PgDn key a few times to read the article's text.**

click a newsgroup to see a list of its articles

click an article to read it

to read a long article, click in the text area and then press PgDn

You can also scroll through the text by using the vertical scroll bar along the right edge of the article. (You can find more information about scrolling in Lesson 1-2.)

5 **Repeat Steps 3 and 4 a few more times. As you select each article, keep an eye on the Unread column in the upper-left section of the window.**

Every time you select an article, the number under the Unread heading next to `news.announce.newusers` decreases by one to reflect that the newsgroup now has fewer unread messages. After each article's text appears in the lower portion of the window, read the text by clicking inside the message area to activate it and then using the PgDn and PgUp keys or the vertical scroll bar to move around the article. Pretty simple, huh?

6 **If you haven't already done so, locate and click an article in the upper-right portion of the window called Answers to Frequently Asked Questions about Usenet (you may see only the first part of the title).**

The text appears in the lower half of your window. This article is the *FAQ* (that is, *Frequently Asked Questions* list) about Usenet newsgroups. The article lists 50 questions at its top and then repeats each question followed by an answer. First read through the list of questions to identify the ones that interest you, and then scroll down the article to read the pertinent answers.

7 **If the** `news.newusers.questions` **newsgroup doesn't appear on your list of subscribed newsgroups, choose File⇨Add Newsgroup from the menu, type** news.newusers.questions **in the box that appears, and press Enter.**

Another newsgroup for people new to the Net appears on your list. Every Internet provider we know carries this newsgroup, too.

8 **Click the** `news.newusers.questions` **newsgroup in the list of newsgroups (if it isn't already selected).**

In this newsgroup, new users ask questions and more experienced people answer them.

Netscape organizes the articles in a newsgroup into *threads*. A thread is an article that begins a discussion, followed by responses to that article, followed by responses to the responses, and so forth. In the list of articles in the upper-right portion of the Netscape News window, Netscape displays the title of the thread (the subject line of the original article) with responses to the original article indented below the original article. Responses to responses are indented further under the articles they respond to — it's like a family tree.

9 **If the articles in the** `news.newusers.questions` **newsgroup aren't sorted by thread, choose Options⇨Mail and News Preferences, click the Organization tab along the top of the Preferences dialog box that appears, and click the Thread News Messages box until it contains a check. Then click OK.**

This command tells Netscape to arrange newsgroup articles by thread.

Sometimes the first article in a thread does not appear, because news servers typically don't keep articles for more than about three days. If the first articles in the thread are older than that, they disappear, leaving the later articles in the thread. You can usually figure out what the earlier articles said, though, because responses frequently quote parts of the original article.

As you just saw, after you select a newsgroup you can read any article in it with just a few mouse clicks. New messages in your newsgroups arrive automatically, so the only hard part is figuring out which articles you want to take the time to read — and that's a skill you'll develop with practice.

Notes:

thread = series of articles that respond to one original article

✓ Progress Check

If you can do the following, you've mastered this lesson:

❑ Open the Netscape News window.

❑ Tell Netscape the name of your Internet provider's news server.

❑ Select a newsgroup.

❑ Read an article.

extra credit

Just the FAQs, ma'am

A *FAQ* is a list of frequently asked questions and their answers. Many newsgroups create FAQs that include the questions that come up over and over and that folks on the newsgroup are sick of answering. If you pose one of these questions, you're likely to get responses that say, *Read the $%#(* FAQ!*

How do you read the FAQ for a newsgroup? If the FAQ appears on the list of articles for the newsgroup, read it like any other article. If you don't see the FAQ among the articles in the newsgroup, go to the news.answers newsgroup. This newsgroup contains the FAQs for many newsgroups that have FAQs, listed in no particular order. Many FAQs are really long and have been divided into several parts. Long FAQs appear as a series of articles, with titles like *alt.backyard.chickens FAQ, Part 2 of 5.*

Lesson 7-2

Listing and Subscribing to Newsgroups

So far, you've explored the news.announce.newsusers and news.newusers.questions newsgroups. These are excellent newsgroups that you should stay tuned to while you're learning the ropes. However, you may be wondering right about now: Where are the other 15,000 newsgroups?

We're glad you asked. You can get an alphabetical list of all top-level newsgroup hierarchies — that is, the first word of each category of newsgroups — by choosing Options⇨Show All Newsgroups from the Netscape News window. You can then double-click a hierarchy to list all the newsgroups it contains. Finally, when you find a newsgroup that interests you, you can subscribe to it with a mouse click.

Displaying and exploring the full newsgroup list

To access all the available newsgroups, you choose Options⇨Show All Newsgroups from the menu. When you see the list of newsgroups hierarchies, you can delve into the hierarchies that look interesting to you.

Follow these steps:

1 Connect to your Internet provider, open the Netscape News window, and maximize the window.

2 Click the Options menu.

A number of options appear, including Show Subscribed Newsgroups (which lists only the newsgroups to which you're subscribed), Show Active Newsgroups (which lists only the newsgroups to which you're subscribed and that have new messages), Show New Newsgroups (which lists only newsgroups that have been created since you last opened the News window), and Show All Newsgroups (which lets you display every newsgroup). The option currently selected is Show Subscribed Newsgroups, as indicated by the bullet to its left.

3 **Click the Show All Newsgroups option.**

Almost all Internet providers carry the seven newsgroup hierarchies described at the beginning of this unit. Some providers also carry lots of other hierarchies, like country hierarchies (with newsgroups about a particular country) and company hierarchies (with newsgroups about a particular company).

The message bar at the bottom of the window starts telling you how much of the data has been received and at what speed (for example, *315K read at 8 bytes/sec*). Within one to six minutes (depending on the speed of your modem and on how busy the news server computer happens to be), the words *Document: Done* appear in the message bar to let you know that the data transfer has been completed. More important, lots of newsgroups are now listed in the upper-left section of your window.

4 **Click anywhere in the newsgroup list, and then use the PgDn and PgUp keys or the vertical scroll bar to move around the alphabetical list.**

You start out by seeing a list of hierarchies — that is, a list that displays the first word of each newsgroup. The asterisk that follows each hierarchy name (for example, alt.* or rec.*) is a placeholder simply meant to remind you that additional words follow the initial word. Similarly, a plus sign and closed folder icon appear to the left of the hierarchy name as additional visual reminders that newsgroups are contained within the listed category.

To the right of each hierarchy name is a number in parentheses that tells you how many newsgroups start with that word. For example, at the time we write this, rec (short for *recreation*) has 604 groups and the popular alt category (short for *alternative* and a catch-all for any topic that falls outside the other hierarchies) has 2,600 newsgroups!

To display the newsgroups within a hierarchy, you can simply click the plus sign to its left. Alternately, you can double-click either the hierarchy's folder or the hierarchy name itself. After you do so, the plus sign turns to a minus sign, the closed folder icon changes to an open folder icon, and the newsgroups within the hierarchy are listed directly below the hierarchy name. Try it!

5 **Press PgDn until you see the rec.* hierarchy, and double-click its name or folder (or click the plus sign to its left).**

Netscape retrieves the data you requested and, after a few moments, displays the names of scores of newsgroups in the rec hierarchy (such as rec.birds, rec.climbing, and rec.skydiving), as shown in Figure 7-3. In addition, it displays the names of many second-level hierarchies, such as rec.arts.* and rec.music.*. To dig deeper into the rec category, open one of these lower-level hierarchies.

6 **Locate the rec.arts.* hierarchy, and double-click its name or folder (or click the plus sign to its left).**

You see additional newsgroups within this narrower category (such as rec.arts.dance and rec.arts.poems). You also see third-level hierarchies, such as rec.arts.books.*, rec.arts.movies.*, and — of course — the wildly popular rec.arts.startrek.*. To see the newsgroups within a third-level hierarchy — or any other hierarchy — you again double-click the hierarchy name.

Of course, you can also go in the other direction and contract hierarchies instead of expanding them. Doing so prevents your newsgroup list from displaying a lot of items you're not regularly interested in. To contract an open hierarchy, simply double-click its name or folder a second time or click the minus sign to its left. Give it a shot!

Notes:

to list a hierarchy's newsgroups, double-click its name or folder or click the plus sign to its left

Figure 7-3: When you double-click the rec.* entry, Netscape displays newsgroups within this hierarchy.

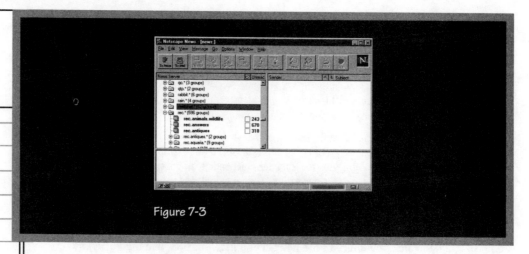

Figure 7-3

7 **Double-click the name or folder of the rec.arts.* hierarchy (or click the minus sign to its left).**

The arts newsgroups list disappears, the open folder icon changes back to a closed icon, and the minus sign changes back to a plus sign.

Finally, restore the list again.

8 **Double-click the name or folder of the rec.arts.* hierarchy (or click the plus sign to its left).**

The list comes back.

You can also list the articles in the upper-left portion of the window by simply clicking the newsgroup's name. Display the text of any article by clicking its heading in the list of articles.

Notice that a box appears to the right of each newsgroup. All you have to do to subscribe to a newsgroup is click this box. That's precisely what you'll do in the next exercise!

Note: You can move the window dividers that separate the newsgroups list in the upper-left part of the window, the articles list in the upper-right corner, and the text of the article in the lower half. For example, if you can't see the full names of some newsgroups with long names, drag the vertical divider between the newsgroups list and the articles list to the right by using your mouse.

Subscribing and unsubscribing to newsgroups

When you decide to read a newsgroup on a regular basis, you *subscribe* to it. Subscribing means that you tell Netscape to include the newsgroup on your list of subscribed newsgroups and to keep track of which articles you've read.

Why subscribe to a newsgroup at all? Well, the list of newsgroups is so huge that you may find it convenient to work with a much shorter list of newsgroups that you're actually interested in. Also, subscribing to a newsgroup lets Netscape keep track of your unread messages.

Out of the more than 15,000 newsgroups available, we recommend that you choose at most ten to read regularly. (We know people who try to follow more than ten newsgroups, and they seldom leave their computers!)

You should still be in the Netscape News window and in the `rec.arts.*` hierarchy. To quickly try out subscribing and unsubscribing to a newsgroup, follow these steps:

1 **Click the box to the right of** `rec.arts.puppetry.`

A check mark appears in the box. You are now subscribed to the newsgroup! To prove it, switch from displaying all newsgroups to displaying only your subscribed newsgroups.

2 **Click the Options menu.**

Notice that a bullet appears next to Show All Newsgroups, indicating that this option is currently selected.

3 **Click the Show Subscribed Newsgroups option.**

Your newsgroup display switches from showing all newsgroups to showing only the ones you're subscribed to, which now include `news.announce. newusers`, `news.newusers.questions`, and (yes!) `rec.arts. puppetry.`

If you're a big puppetry fan, you can stay subscribed to the last newsgroup. Otherwise, quit this newsgroup by clicking its box again. There's no point in cluttering up your list of subscribed newsgroups with newsgroups you don't read.

4 **Click the box to the right of** `rec.arts.puppetry.`

The check mark in the box disappears, indicating that you're no longer subscribed to the newsgroup.

5 **When you're done, choose File⇨Exit to end your session.**

A dialog box appears, asking you to confirm that you want to close all Netscape windows.

6 **Click the Yes button.**

Both the Netscape News and browser windows close.

Browsing down the list of all newsgroups can be fun — Usenet has newsgroups on the most amazingly arcane topics. And when you see an interesting newsgroup, subscribing is easy — just click the box to the right of the newsgroup name.

However, if you don't see the newsgroup you want on your screen and you don't feel like browsing for it, you can instead choose the File⇨Add Newsgroup command, which you used in Lesson 7-1, to display it directly in your News window. When the newsgroup name is displayed, you can subscribe to it by clicking in the box to the right of the newsgroup name.

For example, you may want to try reading the `alt.fan.mozilla` newsgroup, which discusses Netscape Navigator. (*Mozilla* was an early code name for the product.) Not all Internet providers carry `alt` newsgroups, so don't be surprised if it doesn't appear on your list of newsgroups in the `alt.*` hierarchy.

If you type the newsgroup name incorrectly, an error message appears in the bottom part of the Netscape News window. No harm done — just try again!

☑ Progress Check

If you can do the following, you've mastered this lesson:

- ❑ List all top-level newsgroup hierarchies.

- ❑ Expand a hierarchy to display the newsgroups it contains.

- ❑ Subscribe to a newsgroup.

- ❑ Unsubscribe to a newsgroup.

Notes:

Recess

Now that you know how to list and subscribe to newsgroups, you're ready for more advanced instruction. But first, take a stretch. Be sure to disconnect from your Internet provider so that you don't tie up your phone line. Then focus on something far away — out the window, if possible. Focusing on something close up for hours at a time is bad for your eyes!

Lesson 7-3

Searching for Newsgroups of Interest

You can find interesting newsgroups by looking through the list of all newsgroups, but you can miss a lot of interesting ones, too. Isn't there a better way to find the newsgroup you're looking for?

There is! Use the Web! This lesson shows you how to use a Web page to search for newsgroup articles that contain a word or phrase you specify.

The Deja News Research Service has a Web page that can search for newsgroup articles that contain a word or phrase. Follow these steps:

1 **Run Netscape Navigator and connect to your Internet provider.**

If you're already running Netscape and are in the Netscape News window, switch to the Netscape browser window by clicking in the browser window (if you can see it) or choosing Window2⇨0 Netscape from the menu (that's a zero). The Web browser window moves to the foreground.

2 **Click in the Location box, type** dejanews.com, **and press Enter.**

You see the Deja News Quick Search page shown in Figure 7-4.

3 **Click in the Quick Search For box, type a word or phrase (like** cooking **or** baseball **or** xfiles**), and press Enter.**

You see a page listing articles that include the word or phrase you typed. Each article is blue and underlined, which tells you that it's a link. For each article, you see the date it was posted, the article's title, the newsgroup the article was posted to, and the e-mail address of the author of the article. (See Figure 7-5.) Both the title of each article and the e-mail address of its author are links. If more matches than can fit on the page are found, you can click a *next* link near the bottom of the page to see additional matches.

4 **Click the title of an article that looks interesting.**

Deja News displays the article in your browser window. The Newsgroups heading of the article tells you which newsgroup the article comes from.

5 **Press Netscape's Back button to return to the list of articles.**

If the article looks interesting, you may want to return to your Netscape News window and subscribe to the newsgroup.

Pretty cool! If you plan to do more article searching, be sure to add Deja News to your bookmarks by pressing the Backspace button until you return to the Deja News Quick Search page and then pressing Ctrl+D.

Fiddle around a bit with Deja News to research topics near and dear to your heart. When you're content, move on to the next lesson.

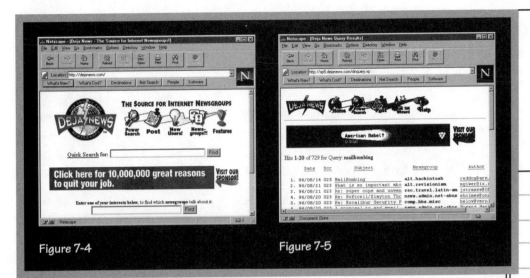

Figure 7-4

Figure 7-5

Figure 7-4: Type a search phrase in the Deja News text box to find newsgroup articles containing the phrase.

Figure 7-5: Deja News lists newsgroup articles that contain the search phrase you entered.

extra credit

Other ways to find newsgroup articles

Two other Web pages that help you search for newsgroups and articles are

▶ **The AltaVista page that you used in Lesson 2-5 to search for Web pages:** Near the top of the page (at `altavista.digital.com`), AltaVista says something like "Search the Web and Display the Results in Standard Form." The words *the Web* appear in a box. When you click in the box, a little menu appears from which you can choose Usenet. Type a word or phrase in the search box and press Enter. When you see a list of articles, click the subject line to read the article. AltaVista displays the newsgroup articles right in your browser window. If you want to read other articles in the newsgroup, look for the newsgroup name in the article header, open the Netscape News window, and use the File➪Add Newsgroup command to display the newsgroup.

▶ **The Liszt page that you used in Lesson ML-3 to search for mailing lists:** Go to `www.liszt.com` and click the Newsgroups button at the bottom of the page. Type a word in the box on the page that appears and press Enter. Liszt searches only the names and descriptions of newsgroups, not in the text of articles. When you see a list of the newsgroups that Liszt found, you can click on the newsgroup name to read the newsgroup in the Netscape News window.

☑ Progress Check

If you can do the following, you've mastered this lesson:

❑ Find newsgroup articles by topic using the Deja News Web site.

❑ Look at the articles that Deja News finds.

Replying to Newsgroup Articles

Lesson 7-4

After you read the articles in a newsgroup for a while, you may be ready to chime in. You have two ways to respond to an article that you read in a newsgroup:

▶ **By e-mail:** If your response is of interest only to the person who posted the original article, if your response is a bit personal and you don't want to share it with the whole newsgroup, or if the original article requested replies by e-mail, respond with an e-mail message directly to the person who wrote the article.

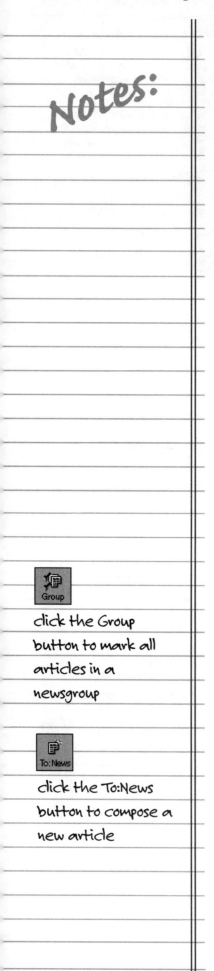

click the Group
button to mark all
articles in a
newsgroup

click the To:News
button to compose a
new article

♦ **With your own article:** If your response is of interest to lots of people who read the newsgroup, you are sure of your facts, and you have time to write a clear, concise response, then respond by posting your own article to the newsgroup. Remember, thousands of people around the world will read your article, so make sure that you really have something to say!

You can also post an article that doesn't respond to another article. If you want to bring up a new topic, you can post a new article.

In this lesson, you learn how to create an article by using the News window's To:News button or the File⇨New News Message command. You then send your article to the misc.test newsgroup, which is designed precisely for the purpose of letting new folks try out their posting skills. Then you respond to your test article by e-mail.

Posting a test article

To get a feel for how to post an article to a newsgroup, follow these steps to send a test message:

1 Run Netscape, connect to your Internet provider, and open the Netscape News window.

Refer to Lesson 7-1 if you don't remember how. You see a list of newsgroups.

2 Choose File⇨Add Newsgroup, type misc.test, and press Enter.

The misc.test newsgroup appears in the upper-left portion of your News window. Because this newsgroup is provided exclusively for the purpose of letting new users test their skills at posting articles, none of the messages in misc.test is really worth reading. To make ignoring the newsgroup's articles easy, you can use a little trick: Click the Group button in the window's Toolbar (or choose Message⇨Mark Newsgroup Read). Doing so marks all the current messages as having been read, which makes finding your own article after you post it easier.

3 Click the Group button to tell Netscape that you have already read (or decided not to read) all the articles in this newsgroup.

All the articles in misc.test lose their boldfacing and green symbols to show that they've been marked as read. Also, the number under the newsgroup's Unread heading disappears. Now start creating your test article.

4 Click the To:News button on the Toolbar (or choose File⇨New News Message).

You see the Message Composition window for writing an article, as shown in Figure 7-6. The window looks like the Message Composition window you used in Unit 5 to compose an e-mail message, except for the headers. Instead of including a Mail To text box for an e-mail address, the window includes a Newsgroups box for the name of the newsgroup to which you want to post the article.

Leave the Cc text box blank unless you want to e-mail a copy of this article to someone (like yourself). The name of the current newsgroup, misc.test, has been automatically inserted in the Newsgroups text box, and the blank Subject text box has been selected.

5 In the Subject box, type Test: Please ignore (or something like that).

The article you're about to post isn't going to be of interest to anyone but you! (Or maybe your mother.) Your signature appears in the message box, the large box in the lower part of the window.

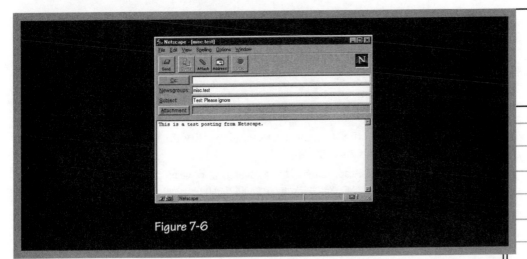

Figure 7-6

Figure 7-6: When you compose a newsgroup article, keep in mind that thousands of people may read it!

6 **Click anywhere inside the message box to select it and then type a message like** This is a test posting from Netscape.

Type whatever you'd like to see when you read the article later.

7 **When the article looks satisfactory, click the Send button (or press Ctrl+Enter or choose File⇨Send Now).**

Netscape posts the article to the misc.test newsgroup.

Your article is winging its way to newsgroup readers all over the world!

If you start composing an article and then think better of it, you can close the Message Composition window by clicking the Close button in the upper-right corner of the window. When Netscape asks whether you're sure that you want to discard your changes, click the Yes button.

> to post an article you've composed, click the Send button, choose File→Send Now, or press Ctrl+Enter

heads up

Rules and regulations for posting articles

All the rules of e-mail Netiquette that you learned in Lesson 5-5 apply to newsgroup articles, too. Follow the rules in the sidebar "Mailing list do's and don'ts" in Unit ML as well, because mailing lists and newsgroups have a lot in common. In addition, follow these rules to avoid getting flamed by angry newsgroupies:

▶ Read a newsgroup for at least a week before posting anything to be sure that your posting is appropriate for the newsgroup.

▶ Read the newsgroup's FAQ before posting anything. (See the sidebar "Just the FAQs, ma'am" earlier in this unit.)

▶ Don't post ads! If you have a product that relates directly to the subject of the newsgroup, you can post a brief article about it *once,* but you'll have better luck if the article is short and informational rather than "salesy" and vague. Be sure to include an e-mail address to which people can write for more information.

▶ Never post an article to a newsgroup you don't read regularly.

▶ Don't post the same article to lots of newsgroups. (This is called *crossposting,* and it's frowned upon.) Sometimes an article is of interest to two or three newsgroups, but think long and hard before you crosspost.

Notes:

Reading the article you posted

In a few minutes, the article you just posted appears in the `worldnet.test` newsgroup. Here's how to see whether your post was sent successfully:

1 In the Netscape News window, click the `misc.test` newsgroup on the newsgroups list.

Netscape retrieves the latest articles, including yours. If your article doesn't appear, wait a few more minutes and try again. (If your article doesn't appear within a half hour, call your Internet provider to find out what's amiss.)

2 Click your article.

The text of your article appears in the lower portion of the News window.

Cool! You posted an article to a newsgroup! When you next have something reasonably interesting and wise to say, consider following the same procedure to post articles to newsgroups that you read regularly.

If you read an article and want to reply to it with any article (because your response is of interest to everyone in the newsgroup), you can post an article in response by clicking the Re:News button on the Toolbar (or choosing Message⇨Post Reply). Netscape displays a Message Composition window for posting a reply to the same newsgroup as the original newsgroup.

Alternately, you can reply to an article privately by sending e-mail to its author. Click the Re:Mail button on the Toolbar (or press Ctrl+R or choose Message⇨Mail Reply). Netscape displays a Message Composition window addressed to the author of the article. Always use e-mail when replying to an annoying, clueless, or downright stupid article — there's no point in embarrassing people in the public arena of a newsgroup.

Forwarding, printing, and saving articles

Here are a few other things you can do with newsgroup articles:

click the Forward
button to forward
an article to
someone by e-mail

▶ **Forward an article by e-mail:** If you see an article that would interest a friend, you can send the text of the article to the friend by e-mail. While displaying the article you want to forward, click the Forward button on the Toolbar, press Ctrl+L, right-click the message text, and choose Forward from the menu that appears, or choose Message⇨Forward. If you want to add your own comments, you may prefer for the text of the article to appear quoted (with each line preceded by a > character); in this case, choose Message⇨Forward Quoted.

Print button

▶ **Print an article:** Click the Print button on the Toolbar, press Ctrl+P, or choose File⇨Print Message(s) to display the Print dialog box. Click OK to print the message.

▶ **Save the article in a text file:** Press Ctrl+S or choose File⇨Save Message(s) As to bring up the Save As dialog box; click the Save as type box and click the Plain Text (*.txt) option; click in the File name box and type an appropriate folder name and filename (for example, **C:\Newsgroups\Tips**); and press Enter.

extra credit

Subscribing to Netscape newsgroups

Netscape Communications maintains its own newsgroups by using its own news server. The Netscape newsgroups are, not surprisingly, in the `netscape.*` hierarchy. Your Internet provider's news server probably doesn't carry the `netscape.*` newsgroups — instead, you have to connect to Netscape's own news server at `secnews.netscape.com`.

To connect to the Netscape news server and subscribe to the newsgroup about Netscape Navigator (it's called `netscape.navigator`), follow these steps:

1. **Run Netscape and connect to your Internet provider. Don't open the News window yet; stay in the browser window.**

2. **Click in the Location box and type** snews://secnews.netscape.com/netscape.navigator **and press Enter.**

   That's *snews* (for "secure news"), a colon, two slashes, the news server name, another slash, and the newsgroup name. Don't type any spaces. When you press Enter, Netscape opens the Netscape News window and adds the `secnews.netscape.com (secure)` news server to your list of news servers. (The newsgroup is marked "secure" because it uses Netscape security features.) Under the news server appears one newsgroup, `netscape.navigator`.

Read and post to the `netscape.navigator` newsgroup as usual. Subscribe to the newsgroup if you plan to read it regularly. Netscape technical support folks can answer your questions about the program.

☑ Progress Check

If you can do the following, you've mastered this lesson:

❏ Post a test article.

❏ Forward an article by e-mail.

❏ Print an article.

❏ Save an article in a file.

Recess

Congratulations! You now know how to read articles in newsgroups, find articles by topic, and post your own articles to newsgroups. You are an amazing person, and we're pleased to know you! Don't get a swelled head, though; you still have to face the Unit 7 quiz!

Unit 7 Quiz

For each of the following questions, circle the letter of the correct answer or answers. Remember, there may be more than one right answer for each question.

1. **A newsgroup:**

   A. Is the staff at a newspaper or radio station.

   B. Is an ongoing discussion, devoted to a particular topic, that takes place on the Internet.

   C. Provides the daily headlines and sports scores with your morning coffee.

   D. Has a name consisting of words, or parts of words, separated by dots.

   E. Consists of articles posted by Internet users around the world.

2. **The major seven newsgroup hierarchies include:**

   A. `news` and `comp`.

   B. `rec` and `misc`.

   C. Doc and Sneezy.

   D. `soc` and `sci`.

   E. Star Trek and Star Wars.

3. **To open a Netscape window, you can:**

   A. Click the Netscape Newsgroups button.

   B. Type **news:** followed by a newsgroup's name in the Location box in the Netscape browser window. (Try it!)

   C. Choose <u>W</u>indow⇨Netscape <u>N</u>ewsgroups.

   D. All of the above.

   E. None of the above; the News window opens automatically when you run Netscape.

4. **To subscribe to a newsgroup:**

   A. Double-click its FAQ.

   B. Double-click its name or folder.

   C. Click the newspaper icon to its left.

   D. Click the blank box to its right.

   E. Choose <u>F</u>ile⇨A<u>d</u>d Newsgroup, type the newsgroup's name in the dialog box that appears, and press Enter.

5. **To list only newsgroups you've subscribed to:**

   A. Click Netscape's Newsgroups button.

   B. Choose <u>O</u>ptions⇨Sho<u>w</u> All Messages.

   C. Choose <u>O</u>ptions⇨Show <u>A</u>ll Newsgroups.

   D. Choose <u>O</u>ptions⇨Show Su<u>b</u>scribed Newsgroups.

   E. Choose <u>O</u>ptions⇨Show A<u>c</u>tive Newsgroups.

Unit 7 Exercise

1. Run Netscape and display the Deja News Web page.

2. Search for something you're interested in, like *chocolate* or *lizards* or *antiques*. Make careful note of the newsgroup.

3. Open the Netscape News window and subscribe to the newsgroup you found.

4. Read the articles for a week or so.

5. Look in the `news.answers` newsgroup for the FAQ on the newsgroup you joined and read the FAQ.

6. When you have a question to ask or want to contribute an answer or comment, post an article to the newsgroup. (Make sure that the question isn't answered in the FAQ.)

7. Continue reading the newsgroup to see how your article looks and what reaction it causes.

Unit 5 Summary

▶ **Telling Netscape Navigator how to send and receive your mail:** To tell Netscape your mail servers and user name, choose Options⇨Mail and News Preferences from the Netscape menu. Click the Servers tab in the Preferences dialog box, fill in the information, and click OK.

▶ **Netscape Mail window:** To read or compose e-mail, choose Window⇨Netscape Mail from the Netscape menu or click the Mail icon (the little envelope in the lower-right corner of the Netscape window).

▶ **Sending e-mail:** Click the To:Mail button on the Toolbar, press Ctrl+M, or choose File⇨New Mail Message from the menu. Enter the address, subject, and text of the message. Then click the Send button on the Toolbar, press Ctrl+Enter, or choose File⇨Send Mail.

▶ **Message Composition window:** Enter the headers in the boxes at the top of the window and the text of the message in the large box in the bottom part of the window.

▶ **Getting your mail:** Netscape downloads your new messages from your Internet provider when you open the Netscape Mail window. To retrieve new messages again, click the Get Mail button on the Toolbar, press Ctrl+T, or choose File⇨Get New Mail from the menu. New messages arrive in your Inbox folder.

▶ **Reading messages:** Click the folder that contains the message in the upper-left section of the Mail window. The messages in the folder are listed in the upper-right sections of the window. To read a listed message, click it; the text of the message appears in the lower part of the Mail window.

▶ **Replying to messages:** Click the Re:Mail button on the Toolbar, press Ctrl+R, or choose the Message⇨Reply command from the menu. Netscape displays a Message Composition window preaddressed to the person who sent you the message.

▶ **Quoting messages:** Remind your correspondent of what he or she said by including parts of the original message in your reply. Quoted material appears with each line preceded by a >. Include only the relevant parts of the message.

▶ **Forwarding messages:** Click the message and then click the Forward button on the Toolbar, press Ctrl+L, or choose Message⇨Forward from the menu. Address the message, add your comments, and send the message.

▶ **Printing messages:** Click the message and then click the Print button on the Toolbar, press Ctrl+P, or choose File⇨Print Message(s) from the menu. When you see the Print dialog box, click OK.

▶ **Deleting messages:** Click the message to select it and then press the Del key, click the Delete button on the Toolbar, or choose Edit⇨Delete Message from the menu. Or drag the message to the Trash folder.

▶ **Following Netiquette:** Don't send unnecessarily angry messages, don't distribute chain letters, and don't believe everything you read! Do check your spelling and do think of your correspondents as real people with feelings and foibles.

Part II Review

Unit 6 Summary

▶ **Address Book:** A list of e-mail addresses with the full names and nicknames of people you write to. Choose Window⇨Address Book to display the Address Book. Address messages by typing a person's nickname or by clicking the Address, Mail To, or Cc button to see the address book list.

▶ **Adding, editing, and deleting addresses:** Choose Item⇨Add User from the Address Book menu bar to add addresses. Click an address and choose Item⇨Properties from the Address Book menu to edit the address. Click an address and press the Del key to delete the address.

▶ **Folders:** Lists of messages. Netscape creates the Inbox, Outbox, Sent, and Trash folders automatically to hold your incoming, outgoing, previously sent, and deleted messages, respectively. Create your own folders by choosing File⇨New Folder from the menu. See the messages in a folder by clicking the name of the folder.

▶ **Moving messages into folders:** Choose Message⇨Move from the menu or drag the message to the folder by using the mouse. To leave a copy in the original folder, choose Message⇨Copy from the menu or hold down the Ctrl key while dragging the folder.

▶ **Attaching a file:** Click the Attach button on the Message Composition window Toolbar, click the Attachment button in the header section of the window, or choose File⇨Attach File to display an Attachments dialog box. Click the box's Attach File button to display an Enter file to attach dialog box. Use the Look in box to specify the file with your mouse, or type the hard disk location and name of the file in the File name box. When you're done, click the current dialog box's Open button, and then click the preceding dialog box's OK button.

▶ **Sending an attached file:** Click the Send button on the Toolbar, press Ctrl+Enter, or choose File⇨Send Mail — in other words, follow the same procedure you use to send e-mail without attachments.

▶ **Getting an attached file:** Open the Netscape Mail window. If the window is already open, click the Get Mail button on the Toolbar, press Ctrl+T, or choose File⇨Get New Mail — in other words, follow the same procedure you use to pick up e-mail without attachments.

▶ **Saving an attached picture that's fully displayed in the message area:** Right-click (that is, click with your *right* mouse button) the picture to pop up a menu. Click the Save Image As option to display a Save As dialog box. Move the folder in which to save the picture, type the filename, and then click the Save button.

▶ **Saving an attached file that's displayed as a box in the message area:** Click the left part of the box (which says something like *Attachment 1* or *Attachment 2* in blue, underlined text) to display an Unknown File Type dialog box. Click the Save File button to display a Save As dialog box. Move the folder in which to save the picture, type the filename, and then click the Save button.

Part II Review

Unit 7 Summary

▶ **Usenet newsgroups:** Usenet is a system on the Internet that includes over 15,000 discussions (newsgroups). You can read and participate in these discussions by using the Netscape News window. Messages distributed via newsgroups are called *articles*. Sending a message to a newsgroup is called *posting an article*.

▶ **Hierarchies:** Groups of newsgroups whose names start with the same word. The seven major hierarchies are rec, soc, talk, sci, comp, news, and misc. The major unofficial hierarchy is alt. Other hierarchies include discussions dedicated to companies, schools, or countries.

▶ **Reading newsgroups:** Select a newsgroup by clicking its name in the upper-left section of the News window. The newsgroup's articles then appear in the upper-right section of the window. To read a listed article, click it; the article's text appears in the lower part of the News window.

▶ **Listing newsgroups:** List all available newsgroups by choosing Options⇨Show All Newsgroups. List only your subscribed newsgroups by choosing Options⇨Show Subscribed Newsgroups. List only your subscribed newsgroups that have new messages by choosing Options⇨Show Active Newsgroups. List only newsgroups that have been created since you last opened the News window by choosing Options⇨Show New Newsgroups.

▶ **Expanding and contracting a newsgroup hierarchy:** To display the newsgroups in a hierarchy, double-click the hierarchy's name or folder or click the plus sign to its left. To hide the newsgroups in a hierarchy, double-click the hierarchy's name or folder a second time or click the minus sign to its left.

▶ **Listing and selecting a newsgroup by typing its name:** To instantly display a newsgroup in the News window, choose File⇨Add Newsgroup, type the exact name of the newsgroup, and press Enter. The newsgroup is immediately listed and selected in the upper-left part of the News window, sparing you from having to wade through hierarchies to find and click it.

▶ **Subscribing and unsubscribing to a newsgroup:** Subscribe to a newsgroup by displaying its name and then clicking the box to its right, which causes a yellow check mark to appear in the box. Unsubscribe the same way; clicking the box a second time makes the yellow check mark disappear.

▶ **Searching for newsgroups:** Use the Liszt Web page at www.liszt.com to search for newsgroups whose names contain a specified word.

▶ **Searching for newsgroup articles:** Use the Deja News Research Service's Web page at dejanews.com or the AltaVista Web page at altavista.digital.com to search for articles that contain specified words or phrases.

▶ **Posting an original newsgroup article:** After you've read a newsgroup for at least a week and have something wise, witty, and wonderful to say, you can post a new article by selecting the newsgroup in the News window, clicking the To:News button to open the Message Composition window, typing a subject heading in the Subject box, pressing Tab to move to the big message area, and carefully typing and editing your message. When you're ready to transmit your message, click the Send button.

▶ **Responding to newsgroup articles:** If what you have to say is of interest primarily to the person to whom you are responding or is private, you can reply to the author by e-mail by clicking the article, clicking the Re:Mail button, typing your message, and clicking the Send button. If your response is of general interest to newsgroup readers, respond publicly in the newsgroup by clicking the article, clicking the Re:News button, typing your response, carefully checking your spelling, grammar, and tone, and clicking the Send button.

Part II Test

The questions on this test cover all the material presented in Part II, Units 5 through 7.

True   False

T   F   1. E-mail is like paper mail because it is written and can be kept for future reference.

T   F   2. E-mail is like the telephone because it's quick, easy, and informal.

T   F   3. dummies@idgbooks.com@ dummies.com is a valid e-mail address.

T   F   4. When composing a message, you can undo the last change you made to your text by pressing Ctrl+Z.

T   F   5. A *flame war* is when countries set forest fires in their enemies' woods.

T   F   6. You can attach only graphics files to messages, not word processing document files.

T   F   7. Before sending an e-mail attachment, you should check that the recipient's mail program can handle MIME attachments.

T   F   8. The Amazon is the largest river in the world.

T   F   9. You can read Usenet newsgroups in the Netscape Mail window.

T   F   10. To test posting an article, you can post it to the misc.test newsgroup.

Multiple Choice

For each of the following questions, circle the correct answer or answers. Remember, there may be more than one right answer for each question.

11. **The Address Book is:**

   A. The little black book you carry around in your jacket pocket.

   B. A feature of Netscape Mail.

   C. Displayed when you choose Window⇨ Address Book from the Netscape Mail window.

   D. A good place to store the e-mail addresses of your friends and coworkers.

   E. Useless.

12. **What does this button do?**

   A. Lets you compose a memo about mail.

   B. Remails the message.

   C. Replies to an e-mail message.

   D. Sends a message back to the person who sent you a message.

   E. The same thing as pressing Ctrl+R.

13. **When addressing an e-mail message:**

   A. You type the addressee's e-mail address in the Mail To box.

   B. You type the addresses of anyone who should receive a copy of the message in the Cc box.

   C. You type the address in the middle of the envelope, with the ZIP code on the last line.

   D. You can type more than one address in the Mail To box, separated by commas.

   E. You can click the Mail To, Cc, or Address buttons to see your Address Book.

14. **Netscape creates the following mail folders automatically:**

   A. E-mail, Phone Calls, and Letters.

   B. Inbox, Outbox, and Shoebox.

   C. Important, Low Priority, and Useless.

   D. Personal, Memos, and Private.

   E. Inbox, Outbox, Sent, and Trash.

Part II Test

15. **To file a message in a folder, you can:**

    A. Print the message, label a new manila folder, stick the printed message in the folder, and shove the whole thing into your filing cabinet.

    B. Select the message and choose Message⇨Move from the menu bar.

    C. Select the message and drag it to a new folder.

    D. Repeat "Message, move!" three times.

    E. Select the message and choose Message⇨Copy from the menu bar. Then delete the message from the original folder.

16. **Which of the following are commonly used methods of attaching files to messages?**

    A. MIME

    B. Uuencoding

    C. Staples

    D. BinHex

    E. Paper clips

17. **To attach a file to an e-mail message:**

    A. Click the Attachment button.

    B. Click the Paper Clip button.

    C. Choose File⇨Attach File.

    D. Type the name of the file in box to the right of the Attachment button.

    E. Choose Attack⇨File.

18. **The following newsgroups are excellent choices for learning about Usenet:**

    A. `news.newusers.questions`

    B. `news.announce.newusers`

    C. `talk.bizarre`

    D. `alt.barney.die.die.die`

    E. `news.answers`

Matching

19. **Match the Netscape Mail window Toolbar buttons with their descriptions:**

     A.   1. Compose a new message

     B.   2. Reply to the current message

     C.   3. Get your new mail messages

     D.   4. Forward the current message to someone

     E.

20. **Match the newsgroup terms with their (newsgroup-related) definitions:**

    A. Usenet   1. Message distributed to a newsgroup

    B. Article   2. Series of messages in which each message is a response to a previous message

    C. Post   3. Decentralized organization that administers newsgroups

    D. Flame   4. Angry or inflammatory message

    E. Thread   5. Transmit an article for distribution to a newsgroup

Part II Test

21. Match these U.S. states with their capitals:

A. Vermont   1. Trenton

B. Indiana   2. Albany

C. New York   3. Albuquerque

D. New Jersey   4. Indianapolis

E. New Mexico   5. Montpelier

22. Match the button with the command that does the same thing:

A.   1. File⇨New News Message

B.   2. File⇨Print Message(s)

C.   3. Message⇨Mark Newsgroup Read

D.   4. Message⇨Forward

Part II Lab Assignment

Step 1: Run Netscape Navigator, connect to your Internet provider, and open the Netscape News window.

Step 2: Find and subscribe to an interesting newsgroup.

You can find a newsgroup by looking through the newsgroup names in the various newsgroup hierarchies or by using the Deja News or Liszt Web page.

Step 3: Find an interesting article.

Step 4: Forward a copy to yourself for future reference.

If you know other people who would be interested, forward the article to them, too.

Step 5 (optional): Send an e-mail message to the author of the article thanking him or her.

Click the Re:Mail button to respond to the article via e-mail. If you have additional information on the topic of the article to add, do so.

Multimedia, Plug-ins, and Creating Web Pages

Part III

In this part . . .

The text and pictures on Web pages can be interesting, it's true — but wouldn't it be cool to be able to listen to sound clips — perhaps up-to-the-minute news reports or play-by-play sportscasts? And what about watching video clips? Netscape can play both sound and video clips with help from *plug-ins,* add-on programs that expand the things that Netscape can do. In Unit 8, you learn all about plug-ins and install and use a bunch of plug-ins stored on the *Dummies 101* CD-ROM. By the end of Unit 8, you'll be watching video and recalculating spreadsheets on Web pages, as well as adding a spell-checker to your Netscape Mail and News windows.

Unit 9 takes you one step further — making your *own* Web pages. Netscape Navigator Gold includes a powerful Web page editor, and you learn to make pages that contain text, pictures, and hypertext links.

Extending Netscape's Capabilities by Using Plug-ins

Objectives for This Unit

✓ Getting acquainted with Web buzzwords like *Java, applets, plug-ins,* and *helper apps*

✓ Learning how to extend Netscape's capabilities by using plug-ins

✓ Installing and using plug-ins that let you hear sounds, see movies, and check your spelling in Netscape — and lots more!

on the CD

◗ Shockwave plug-in

◗ VDOLive plug-in

◗ ASAP WebShow plug-in

◗ Word Viewer plug-in

◗ Formula One/NET plug-in

◗ Ichat plug-in

◗ CyberSpell plug-in

If you've followed along with Units 1 through 7 in this book, you are now a fully qualified Netscape user. You can browse the Web, send and receive e-mail, and read Usenet newsgroups. So what else is there?

Well, as the World Wide Web has gotten more popular and browsers (especially Netscape) have become so widely used, several new developments let Web pages do more than just present text and graphics. You may have run into these buzzwords:

◗ Helper applications

◗ Plug-ins

◗ Java applets

In this unit, you learn what these buzzwords mean, and you use one of them extensively — you install various plug-ins to extend the capabilities of Netscape. Using plug-ins, you can watch movie clips, listen to sound clips, and add a spelling checker to the Netscape Mail and News windows.

Lesson 8-1

Introduction to Fancy Web Terminology, and Why Plug-ins Are Cool

The technical folks who make browsers and Web pages have taken two approaches to making the Web a more exciting place to be:

- They have made Web pages more elaborate by using things called *Java applets*.

- They have made Web browsers like Netscape more powerful by creating new versions, adding helper applications, and adding *plug-ins*.

To be a true Netscape expert, you should know how each of these methods gives your copy of Netscape more power.

Making smarter Web pages

Most Web pages include text and pictures. Some new Web pages include little programs, called *applets* (a nickname for cute little *appl*ication programs), as part of the Web page. Because Web pages can be viewed by Web browsers that run on DOS, Windows, Macintoshes, or other systems, applets must be written in a language that any browser can understand and run. The language used for writing Web page applets is *Java*, a language based on the C++ programming language and created by Sun Microsystems.

The Windows 95 version of Netscape 3.0 can run Java applets, and you may run into Web pages that contain them. Windows 3.1 users are out of luck — perhaps a later version of Netscape for Windows 3.1 will support Java. (And don't think that switching to Netscape's arch-rival Microsoft Internet Explorer will help — its Windows 3.1 version doesn't handle Java applets, either!)

Note: Java applets can create additional Netscape windows, so you can end up with several Netscape windows on-screen. Some of these windows don't have menu bars, so to close them you have to click the Close button or press Alt + F4.

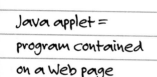

Java applet =
program contained
on a Web page

For example, ESPN (the sports network that runs one of the most-visited Web sites on the Internet) provides a Java applet that displays a small window displaying the latest sports scores on your screen. To see it (if you have Windows 95), follow these steps:

1 **Run Netscape and connect to your Internet provider.**

2 **Type** www.espn.com/index.java.html **and press Enter.**

You see the ESPN front page, with lots of interesting articles and late-breaking sports news. Near the top of the page is the ScorePost, a box that displays a new sports score or headline every few seconds.

3 **Display the ScorePost box in its own window by clicking the Display on desktop button.**

The ScorePost box appears in its own ESPN SportsZone ScorePost window, as shown in Figure 8-1.

4 **When you're done watching sports headlines, close the ESPN SportsZone ScorePost window by clicking the Close button or pressing Alt+F4.**

heads up

If you're at work, you should know that people have gotten into trouble for keeping the ScorePost window open during office hours. Keep your mind on your work!

Figure 8-1

Figure 8-1: This Java applet displays a little window and updates the information in it every few seconds.

Notes:

Unless you're an accomplished programmer, you probably don't have any interest in writing Java applets, but if you do, get a copy of *Java For Dummies* by Aaron E. Walsh (published by IDG Books Worldwide, Inc.).

extra credit

What's the deal with Java?

Netscape (the Windows 95 version, anyway) can run Java applets. In English, this statement means that if a Web page includes a little program written in the Java programming language, Netscape can run the little program right on your computer. Java applets can make raisins dance or messages scroll by, or look up the prices of items you're ordering.

However, what's to stop a Java applet from deleting files on your hard disk or forwarding the messages in your e-mail inbox to someone else? Netscape's programmers and people at Sun Microsystems, the folks who invented Java, designed controls that prevent Java applets from doing anything destructive. However, rumors about ways to write sneaky Java applets that can do damage surface from time to time.

Windows 3.1 users don't have to worry — the Windows 3.1 version of Netscape 3.0 can't run Java applets. If you use Windows 95 and have security concerns about programs running on your computer without your permission, you can turn off Netscape's capability to run Java applets:

1. **Choose Options⇨Network Preferences from the menu in the Netscape browser, Mail, or News window.**

2. **Click the Languages tab along the top of the Preferences window that appears.**

3. **Click the Enable Java and Enable JavaScript boxes until neither one contains a check. Then click OK.**

   Now Netscape refuses to run any Java applets when you load Web pages that contain them.

Making smarter Web browsers

NCSA Mosaic was the first Web browser that could display both text and pictures, and Netscape can, too. Then someone had the bright idea of letting Web browsers use *helper applications*, separate programs that allow the browser to handle other things, like sound and video. In Lesson 4-2, you learned to extend the capabilities of Netscape by installing helper applications. You set up WinZip to be a helper application that takes a compressed zip file that you download from the Web and enables you both to view the contents of the file and to decompress the contents to make them useable again.

helper application = program that Netscape runs when a Web page contains information Netscape can't display

The new, cool way to make Netscape smarter is to add new pieces of software to it. These pieces of software are called *plug-ins*, and they are programs designed to "plug in" to Netscape to give it new capabilities. Lots of companies have jumped on the plug-in bandwagon, writing plug-ins in these general categories. Unlike helper applications, plug-ins don't run by themselves. Instead, they become part of Netscape, enabling Netscape to display new kinds of information in the Netscape browser window or adding new commands to Netscape menus:

> ◆ **Audio** plug-ins allow Netscape to play sounds that are stored as part of Web pages. For example, you can listen to news shows from National Public Radio by going to NPR's Web site at www.npr.org. Lesson 8-3 explains how to use two audio plug-ins, RealAudio and LiveAudio.

> ◆ **Video** plug-ins let you play little movies on Web pages. See Lesson 8-4 for how to use two video plug-ins: LiveVideo and QuickTime. You also see Shockwave, a plug-in that shows movies, plays audio clips, and lets you interact with Web pages.

> ◆ **3D and virtual reality** plug-ins let you wander around in 3D "virtual reality worlds." See Lesson 8-5 for how to use the Live3D plug-in.

> ◆ **Document viewers** let you see various types of documents — Lesson 8-6 explains how to use the Word Viewer, ASAP WebShow, and Formula One/NET plug-ins to see Microsoft Word documents, Excel spreadsheets, and slide shows right in the Netscape browser window.

> ◆ **Miscellaneous** other plug-ins give Netscape other useful capabilities. In Lesson 8-7, you learn to use the Ichat plug-in to participate in live chats on Web pages. You also install a trial version of the CyberSpell plug-in to check the spelling of messages you send from the Netscape Mail and Netscape News windows.

At the time we wrote this book, Netscape came bundled with several plug-ins. You can check the Netscape home page (home.netscape.com) to find out what Netscape is including with its program now. It also lists plug-ins from other companies — over 100 plug-ins are available.

This unit describes a wide variety of plug-ins, including plug-ins from each of the categories we just listed. Of course, you probably aren't interested in every plug-in we describe. Not everyone needs to see spreadsheets in Web pages, participate in online chats, or watch movie clips. On the other hand, why not try them all?

Some of the plug-ins described in this unit are part of Netscape 3.0 and higher, and the others are stored on the CD-ROM that came with this book. Many plug-ins are *shareware* programs, which means that if you install them and decide to use them after trying them out, you are obligated to send a registration fee to the authors of the programs. Others are *freeware*, which means that they are yours to use for free. Still other plug-ins are available as *demos*, which expire (stop working) after a certain number of days. If you want to continue using the plug-ins, you have to buy them.

on the CD

In this unit, we walk you through installing and using all the plug-ins on the *Dummies 101* CD-ROM, as well as some plug-ins you can download from the Internet. If you want to use plug-ins, read Lesson 8-2, which explains the general procedure for installing plug-ins. Then read the rest of the lessons in this unit, picking and choosing the plug-ins you want to try.

heads up

Caution: In this unit, you use new technology in the form of a raftload of plug-in programs. Not everything will work perfectly. Some plug-ins work better than others, some don't work very well with Windows 3.1, and some

---

plug-in = program
that extends
Netscape's
capabilities by
displaying new kinds
of info or by adding
new commands to
Netscape's menus

try the plug-ins on
the Dummies 101
CD-ROM

☑ **Progress Check**

If you can do the following, you've mastered this lesson:

❑ Understand the difference between Java applets, helper applications, and plug-ins.

❑ Know what kinds of things plug-ins can do.

❑ Imagine what interesting Web pages you'll encounter when your copy of Netscape can play sounds, show video clips, and fly through virtual worlds.

may work a little differently from our descriptions. Just try things out and see what happens. Plan on visiting the Web sites for the plug-ins we describe to find out what's happened since we wrote this book. In many cases, newer versions of plug-in programs will be available for downloading.

extra credit

What's the difference between helper applications and plug-ins?

A *helper application* is a program that runs by itself, even when Netscape isn't running, to display or play files that are stored in a particular format. For example, you can run WinZip (described in Lesson 3-2 and installed as a helper application in Lesson 4-2) to compress and decompress files in the zip file format. WinZip is a regular Windows program, not originally designed to work with Netscape. What makes WinZip a helper application is that you can tell Netscape to run it automatically when it encounters zip files.

You can tell Netscape to run a helper application when it runs into a file in a format that Netscape can't handle on its own. For example, you can tell Netscape to run WinZip whenever it encounters a zip file.

In contrast, a *plug-in* is a program that can work only as part of Netscape; you can't run the program on its own. For example, the VDOLive plug-in doesn't do anything by itself. When installed as part of Netscape, however, it can play video clips. Plug-ins extend the capabilities of Netscape by enabling it to display or play new types of files or even by adding new commands to Netscape menus. Plug-ins enable Netscape to display new kinds of information right in the Netscape window.

Some plug-ins work with helper applications. For example, the RealAudio plug-in works with the standalone RealAudio Player program to play RealAudio-format sound files. Luckily, exactly how plug-ins work doesn't matter — the main thing is that they let Netscape do all kinds of cool things.

Installing Plug-ins

Lesson 8-2

Before you can use a plug-in, you have to install it, which means both copying the program file to your hard disk and telling Netscape about the plug-in. This lesson describes how to find out what plug-ins you already have installed, how to install the plug-ins stored on the *Dummies 101* CD-ROM, and how to install plug-ins that you download from the Web.

Which plug-ins do you have?

You can ask Netscape for a list of the plug-ins that you have installed by choosing Help⇨About Plug-ins. You see a list that looks like Figure 8-2. After you're done looking at the list, click Netscape's Back button.

choose <u>H</u>elp→About <u>P</u>lug-ins to see a list of installed plug-ins

The LiveAudio, LiveVideo, Live3D, and QuickTime plug-ins are included in the standard version of Netscape; look on your plug-in list for them. For reasons we can't fathom, the LiveVideo plug-in is called NPAVI32 Dynamic Link Library on this list — if you see that name on your list, you've got LiveVideo. If you don't have these plug-ins, see Lesson 1-1 for how to get the current version of Netscape.

Figure 8-2: Netscape can display a list of the plug-ins you've installed so far.

Figure 8-3: Click the button for the plug-in you want to install.

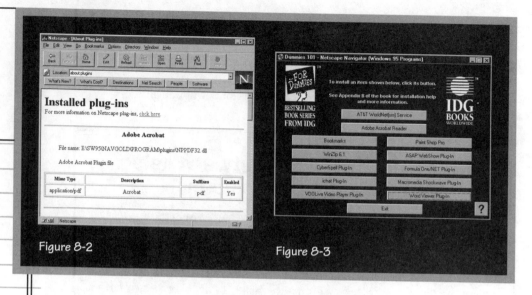

Figure 8-2   Figure 8-3

Notes:

The rest of the plug-ins described in this unit come from the *Dummies 101* CD-ROM and/or can be downloaded from the Web.

Installing plug-ins from the CD-ROM

on the CD

After you install Netscape Navigator 3.0 or later, follow these steps to install any of the plug-ins stored on the CD-ROM that comes with this book:

1 If you're running Netscape, exit.

You aren't supposed to install plug-ins while Netscape is running.

2 Find the *Dummies 101* CD-ROM and insert the disc, label side up, into your CD-ROM drive.

If you're using Windows 95, the Installer program should run automagically and display the window shown in Figure 8-3. If this occurs, skip to Step 5.

3 If the Installer window does *not* appear: If you've already created a *Dummies 101* Installer icon, double-click the icon. Or if you're using Windows 95, click the Start button and choose Programs➪ Dummies 101➪Dummies 101 - Netscape Navigator Installer.

You see the Installer window shown in Figure 8-3. Skip to Step 5.

4 If you *haven't* created a *Dummies 101* Installer icon yet, take a quick detour to Appendix B and follow the directions in the "Running the *Dummies 101* Installer Program" section. After you're done, double-click the icon to bring up the Installer window. Or if you're using Windows 95, click the Start button and choose Programs➪ Dummies 101➪Dummies 101 - Netscape Navigator Installer.

You see the Installer window shown in Figure 8-3.

5 Click the button for the plug-in you want.

The plug-in's installation program runs.

6 Follow the instructions that appear on your screen.

The instructions are different for each plug-in. After you complete the installation, you see the Installer window again.

7 Run Netscape and test the plug-in.

If the plug-in works properly, you're set. Otherwise, see Lesson 9-8, "Uninstalling a Plug-In."

8 **After you're done installing plug-ins, close the Installer window by clicking its Exit button.**

Installing plug-ins that you download

Another source of plug-ins is the Internet itself. You can download many shareware, freeware, and demo versions of plug-ins right from the Web. Three excellent sources of plug-ins are

- **Netscape Web site,** at `home.netscape.com`
- **Tucows (The Ultimate Collection Of WinSock Software),** at `www.tucows.com`
- **The Consummate WinSock Applications List,** at `www.cwsapps.com`

Here's how to install a plug-in that you download from the Net:

1 **Download the plug-in program from the Netscape Web site, from a Web site that lists Netscape plug-ins, or from the developer's Web site.**

Make a note of the folder in which you store the file you downloaded.

2 **Exit Netscape.**

You can't install a plug-in while Netscape is running.

3 **Run Windows Explorer or My Computer (in Windows 95) or File Manager (in Windows 3.1).**

4 **Find the file that contains the plug-in program and double-click the program name.**

The installation program runs.

5 **Follow the instructions on-screen.**

Some plug-ins come with text files (usually named Readme.txt) with additional information about installing the plug-in.

After you install plug-ins

Installing a plug-in puts one or more files in the plugins subfolder of the Netscape Program folder. The filenames start with *np* (for Netscape Plug-in) and have the filename extension *dll* (the Windows standard extension for add-on programs). Installation may also place other files in other folders. Some plug-ins come with standalone programs that do part of their job. For example, the RealAudio plug-in (which plays sound clips from the Web) includes the RealAudio Player, a standalone program. The plug-in requires the standalone player to work.

heads up

Be sure to install one plug-in at a time. After you install a plug-in, run Netscape and see whether the plug-in works. Also see whether similar plug-ins or helper applications have stopped working.

Note: Plug-ins and helper applications may conflict with each other. For example, if you previously installed a helper application to play audio clips, the helper application may stop working when you install an audio plug-in. Our advice is to install plug-ins one at a time and test Netscape after each one. If Netscape, a plug-in, or a helper application stops working, you may need to uninstall the last plug-in you installed. To uninstall plug-ins, see Lesson 8-8.

download shareware and freeware plug-ins from the Web

install one plug-in at a time

Figure 8-4: You need another plug-in to deal with some of the information on this Web page. Do you want it?

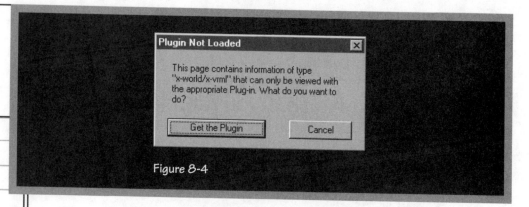

Figure 8-4

Plug-ins are usually designed to work with a particular version of Netscape. The plug-ins on the CD-ROM in the back of this book are designed to work with Netscape 3.0. If you've got a newer version of Netscape, you may need to get a newer version of some plug-ins. Check the Netscape home page or the Web site for the plug-in — we tell you where to get more information about each plug-in we describe. When you upgrade your Netscape program, you may need to reinstall your plug-ins.

extra credit

"Plugin Not Loaded"

When you are at Netscape's own Web site or a site run by a company that makes plug-ins, you may encounter a window like the one shown in Figure 8-4, asking whether you want to download a plug-in. This window may appear when you open a Web page that contains information that requires a plug-in you don't have. In Figure 8-4, Netscape needs a plug-in that can handle x-world/x-vrml information — a 3D virtual reality world that you'll learn more about in Lesson 8-5.

Unfortunately, the window doesn't tell you exactly which plug-in it plans to download. If you want to go ahead and get the suggested plug-in, click Get the Plugin and follow the instructions that appear. If you'd rather not, click Cancel.

☑ **Progress Check**

If you can do the following, you've mastered this lesson:

❑ Know where plug-ins come from.

❑ Know the usual steps to install a plug-in.

Lesson 8-3

Listening to the Web with RealAudio and LiveAudio

RealAudio plays sound clips while you download them

RealAudio is a plug-in that lets you play audio clips as you download them from the Web. Unlike some other audio players, you don't have to wait until you receive the entire audio file before starting to play it. RealAudio can start playing the beginning of the audio file while continuing to download the rest of the file (the cool term for this capability is *streaming audio*). No waiting! RealAudio consists of two parts: the standalone RealAudio program, which plays sound files, and the RealAudio plug-in, which connects the RealAudio Player to Netscape.

RealAudio comes from a company named Progressive Networks and plays files in RealAudio format, which have the filename extension *ra* or *ram*. The plug-in isn't on the *Dummies 101* CD-ROM; we tell you how to download the latest version from the Progressive Networks Web site.

LiveAudio, which comes with Netscape, is similar to RealAudio but plays sound clips in most standard formats other than the RealAudio format (including the AIFF, AU, MIDI, and WAV formats, if you care). If you installed the standard version of Netscape, you probably have LiveAudio installed already.

You want to have both the RealAudio and LiveAudio plug-ins installed so that you can hear all sound clips that you encounter on the Web.

heads up

To use RealAudio or LiveAudio, you need at least a 14,400 bps connection to the Internet. A 2,400 or 9,600 bps connection doesn't cut the mustard — the data arrives too slowly to be played correctly, and the sound quality is terrible. You also need a computer with at least 8MB of memory (RAM) and a Windows-compatible sound card and speakers. Otherwise, how can you hear anything? The RealAudio program takes about 2MB of disk space.

Installing the RealAudio plug-in

You can download the RealAudio plug-in from the RealAudio Web site at www.realaudio.com. For information about downloading files from the Web, see Lesson 3-2.

After you download the file — and, if necessary, used WinZip to decompress it — double-click a file named something like Setup.exe, Install.exe, or RealAudio.exe to kick off RealAudio's installation program. Follow the prompts that appear on your screen to perform the installation. RealAudio has two components, a standalone player and the actual plug-in, so you'll probably be asked whether you want to configure RealAudio to work with Netscape (referring to the standalone program) and whether you want to install the RealAudio plug-in in Netscape (referring to the plug-in). In both cases, answer *yes*.

When the installation is complete, you see a RealAudio folder on your desktop (under Windows 95) or a RealAudio Program Group (under Windows 3.1). Either way, you see icons for several sample sound files, an information text file named Readme, and the standalone RealAudio program. You don't need to run the standalone program because you use RealAudio from Netscape. Another icon lets you uninstall the RealAudio program in case you decide not to use it.

To try out your RealAudio player, double-click one of the sample icons in the RealAudio folder or Program Group. In response, the standalone RealAudio player should run and play the sounds in the file you selected. If this occurs, you're set. If you don't hear anything, however, make sure that your PC's sound card and speakers are working properly. If that doesn't do the trick, find a solution in the RealAudio information file by double-clicking the Readme icon and reading the document that appears.

Using RealAudio to listen to the radio

To try the RealAudio plug-in, go to the NPR home page and play some news:

1 **Run Netscape and connect to your Internet provider.**

2 **Click in the Netscape browser window's Location box, type** www.npr.org, **and press Enter.**

You see a list of the audio stories offered by National Public Radio.

Notes:

LiveAudio plays a wide variety of sound formats

NPR news is available anytime

Figure 8-5: You can control the RealAudio Player with buttons like the ones on your VCR.

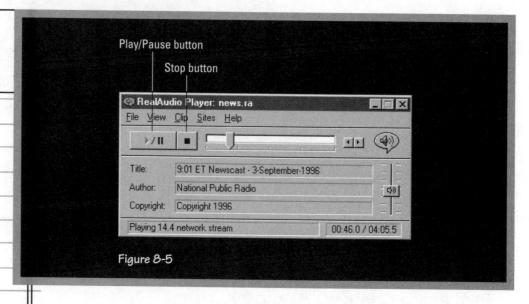

Figure 8-5

3 Click the link under the Breaking News heading.

Or click the link under the NPR Audio Story of the Day heading or any other link that looks interesting.

NPR offers its news stories in two formats, RealAudio 1.0 (14,400 bps) and RealAudio 2.0 (28,800 bps). The 2.0 version gives you better sound quality, but you can use it only if your computer, modem, and Internet provider's phone connection are fast enough — your phone connection must be 28,800 bps or faster, and your computer must be a 486 or Pentium that runs at a minimum of 66 MHz. If you're not sure, you can try both to see which sounds better on your system.

4 Click a link that activates a RealAudio file.

A Viewing Location box appears briefly. Then the RealAudio Player window appears, as shown in Figure 8-5, and the news begins!

Depending on the speed of your computer and Internet connection and what other programs are running on your computer, the sound may be terrific, or it may be choppy and crackly. Exit other programs if you're getting lousy sound.

5 To stop the sound clip for a moment, click the Play/Pause button. To start it again, click the same button again.

When you pause and restart the sound clip, the news picks up where you left off.

6 To stop the sound clip for good, click the Stop button.

Now if you click the Play button, the sound clip starts over at the beginning.

You don't have to close the RealAudio window if you plan to play more sounds later. Click in the Netscape window to return to your browser.

Here are some Web sites that carry RealAudio sound files:

- The **RealAudio** home page (www.realaudio.com) has links to sites you can try.

- **Timecast** (www.timecast.com) is a daily listing of radio programs on the Web. The page lists news, sports, entertainment, and business stories on the Web. One button lists live stories on the Web right now.

click the VCR-like buttons to stop, start, and pause the sound

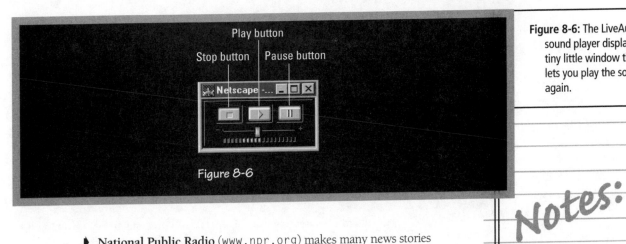

Figure 8-6

Figure 8-6: The LiveAudio sound player displays a tiny little window that lets you play the sound again.

Notes:

◆ **National Public Radio** (www.npr.org) makes many news stories from *Morning Edition, All Things Considered, Fresh Air, Car Talk,* and other programs available via RealAudio files.

◆ **ESPN** (www.espn.com) carries live sportscasts, along with an amazing array of sports news. Click the Live Audio button on its home page.

Installing the LiveAudio plug-in

LiveAudio comes with the standard version of Netscape 3.0. Choose Help⇨About Plug-ins from the Netscape menu to see whether LiveAudio is listed among your plug-ins. If you don't have LiveAudio, see Lesson 1-1 for suggestions on how to upgrade your copy of Netscape to the current version.

Playing sounds with LiveAudio

How about playing a sound clip with LiveAudio?

1 **Run Netscape and connect to your Internet provider.**

2 **Click in the browser window's Location box, type** www.dailywav.com, **and press Enter.**

You see the Daily.WAV Web page, which offers a different WAV (sound) file each day. If the Daily.WAV site doesn't respond, check out the Rock & Roll Hall of Fame at www.rockhall.com. Look around to find sound files — we found some by clicking The 500 Songs and clicking the name of a band.

3 **Click the WAV of the day or any other sound file (WAV, AU, MIDI, or AIFF) that looks interesting.**

Netscape downloads the WAV file and then plays it. While the file is down-loading, a tiny Netscape window appears. Then you see a little tape player in the window (see Figure 8-6) and hear the sound clip.

Downloading the sound file may take several minutes, during which time the tiny Netscape window remains gray and lifeless. Just sit tight — the file arrives sooner or later.

4 **To play the clip again, click the Play button.**

5 **When you're done listening to the sound clip, close the window.**

If you don't close the little Netscape window that plays the sound clip, it stays open until you exit Netscape. Netscape opens another little window for each sound you download, which can clutter up your screen and computer's memory.

☑ **Progress Check**

If you can do the following, you've mastered this lesson:

❑ Install the RealAudio and LiveAudio plug-ins.

❑ Listen to a sound clip on a Web page.

Sometimes the LiveAudio sound player appears right in the Web page and has a different look.

To find Web sites that include sounds that your LiveAudio plug-in can play, go to the Yahoo! page (at www.yahoo.com) and look around. We found lots of sounds by choosing Entertainment, then Music, then Listening_Booth, and then Archives.

Recess

Your ears must be ringing from all this plug-in excitement! Get up and walk around for a few minutes to clear your head.

Lesson 8-4

Watching Movies with LiveVideo, QuickTime, and Shockwave

Wouldn't it be cool if Web pages could contain video right on the page? Well, they can! This lesson describes how to install and use three plug-ins that play video clips in the Netscape window:

▶ **LiveVideo** is a plug-in that plays movies in a standard video format used on the Web — AVI files. LiveVideo has to wait until the whole video clip downloads before it can start to play the clip. The plug-in comes free with the standard version of Netscape, so the price is right. See the Netscape home page (home.netscape.com) for more information about LiveVideo.

▶ The **QuickTime** plug-in plays movies in another standard format called (amazingly enough) QuickTime, a format invented by Apple Computer. QuickTime movies are stored in files with the extension MOV. The QuickTime plug-in comes with Netscape, but you need the QuickTime Player for Windows, a standalone program from Apple (available from the Web page quicktime.apple.com), to use it.

▶ **Shockwave** is a particularly cool plug-in because it can play sounds, show movies, and interact with you all at once. "Shocked" Web pages (pages that use Shockwave) can be interactive, allowing the Web page to change as you move your mouse pointer around. An advantage of Shockwave is that the files to be downloaded to your computer are usually much smaller than files in other video or animation formats. Audio files start playing before they are completely downloaded, because Shockwave uses RealAudio to play sounds.

Shockwave is popular among Web page developers because they can use one program — Macromedia Director — to create video, audio, and animated material for Web sites. Its Web page is at www.macromedia.com.

Shockwave plays video, audio, and animations and lets you interact with the Web page

heads up

One problem with playing movies from the Web is that the files that contain them are *BIG*. A three-minute movie preview may take up 10MB on disk. Files this large take forever to download, especially if you don't have a fast modem.

Notes:

So don't plan on watching long movies — few are available on the Web, anyway. The movies you find on the Web are moving pictures that last seconds or perhaps minutes. You view them in a little tiny window within the Netscape window, usually about two inches square.

Note: This lesson describes the version of the Shockwave plug-in on the CD-ROM in the back of this book. However, before you install it, consider going to the Shockwave site at www.macromedia.com to find out whether a newer version is available.

Installing LiveVideo and QuickTIme

The LiveVideo and QuickTime plug-ins are preinstalled in Netscape 3.0 and higher. Before you can use the QuickTime plug-in, however, you have to install a standalone program called QuickTime for Windows Movie Player, which works in conjunction with the plug-in. If you got your copy of Netscape 3.0 or higher from a CD-ROM, your CD-ROM probably has the QuickTime standalone program on it as well. Otherwise, follow these steps to download and install the QuickTime Player:

1 **Run Netscape and connect to the Internet.**

2 **Click in the Location box, type** quicktime.apple.com, **and press Enter.**

You go to the QuickTime Web site. This site is very busy; you may have to try several times before you get through.

3 **Find the QuickTime for Windows Player and download the file.**

Follow the instructions on the Web pages. Make a note of the folder into which you download the file.

If you can't find the program, or if the Web site is too busy for you to connect, go to the Tucows site (www.tucows.com) and find the program — it's listed under Non-Internet Programs.

4 **Disconnect from the Internet and exit Netscape.**

5 **In Windows 95, run My Computer or Windows Explorer, find the file you just downloaded (it's probably called Qt32.exe), and double-click the filename.**

In Windows 3.1, run File Manager, find the file you just downloaded (it's probably called Qt16.exe), and double-click the filename.

The QuickTime installation program runs.

6 **Follow the instructions on-screen.**

After installing the QuickTime Player, the installation program instructs you to press the spacebar to run a movie, which calibrates the player.

1 **Press the spacebar to start the calibration movie.**

You see the Movie Player window and a little animated QuickTime logo with zoomy sound effects.

2 **Close the movie window and the Movie Player window.**

Windows 95 users can click the Close button in the upper-right corner of each window, and Windows 3.1 users can double-click the Control-menu box (the little gray minus-sign button) in the upper-left corner of each window.

Notes:

right-click the video
image to see
commands

QuickTime logo

The QuickTime installation creates a desktop folder (in Windows 95) or a Program Group (in Windows 3.1) that contains icons for the movie player, a picture viewer, and other files. You don't need to use these icons — Netscape runs the movie player when you find a QuickTime movie on the Web.

For updates to LiveVideo, see the Netscape Web site at home.netscape.com. For more information about QuickTime, see the QuickTime Web pages at quicktime.apple.com.

Watching AVI movies with LiveVideo

When you display a Web page that contains a movie clip, the link usually tells what kind of movie it is (QuickTime, AVI, MPEG, or other format), how long the clip is (in minutes and seconds), and how big the file is (in megabytes, or MB). Click the link to download the movie — the QuickTime plug-in can play QuickTime files, and the LiveVideo plug-in can play AVI and MPEG formats. The status bar at the bottom of the Netscape window tells you how far the download has gotten and how long you have to wait.

When you're watching a movie in AVI format with the LiveVideo plug-in, click the movie image to stop it and then click it again to resume playing it. Alternately, you can click the movie image with the right mouse button to see a menu of commands that includes Play, Pause, Rewind, Fast Forward, Frame Back, and Frame Forward.

Watching QuickTime movies

When you see the QuickTime logo, Netscape is downloading a QuickTime movie. After the movie downloads, you can play it by using the Play button (the usual right-pointing triangle). Right-clicking the image shows a menu of options that includes Play, Rewind, and Save Movie. Choose Save Movie and choose a location for the file if you want to play the movie later without downloading it again.

Installing Shockwave

Follow the steps in Lesson 8-2 to install the Shockwave plug-in from the *Dummies 101* CD-ROM.

Looking at "shocked" pages

Try out the Shockwave plug-in by going to its home page at www.macromedia.com/shockwave. If you have a choice between the "shocked" (with Shockwave) or "unshocked" (without Shockwave), choose the shocked page. Macromedia selects a "Shocked Site of the Day" that is a good example of the things you can do with Shockwave.

You can find other "shocked" pages at the following sites:

◆ *Citi:Zen Magazine* (www.citizenmag.com) is an online magazine that uses Shockwave effects. You have to wait a few minutes for the magazine to download before you can see anything.

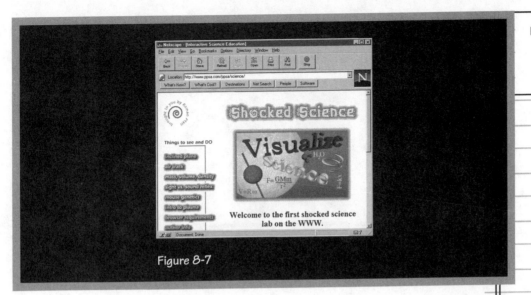

Figure 8-7

Figure 8-7: On the Shocked Science page, mice fly and electrons circle atomic nuclei.

- Shocked Science (`www.ppsa.com/ppsa/science`) is an online science lab that uses Shockwave to help people visualize science (see Figure 8-7). The Web site is by Raman Pfaff, a physicist who is trying to use multimedia and the WWW for science education.

- Paramount Pictures (`www.paramount.com`) has some animated stuff from its movies.

- *Mission Impossible* (`www.missionimpossible.com`) is the Web site for the classic television show and recent movie. Be sure to choose the Shockwave version of the mission site.

- *Dragonheart* (`www.mca.com/universal_pictures/dragonheart`) is another movie site. Click the link that says "Got Shockwave? Try this!" This one takes a few minutes to download.

Some of these sites may have closed by the time you read this (especially the ones dedicated to recent movies). You can look for other sites by starting at Yahoo! (`www.yahoo.com`), clicking the Computers and Internet link, and searching for "shockwave" or "shocked."

Finding all kinds of movies

Here are places you can look for movies on the Web:

- Go to the MovieLink Web site at `www.movielink.com`, which can help you find out what movies are playing in your area (if you live in a metropolitan area, anyway). MovieLink also includes previews of hundreds of movies, in both AVI and QuickTime format.

- Try typing **disney** or **paramount** or **abc** or **mca** or **foxnetwork**, or the name of another movie or television company, in the Location box in the Netscape window. Netscape adds *www.* to the beginning and *.com* to end and tries to connect to the Web site. You never know what you'll see, but it's fun to try guessing the Web addresses of major companies!

- Go to the Yahoo! page, and choose Entertainment and then Movies. Look around. Among the information about movies may be a few film clips.

☑ Progress Check

If you can do the following, you've mastered this lesson:

❑ Install the QuickTime for Windows movie player.

❑ Play a movie clip on a Web page (usually after a long wait).

❑ Look at "shocked" Web pages.

Figure 8-8: VDOLive shows the best picture it can within the limitations of the speed of your Internet connection.

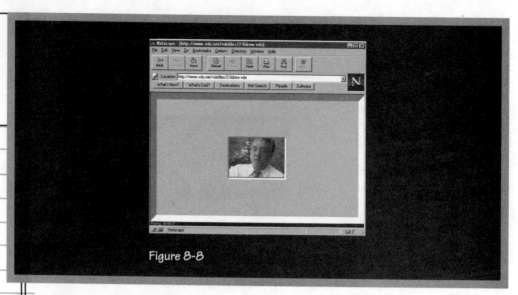

Figure 8-8

Notes:

extra credit

VDOLive: Video without the wait

VDOLive is a plug-in that can start playing a movie clip (stored in the special *vdo* format) while the video file is still downloading — a technique that's referred to as *streaming video*. Instead of waiting 10 or 20 minutes for a movie clip to download, you wait only 10 or 20 *seconds* while the first part of the movie arrives; then the movie starts to play!

Although streaming video is a great idea, the execution still has some kinks. Unless you have a super-fast Internet connection (such as an expensive ISDN or T1 connection that bypasses normal phone lines), you can't download video data as quickly as you can watch it, so what you typically see isn't full-motion video so much as jerky pictures accompanied by sound. On the other hand, this approach spares you from having to wait a long time for a video clip and then discover, after it's finally downloaded, that you aren't interested in its contents.

You can install the VDOLive plug-in from the CD-ROM that came with this book. For instructions on installing VDOLive, see Lesson 8-2.

After you install the VDOLive plug-in and the VDOLive Player (the helper application that actually plays the movie), go to the Web site at `www.vdo.net`. Click the VDOLive Gallery to see some sample video clips. Follow the links until you find an interesting-looking movie — the VDOLive Gallery lists hundreds of Web sites that use VDOLive to download video. After you choose a video clip to download, nothing seems to happen for a minute or two; then you see the rotating VDOLive logo. Finally, the file begins to arrive, and the movie begins playing in a small window within the Netscape window (see Figure 8-8). When the video clip is over, you return to the previous Web page.

You can make the picture bigger by right-clicking the picture and choosing Zoom In/Out from the menu that appears. Do the same thing again to make the picture its original size. If you want to stop the movie before the end, right-click the picture and choose Stop from the menu that appears.

Lesson 8-5   Wandering in Cyberspace with Live3D

Have you heard of *virtual reality* (or *VR*)? Well, virtual reality is reality that isn't really real — a fake world that looks real and feels like you're really inside it. The earliest virtual reality implementation was the storyteller, starting

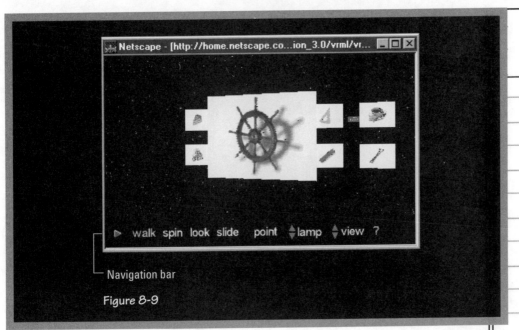

Navigation bar

Figure 8-9

Figure 8-9: The Live3D plug-in displays a virtual reality world in its own window.

thousands of years ago. You could close your eyes while listening to the story and imagine that you were in it. Virtual reality progressed through books, radio, and television, and one of its latest incarnations is on the Web.

Virtual reality objects on Web pages — called *worlds* in the technical vernacular — at first look like regular pictures. But you can "enter" these pictures and move around within them! As you do so, the picture changes. If you look up, you're see what's above you; if you look to your side, you see another part of the picture that wasn't visible initially. That's why virtual reality is also called *3D* — it's like being in a three-dimensional world.

Web pages that contain virtual worlds are written in a special language called *VRML* (Virtual Reality Modeling Language), and files in this format have the extension WRL. Netscape doesn't understand VRML, but Netscape 3.0 and up includes a plug-in named Live3D that does.

Figure 8-9 shows a virtual reality world as displayed by Live3D. The navigation bar — the row of words along the bottom of the window — provides commands for moving around in the world.

Here are things you can do in Live3D:

▶ **Walk forward:** To move yourself forward into the scene, hold down the left mouse button while you move the mouse (this action is called *dragging*). If you go too far, you can drag the mouse backward to go back.

▶ **Turn:** To turn, or spin, hold down the right mouse button while you move the mouse. The scene changes as though you were turning your head.

▶ **Take a closer look:** To zoom in on something, hold down the Ctrl key while you click. You zoom toward the thing you clicked. To get closer yet, Ctrl+click again.

▶ **Go to a predefined viewpoint:** The creator of the virtual world may have chosen some particularly useful or good-looking positions and saved them as *viewpoints*. The view you see when you enter the world is called the *entry view,* and it's always one of the predefined viewpoints.

virtual world = 3D
virtual reality object
on a Web page

VRML = virtual
reality modeling
language, the
language virtual
worlds are written in

drag the mouse to
move around the
virtual world

drag the mouse
using the right
button to turn your
virtual head

To see a list of viewpoints and move to one of them (a useful move if you're totally lost), right-click anywhere in the virtual world and choose Viewpoints from the menu that appears. Then choose a viewpoint from the list.

If the virtual world appears in its own window, when you are done exploring it you can close the window that displays it by clicking the Close button (in Windows 95) or double-clicking the Control-menu box (in Windows 3.1).

Live3D lets you do lots of other things in a virtual world, like turning your headlights on and off, as well as controlling how you move and how much detail you see. For more information about Live3D, go to the Netscape home page (home.netscape.com) and click the Assistance button.

Finding worlds to explore

The best way to find virtual worlds on the Web is to use the Web:

- **Proteinman's Top Ten VRML Worlds** (www.clark.net/theme/proteinman): What more can we say?

- **Virtus VRML Site of the Week** (www.virtus.com/vrmlsite.html): Virtus, a company that makes a bunch of VRML-related products, chooses a new favorite virtual world each week.

- **Aereal Boom** (www.aereal.com/boom): This Web site has a database of virtual worlds and takes you to one. You try out the world, rate it (from one to five stars), and jump to another virtual world.

- **Yahoo!** (www.yahoo.com): You can find listings of virtual words by choosing Computers and Internet, then World Wide Web, and then Virtual Reality Modeling Language (VRML). You find lists of worlds on the Web as well as Web pages with information about creating virtual worlds and using VRML plug-ins.

Recess

Now that you've spent time exploring virtual worlds, maybe it's time to get out into the real world for a while. Talk a walk and admire the sky — no virtual world can duplicate that!

☑ Progress Check

If you can do the following, you've mastered this lesson:

❑ Enter a virtual world by using Live3D.

❑ Move around inside a virtual world. (Wow! Tell your friends!)

❑ Find other virtual worlds to explore.

Lesson 8-6

Viewing Documents with ASAP WebShow, Word Viewer, and Formula One/NET

plug-ins let Netscape display many kinds of files

Before there were Web pages, people stored information in lots of other formats, like word processing documents, spreadsheets, and slide show presentations. Using plug-ins, you can look at some of these kinds of information in your Netscape window. For example, suppose someone used a presentation program to make an impressive slide show. Using ASAP WebShow, the presentation can appear in a Web page.

on the CD

In this unit, you try these plug-ins, which are all on the *Dummies 101* CD-ROM:

- **ASAP WebShow,** from Software Publishing Corp. (www.spco.com/asap/asapwebs.htm), displays slide show presentations created by Microsoft PowerPoint or ASAP WordPower. It uses the RealAudio Player (described in Lesson 8-3) to play audio along with the presentation. Web page creators like WebShow because it can display slide shows created with Microsoft PowerPoint (a very popular presentation program) on Web pages.

- **Word Viewer,** from Inso Corp. (www.inso.com), displays Microsoft Word documents in the Netscape window.

- **Formula One/NET,** from Visual Components (www.visualcomp.com) displays Web pages that include spreadsheets.

heads up

There's one big difference among the plug-ins you meet in this lesson: ASAP WebShow and Formula One/NET display only Web pages that were set up to include WebShow presentations and Excel spreadsheets — you can't use them to display your own WebShow presentations or spreadsheets (if you have any). On the other hand, you *can* use Word Viewer to view Word documents from your own hard disk.

Watching slide shows with ASAP WebShow

Install the ASAP WebShow plug-in from the *Dummies 101* CD-ROM, following the instructions in Lesson 8-2. If no license agreement window appears, press Alt+Tab until it comes into view. The second dialog box that appears during the installation has a checkbox in the lower-left corner that lets you install the ASAP WordPower Player for use with programs other than Netscape. If you don't plan to use any other programs to look at ASAP WebShow presentations (we don't), click this box to remove the check.

To look at a presentation by using ASAP WebShow, go to its home page at www.spco.com/asap/asapwebs.htm and go to the ASAP WebShow Gallery. You can also search for pages that contain the phrase *ASAP WebShow* by using Yahoo, AltaVista, or your favorite Web search page.

Viewing Word documents with Word Viewer

You can use Word Viewer to look at any Microsoft Word 6.0 or 7.0 document on your own computer as well as documents that are incorporated into Web pages. Install the plug-in from the CD-ROM in the back of this book by following the instructions in Lesson 8-2. When the installation program offers to install the plug-in somewhere other than the Netscape plug-ins folder, don't do it! Just click <u>N</u>ext.

If you have any Word documents on your hard disk, follow these steps to see the document in the Netscape window:

1   Run Netscape.

You don't need to connect to your Internet provider.

Notes:

2 **Choose the File⇨Open File in Browser command from the Netscape browser menu (or press Ctrl+O).**

You see the Open dialog box.

3 **In Windows 95, click in the Files of Type box and choose Microsoft 6 and 95 (*.doc) from the menu that appears.**

In Windows 3.1, click in the List Files of Type box and choose Microsoft Word (*.doc) from the menu that appears.

Now the dialog box lists the Word documents in the current folder.

4 **Move to a folder that contains your documents and double-click a document.**

The document appears on-screen, looking just as it does in Microsoft Word.

5 **If you want to print the document, choose File⇨Print from the menu and click OK on the dialog box that appears.**

6 **When you're done looking at the document, return to browsing Web pages.**

For example, connect to the Net and click one of your bookmarks; the Word document is replaced by a Web page in your browser window.

If you find Word Viewer useful, you may want to get Quick View Plus, which can display over 200 formats, including Microsoft Works, WordPerfect, Lotus 1-2-3, Microsoft Excel, QuattroPro, Microsoft Access, dBASE, FoxBase, Paradox, PowerPoint, and zip files. With the plug-in, you can view and print files in any of these formats right in your Netscape window, without having the programs loaded on your hard disk. Go to the publisher's Web page at www.inso.com to find out more. When we wrote this book, Inso Corp. offered a 30-day free trial of Quick View Plus, and a permanent license to use the program cost $49.

Displaying spreadsheets by using Formula One/NET

To install the Formula One/NET plug-in from the *Dummies 101* CD-ROM, follow the instructions in Lesson 8-2. When the installation program asks where to install the plug-in, it suggests the Program folder in the Netscape program folder. Take its suggestion and click Next. When the program asks where to install samples, choose any folder where you wouldn't mind storing some sample Web pages. Make a note of where you told the program to store the sample pages so that you can look at them later in this lesson.

Unlike Word Viewer, Formula One/NET doesn't let you open your own files in Netscape. Instead, Formula One/NET gives Netscape the capability to display Web pages that include customized spreadsheet objects. For example, a stock brokerage may create Web pages that include spreadsheets analyzing the performance of stocks or mutual funds.

The plug-in comes with a sample page that you can try:

1 **Run Netscape.**

You don't need to connect to your Internet provider.

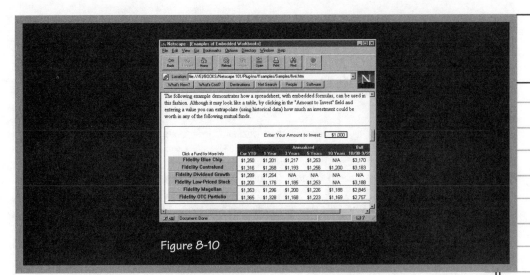

Figure 8-10

Figure 8-10: Web pages can contain spreadsheets that really work!

2 **Choose File⇨Open File from the Netscape browser menu (or press Ctrl+O).**

You see the Open dialog box.

3 **Move to the folder in which you told the Formula One/NET installation program to store its sample Web pages and then move to the Sample folder you find there.**

The folder contains one Web page, named live.htm.

4 **Double-click the live.htm filename.**

Netscape loads the Web page from your hard disk.

5 **Scroll down the page, reading the instructions and playing with the spreadsheets.**

You can type numbers, labels, and formulas in the first spreadsheet, which starts out empty. Figure 8-10 shows a sample spreadsheet.

type numbers in the spreadsheet, and the Web page calculates the answer

To find other Web pages that use Formula One/NET to include spreadsheets, use Yahoo! (www.yahoo.com), AltaVista (altavista.digital.com), or another Web search site to search for "Formula One/NET." We found these (remember that these Web pages may have moved or disappeared by the time you read this):

▶ **Airdrie Calculators** (www.med.ucalgary.ca/saran/airdcalc.htm): These interesting health-related pages are by the Airdrie Medical Clinic in Calgary, Canada. They include the Aerobics Calculator (enter your height and weight, and this Web page calculates your target pulse range for aerobic exercise), the ADHD Calculator (answer the questions to determine whether you child has ADHD, or Attention Deficiency Hyperactivity Disorder), the Gestation Calculator (pregnant? use the Web to calculate your due date!), and The Hot Stuff on a Hot Kid page (figure out how much Tylenol to give a feverish child).

▶ **Guess which countries provide the fastest growing export markets** (www.coopers.co.uk/middlemarket/barometer/spreadsheet): Coopers & Lybrand UK, a division of a huge accounting firm, created a Web page that uses the Formula One/NET spreadsheet and graphics to test your knowledge of world economics.

☑ Progress Check

If you can do the following, you've mastered this lesson:

❏ Install the ASAP WebShow, Word Viewer, and Formula One/NET plug-ins.

❏ Look at ASAP WebShow presentations.

❏ Display any Word document in your Netscape window.

❏ Look at Web pages that include spreadsheets by using the Formula One/ NET plug-in.

extra credit

Looking at PDF files with the Acrobat Reader plug-in

Acrobat Reader from Adobe Systems displays files stored in the *pdf* format (short for *Portable Document Files*), which is becoming a standard format for distributing documents that include both text and graphics. In fact, because we couldn't squeeze all the information we want to give you into the pages of this book, we include three files in pdf format on the *Dummies 101* CD-ROM: wnet95.pdf (which contains instructions for installing AT&T WorldNet Service for Windows 95), wnet31.pdf (which contains instructions for installing AT&T WorldNet Service for Windows 3.1), and maillist.pdf (which contains a companion unit to Unit 7 that explains how to join e-mail mailing lists). In addition, we include the standalone Acrobat program on the CD-ROM so that you can easily read these files. (For more information, see Appendix B.)

Abode also makes a plug-in version of its Acrobat program, which lets you read pdf files from within your Netscape window. You can download this plug-in from www.adobe.com and then install it by following the instructions in Lesson 8-2. After you do so, try out the plug-in by choosing File⇨Open File or pressing Ctrl+O from the Netscape browser window to display an Open dialog box. Click in the Files of Type box and choose Acrobat (*.pdf) from the menu that appears; the pdf files in your current folder are listed. Move to a folder that contains a pdf file you want to view, and then double-click the filename. You see the file in your browser window; you also see a new Toolbar near the top of the window that contains buttons to help you use Acrobat (as shown in Figure 8-11). Click the VCR-like buttons on the Acrobat Toolbar to move from page to page. When you're done, return to browsing Web pages as usual (for example, click the Back button to return to the preceding Web page).

For more information, read the Acrobat manual, which is in the file Help-r.pdf. This file is stored in the same folder at the Acrobat standalone program, usually in C:\Program Files\Acrobat\Help (under Windows 95) or C:\Acrobat\Help (under Windows 3.1).

Lesson 8-7

Two More Cool Plug-ins: Ichat and CyberSpell

Two other plug-ins are too interesting to omit:

▸ **Ichat** lets you participate in live "chats," in which you and others can type messages to each other. Several Web sites use Ichat to set up *chat rooms,* that is, chats on various topics. You can also use the Ichat plug-in to participate in Internet Relay Chat (IRC), a widely used chat system. The Ichat plug-in comes from a company also named Ichat, at www.ichat.com. (Unfortunately, no Windows 3.1 version of Ichat is available as we write this book. If you use Window 3.1, you can check the Ichat site periodically to see whether such a version has become available; or you can simply opt to use a standalone program for chat, such as the excellent mIRC program, which you can download from www.mirc.co.uk.)

▸ **CyberSpell** adds a spelling checker to the Message Composition window you see when you want to send an e-mail message or post an article to a Usenet newsgroup. CyberSpell comes from Inso Corp., the same people who created the Word Viewer you saw in Lesson 8-6 — see the Web site at www.inso.com for more information.

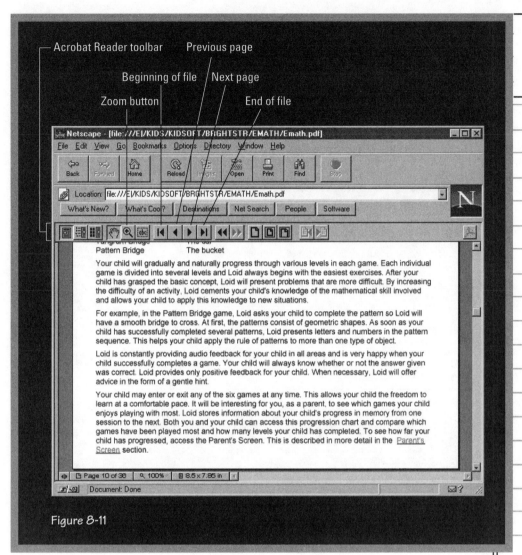

Figure 8-11: When you view a pdf file in Netscape, an Acrobat Toolbar appears in your browser window.

Acrobat Reader toolbar   Previous page

Beginning of file / Next page

Zoom button   End of file

Notes:

Figure 8-11

Both the Ichat and the CyberSpell plug-ins are on the CD-ROM that comes with this book. The CyberSpell plug-in is a 30-day trial version, so if you decide that you want to keep using it, you have to pay its publisher (at the time we write this, the price is $24.95). Otherwise, use it for 30 days and then uninstall it after it stops working.

Chatting on the Web

If you use Windows 95, you can install the Ichat plug-in from the *Dummies 101* CD-ROM by following the instructions in Lesson 8-2. (Currently, no version of Ichat for Windows 3.1 is available.)

Ichat lets you participate in two kinds of online conversations:

- **Ichat-enabled Web pages** (that is, Web pages that have Ichat chat rooms in them), mainly on Ichat's own Itropolis Web site

- **Internet Relay Chat (IRC),** an Internet-wide system of chat channels used by thousands of people all over the world

Ichat lets you connect to Ichat chat rooms or to Internet Relay Chat

Figure 8-12: When you are ready to participate in a conversation, type a message in the text box near the bottom of the Netscape window.

Ichat toolbar

Click here to type a message   Chat messages   Participants

Icons for other chat rooms

Figure 8-12

For either type of chat, go to the Ichat home page at www.ichat.com to find out how to use the plug-in and find some people to chat with. (*Note:* Be sure to install the Shockwave plug-in, described in Lesson 8-4, before starting to chat, because many Ichat chat rooms have Shockwave-style multimedia information in them, too.)

The last time we visited the Ichat Web site, it worked like this (but the designer of a chat site may set things up differently):

1 **Run Netscape and connect to your Internet provider.**

2 **Click in the Location box, type** www.ichat.com, **and press Enter.**

You see the Ichat home page.

3 **Click the Chat sites or Featured chat sites link.**

You see a list of Ichat sites. Each site has one or more Web pages that contain Ichat chat rooms. Some sites are for general chatting, and others concentrate on particular topics.

4 **Click a site.**

The Ichat plug-in takes over and connects to the chat room. You may need to log in before you can enter a chat room. Or you may have to select which chat room you want by clicking a room name or a picture — for example, clicking a picture of a bar might take you to an informal social chat room.

Notes:

When you're in an Ichat chat room, your Netscape window looks something like Figure 8-12, depending on how the chat room is designed. The upper part of the window usually shows information about the room you're in, which may include links to adjoining rooms. The lower part of the window shows the conversation in progress and (in the lower-right corner) a list of the people in the room.

5 **Watch the conversation for a while. If icons appear for other chat rooms, you can click an icon to leave the room you're in and move to the room you click.**

6 **When you want to say something, click in the box at the bottom of the window, type a message, and press Enter.**

7 **When you're done, just go to another Web page in any of the usual ways.**

You may want to click the Back button on the Netscape Toolbar a few times to return to the list of chat sites.

The last item on the Chat Sites list is IRC chat, which takes you to Internet Relay Chat. You have to select an IRC server (the Internet host computer you want to connect to as your IRC "switchboard") and an IRC channel (chat room) before you click the Connect to IRC button. Unlike Ichat chat rooms, IRC channels aren't decorated with graphics — the whole Netscape window shows the conversation and the list of participants, instead of just the lower half of the window.

For more information when you're using the Ichat plug-in, click the Help button, the last button on the Ichat toolbar.

Ichat Help button

Adding a spelling checker

on the CD

You can install the CyberSpell plug-in by following the instructions in Lesson 8-2. After you do so, CyberSpell is added to your StartUp folder (under Windows 95) or StartUp Program Group (under Windows 3.1) so that it runs automatically whenever you start up Windows. You can tell that CyberSpell is active by the tiny CyberSpell icon that appears in the tray on the right end of the Taskbar (under Windows 95) or by the minimized CyberSpell icon that appears near the bottom of the screen (under Windows 3.1).

When you use Netscape to compose either an e-mail message or a Usenet newsgroup article, you see the Message Composition window. (Jump back to Lesson 5-2 to review how to use it.) When CyberSpell is running, the menu bar in the Message Composition window contains an extra command: Spelling. After you type the text of the message you want to send, choose Spelling⇨Quick Spell from the menu. You see the CyberSpell dialog box shown in Figure 8-13, showing a misspelled word and some suggested corrections. Choose the correct word from the Suggestions list, or type the correct word and then click Change.

The Spelling⇨Quick Spell command catches spelling errors, repeated words, and capitalization errors. If you want CyberSpell to look for punctuation, numeric format, date format, and some grammatical errors, choose Spelling⇨Power Spell instead.

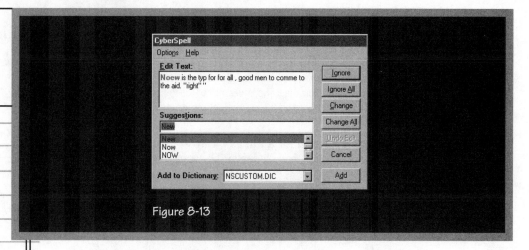

Figure 8-13

☑ Progress Check

If you can do the following,
you've mastered this lesson:

❑ Install the Ichat and
CyberSpell plug-ins.

❑ Use Ichat to participate in
online chats (Windows 95
only).

❑ Check your spelling with
CyberSpell.

The CyberSpell program prefers to run all the time, but you can turn it off. To exit CyberSpell:

▶ In Windows 95, press Ctrl+Alt+Del to display the Close Program dialog box, select Cyber32 from the list, and click the End Task button. To restart the program, click the Start button on the Taskbar and then choose Programs➪CyberSpell➪CyberSpell.

▶ In Windows 3.1, press Ctrl+Esc to display the Task List dialog box, click the CyberSpell entry to highlight it, and click the End Task button. To restart CyberSpell, double-click the CyberSpell icon in the CyberSpell Program Group.

If you try to use CyberSpell after 30 days, you see a message telling you that the program has expired but that you can make it useable again by getting an unlock code over the phone. If you want to buy the program, grab a credit card, click the Unlock button, and follow the instructions that appear. (Also, be sure to disconnect from the Internet — CyberSpell makes a direct toll-free call to its publisher's own computer to process your order.)

Lesson 8-8   Uninstalling a Plug-in

Just because you install a plug-in doesn't mean that you want to keep it forever. For example, you may find that a new plug-in interferes with the operation of another plug-in you've been using, forcing you to eliminate one of them. On the other hand, you may decide that a plug-in simply isn't very useful — or just isn't as good as another plug-in you recently discovered that does the same thing. Even if you have no problems with a plug-in, you may eventually want to remove, or *uninstall,* it so that you can install a new and improved version of it.

You can remove a plug-in in several ways. This lesson covers using the plug-in's own uninstall program, using the Windows 95 Add/Remove Program utility, and deleting the plug-in manually.

Note: Before uninstalling a plug-in, make sure that Netscape is *not* running. Otherwise, you may encounter problems trying to remove a plug-in that Netscape is in the process of using.

Using the plug-in's uninstall program

If your plug-in is typical, it includes a program in its folder or program group whose sole purpose in life is to uninstall the plug-in. Look for such a program, which has the word *uninstall* or *remove* as part of its name. If you find it, double-click the program's icon and then follow the prompts that step you through removing the plug-in.

After the operation is completed (it typically takes less than a minute), check for superfluous items that may remain, such as the uninstall program itself, and the folder or Program Group that held the plug-in's files. Manually delete each leftover item by clicking it to select it and pressing the Del key (and, if necessary, clicking a Yes button to confirm the deletion). Alternately, if you're using Windows 95, you can right-click each item and then click the Delete option from the menu that appears. Continue deleting until everything related to the plug-in is gone.

Using the Windows 95 Add/Remove utility

If you don't find an uninstall program among the plug-in's files and you're running Windows 95, you may be able to eliminate the plug-in by using the Control Panel's Add/Remove Programs utility. To try this option, follow these steps:

1 **Click the Windows 95 Start button in the bottom-left corner of your screen and choose Settings⇨Control Panel from the menu that appears.**

A window with a variety of icons appears. Locate the Add/Remove Programs icon.

2 **Double-click the Add/Remove Programs icon.**

A dialog box listing the programs that are installed on your system appears.

3 **Scroll through the list of programs until you find the name of your plug-in.**

If your plug-in *isn't* listed, click the Cancel button, click the Control Panel's Close button to exit the window, and skip to the next section, "Removing a plug-in manually."

4 **Click the line containing the name of your plug-in to select it.**

The line is highlighted.

5 **Click the Add/Remove button.**

You're asked to verify your decision to remove the software.

6 **Click the Yes button.**

The process of removing the plug-in's files begins. Respond to any prompts as needed until all the program and data files are removed.

7 **Click the dialog box's OK button.**

The dialog box closes.

8 **Click the Control Panel window's Close button.**

The Control Panel closes.

9 **If any traces of the installation (such as an empty folder) remain, delete each item manually by clicking it with your *right* (not left) mouse button to pop up a menu and then clicking the menu's Delete option.**

Notes:

extra credit

Talking on the Net with CoolTalk

Netscape 3.0 and up includes CoolTalk, a separate program that lets you use the Internet like a phone. CoolTalk allows you to make phone calls to anywhere in the world without incurring long-distance phone charges. (Or that's the idea, anyway; this category of Internet software is still in its infancy, so it may not always work as smoothly as you'd like it to.)

To use CoolTalk, you need a sound card installed in your computer and speakers attached to the sound card (the same equipment you need to hear LiveAudio or RealAudio sound clips from the Web). In addition, you need a microphone attached to your sound card so that you can do your part of the talking.

To run CoolTalk, connect to the Internet and then double-click the CoolTalk icon in your Netscape folder or Program Group. (Alternately, click the Windows 95 Start button and choose Programs➪Netscape Navigator➪CoolTalk.) The first time you run CoolTalk, a Setup program guides you through tailoring the program for your system. If you have trouble during this process, check out the live.netscape.com for information, or send e-mail to cooltalk_support@netscape.com.

When CoolTalk is running, it looks like Figure 8-14. Explaining how to use CoolTalk is beyond the scope of this book, but you can get more information by choosing Help➪Help Topics from the program's menu. You might also consider buying a book that covers the subject, such as *Internet Telephony For Dummies* by Daniel D. Briere and Patrick J. Hurley (IDG Books Worldwide).

Note: CoolTalk requires Microsoft Video for Windows (Msvideo.dll). This program is included as part of Windows 95, but if you use Windows 3.1 and see an error message about Video for Windows when running CoolTalk, you need to get and install the program, which you can find on various sites on the Web. (For example, as we write this, it's available at URL ftp://ftp.microsoft.com/softlib/mslfiles/wv1160.exe.) After you download the file, move to the folder that contains it, double-click the file's name (which causes the single compressed file to expand to lots of files), press F5 to refresh the file list, and double-click the file named Setup.exe. Finally, follow the setup instructions that appear to install the program.

Removing a plug-in manually

If all else fails, you can remove a plug-in's components yourself, piece by piece.

A typical plug-in consists primarily of a single file that resides in a plugins subfolder contained within your Netscape Program folder. The plug-in's name ends with a period and the letters *dll* (short for *Dynamic Link Library*). Most Netscape plug-ins have names that begin with the letters NP (short for *Netscape plug-in*). You can find the exact location and filename of the plug-in by choosing Help➪About Plug-ins.

For example, if your Netscape folder is named *Netscape,* your primary plug-in file is probably located in the subfolder Netscape/Program/plugins and has a filename that ends with dll. To double-check, run Netscape, choose Help➪About Plug-ins, and locate the entry for the plug-in you're interested in. Included in the data you'll see are the names of the folder and file that contain the plug-in. (The filename is probably similar to the name of your plug-in; for example, the LiveAudio plug-in lives in a file named Npaudio.dll.) Write down the information and then exit Netscape.

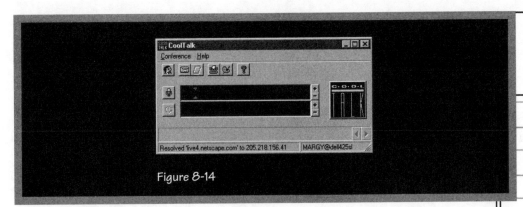

Figure 8-14

Figure 8-14: CoolTalk lets you talk on the phone over the Internet, with no long-distance charges.

Notes:

To eliminate the plug-in file, move to the appropriate folder by using My Computer or Windows Explorer (under Windows 95) or File Manager (under Windows 3.1), and look for the filename you've identified. When you locate the file, click it to select it and press the Del key to delete it. If a dialog box asking you to confirm the deletion appears, click the Yes button.

Next, look for a folder or Program Group that has a name similar to the plug-in's. (For example, if you're using Windows 95, click the Start button, click Programs, and look for the name of the plug-in among the list of programs.) If you locate such a folder or Program Group, eliminate each item in it by clicking and pressing Del, and then remove the folder or Program Group itself by clicking it and pressing Del. Alternately, if you're using Windows 95, you can right-click each item and then click the Delete option from the menu that appears.

heads up

If you're worried about deleting files, you may prefer to move the plug-in files to another folder for a while and then run Netscape to make sure that everything (except the plug-in) still works. If Netscape and the other plug-ins work fine, *then* delete the files.

When you're done, you have removed all traces of the plug-in, freeing up space on your hard disk for new and improved plug-ins!

☑ Progress Check

If you can do the following, you've mastered this lesson:

❑ Uninstall a plug-in that you've decided not to use.

Unit 8 Quiz

For each of the following questions, circle the letter of the correct answer or answers. Remember, each question may have more than one right answer.

1. **A Netscape plug-in is:**

   A. A program that allows you to plug Netscape into a wall socket so that it doesn't have to run off batteries.

   B. A program that extends the capabilities of Netscape.

   C. A program that lets you view additional kinds of information in the Netscape window.

   D. A program that can add new commands to Netscape's menus.

Notes:

2. **A Java applet is:**

    A. A small program embedded in a Web page.

    B. A program that lets a Web page do something fancy.

    C. A small program written in the Java programming language.

    D. A small apple with added caffeine.

3. **To hear sound clips on Web pages, you need:**

    A. A plug-in that can play audio files, like LiveAudio or RealAudio.

    B. A sound card.

    C. Speakers.

    D. A radio receiver that can pick up the Web radio station.

4. **A shocked Web page is:**

    A. X-rated.

    B. Equipped with multimedia information that requires the Shockwave plug-in.

    C. Stunned that you don't have the Shockwave plug-in.

    D. A page that has sustained an electrical current of 110 volts.

5. **When exploring a virtual world, you can:**

    A. Move forward and backward.

    B. Turn from side to side.

    C. Move to predefined viewpoints.

    D. Plant your flag in the soil and claim the world for the Queen of England.

Unit 8 Exercise

1. Run Netscape, connect to your Internet provider, and go to the Tucows Web site at `www.tucows.com`. (If you can't get through, go to the Consummate WinSock Applications Web site at `www.cwsapps.com`.)

2. Find the Web page that lists Netscape plug-ins for the version of Windows you're using.

3. Find a plug-in that looks like fun.

4. Download the plug-in.

5. Install the plug-in (be sure to exit Netscape first).

6. Try out the new plug-in. To find out how, you may need to go to the home page for the plug-in (which is displayed on the Tucows or Consummate WinSock Applications page from which you downloaded the plug-in).

7. If the plug-in is disappointing, uninstall it.

Creating Your Own Web Pages

Prerequisites
◗ Browsing the Web (Units 1, 2, and 3)

Objectives for This Unit

✓ Opening the Editor window in Netscape Navigator Gold

✓ Creating a Web page

✓ Entering and formatting Web page text

✓ Saving a Web page

✓ Retrieving an existing Web page

✓ Creating links and bulleted lists in a Web page

✓ Adding pictures to a Web page

✓ Getting your Web pages up on the Internet

on the CD

◗ Mounts.gif (picture of mountains)

◗ Fern.gif (picture of ferns)

◗ Rainbow.gif (picture of a rainbow)

As you've worked through this book, you've probably seen and enjoyed hundreds of interesting Web pages. Cruising the Net is a terrifically rewarding skill, and you may be perfectly happy with using the Web just as an information and entertainment resource (similar to the way you use magazines, radio, and television).

Cruising isn't the only way you can interact with the Web, though; you can also publish your *own* Web pages. Doing so allows you to reach out and communicate with the tens of millions of other people on the Net.

To compose your pages, you can use the editing features that are included in Netscape Navigator Gold Version 3.0 or higher. If you're currently using the Standard edition of Netscape 3.0, turn to Lesson 1-1 for information about how to obtain Netscape Gold. The only difference between the two editions is that Netscape Gold has the extra capability of letting you create, edit, and transmit your own Web pages.

To get your Web pages online, you need to obtain disk space on a computer that constantly communicates with the Web, or a *Web server*. Many Internet providers offer such disk space as part of their service to their subscribers. Alternately, you may be able to obtain disk space on a Web server through a company you're affiliated with or through a nonprofit organization (see Lesson 9-4 for details). When your pages are ready to be unveiled to the public, you can use Netscape Gold to copy them from your PC to the Web server you've selected via the Web. You can also use Netscape Gold to edit and recopy your files at any time, which means you can update your Web pages as often as you want.

Netscape Navigator Gold includes a Web page editor

If the prospect of publishing your own material on the Web sounds appealing — and if you're willing to learn a bit of technical stuff involving how Web pages are put together — then this unit is for you.

Lesson 9-1 Creating a Web Page

Creating a Web page is not hard, but you should understand a few things about how pages are constructed before you get started.

A Web page actually consists of several files. The foundation of the page is its text file, which contains (as you may have guessed) the page's text. In addition, this file holds the names of other files to be incorporated into the page (such as picture and sound files) and special codes that direct how the text and other elements should be formatted and arranged on the page.

The formatting codes are called *tags,* and they come from a computer language called *HTML* (short for *Hypertext Markup Language*). In fact, the main job of all Web browsers — including Netscape Navigator — is to correctly interpret HTML tags and use them to display each Web page precisely as its designer intended it to look. Browsers perform this "page construction" on the fly every time you access a new Web page; they simply do it so quickly that you're normally not aware that it's happening.

This structure means that you can create a Web page by typing text and appropriate HTML codes into any word processor that saves documents in a *plain text* (also known as *ASCII*) format. Some people simply use the Windows Notepad program to create their Web pages (naming each text file with the extension HTM to identify it as an HTML document). However, taking this approach requires a strong understanding of HTML codes — such as knowing you have to enclose a word in `<B>` and `</B>` tags to boldface it and knowing that to place a link on a page you have to use the format `<A HREF= "http:/ /www.yoururl.com"></A>`.

Learning HTML inside-out is useful if you need to create fancy effects or exercise super-precise control over your Web pages. For most of us, though, life is too short to memorize a bunch of HTML codes. Fortunately, Netscape Navigator Gold provides an alternative; by using its Editor window, you can format Web pages with menu commands and Toolbar buttons. The Editor window then automatically (and invisibly) converts all your instructions into HTML tags for you, so you never have to deal with the programming language directly.

To begin creating a Web page with Netscape Navigator Gold — which we refer to as just plain *Netscape* for the rest of this unit — you choose File⇨New Document from the menu. This command offers you three choices:

- **Blank:** Lets you create a Web page from scratch.
- **From Template:** If you're connected to the Net, takes you to a Web page on the Netscape Communications site that contains a bunch of sample (or *template*) Web pages that you can use as jumping-off points. After you download a sample Web page, you can edit it to display your own information and revise its look to your tastes, which can sometimes be faster and easier than starting from a blank page.

Margin notes:

HTML = Hypertext Markup Language, the language Web pages are written in

to create a Web page, first choose File→New Document

▶ **From Wizard:** If you're connected to the Net, takes you to an interactive program on the Netscape Communications site that steps you through the process of creating a very simple Web page.

In this lesson, you start with an empty Web page by choosing File⇨New Document⇨Blank. You then type the information you want to appear on your page, edit how your text is formatted, and save your page to your hard disk. We don't step you through using the From Templates and From Wizard options, but after you master the basic skills that are covered in this unit, you can try out those options on your own.

Note: Before you start composing Web pages, you should create a folder devoted to storing your Web files. For example, if you use Windows 95, you can double-click the My Computer desktop icon, double-click the icon representing your hard drive, choose File⇨New⇨Folder from the menu, type the name of the new folder (for example, **Web Pages**), and click anywhere outside the folder to save your changes. If you use Windows 3.1, you can run File Manager, choose File⇨Create Directory from the menu, and then type the name of the new folder (for example, **WebPages**).

store your Web pages in a separate folder

Opening the Netscape Editor window

Here's how to get started making a Web page:

1 **Run Netscape, but don't bother to connect to the Internet.**

You don't have to be connected to the Internet to create a Web page. Initially, you can simply store the page on your PC's hard disk.

2 **Choose File⇨New Document⇨Blank from the menu.**

The Netscape Editor window appears, as shown in Figure 9-1. The window has three Toolbars full of buttons for you to use: the Character Format Toolbar (at the top in Windows 95, but at the bottom in Windows 3.1, for reasons known only to the programmers at Netscape), with buttons that let you do such things as italicize and boldface your text and change your text's size and color; the File/Edit Toolbar (in the middle in Windows 95, but at the top in Windows 3.1), with buttons that let you open, edit, search, print, and save your Web page, as well as display the page in a browser window; and the Paragraph Format Toolbar (at the bottom in Windows 95, but in the middle in Windows 3.1), with buttons for creating bulleted or numbered lists, indenting text, and aligning text.

File→New Document→Blank creates a blank Web page

Note: You can identify any button simply by resting your mouse pointer on it. After about a second, a small box that displays the name of the button appears.

3 **If any of the three Toolbars isn't currently displayed, click the Options menu.**

You see options that include Show File/Edit Toolbar, Show Character Format Toolbar, and Show Paragraph Format Toolbar, each of which should have a check mark to its left to indicate that it's currently turned on. If a check mark is missing from any of these three options, click the option to turn it on.

use the Options menu to control which Toolbars appear

The Netscape browser window remains open while you're using the Netscape Editor. If you want inspiration while creating a Web page, or if you need to search the Web for information associated with your page, you can always connect to the Internet, click on the Netscape browser window, and cruise the Net!

Figure 9-1: The Netscape Editor lets you create and revise Web pages.

Notes:

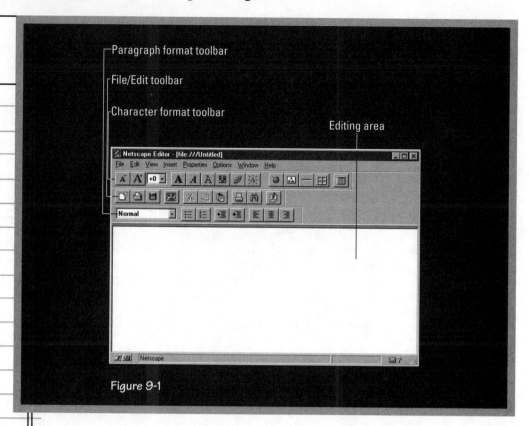

Figure 9-1

Composing text for your Web page

The Editor window works like a word processor, letting you enter, edit, and format text and graphics. Instead of creating a document to be printed on paper, however, the Editor is designed to turn your information into a Web page that can be displayed by Netscape and other browser programs.

Follow these steps to type some text into the Editor:

1 **Click in the editing area — that is, the big blank box below the three Toolbars.**

A large, blinking *cursor* appears in the upper-left corner of the editing area, waiting for you to type something. As in a word processor, the cursor shows where your typing will appear in your document.

2 **Type a few words that you want to use as the title of your Web page.**

You may want to call it *John Smith's Home Page, The John Smith Page,* or *All About John Smith.* (You may even prefer to use your own name!)

If you make a typo or change your mind about what you've typed, you can use the keys listed in Table 9-1 to move around your document and correct your errors.

type in the editing area to add text to your Web page

Table 9-1   Keystroke Shortcuts for Editing Web Page Text

Keystroke	What It Does
Home	Moves your cursor to the beginning of the current line
End	Moves to the end of the current line
Ctrl+Home	Moves to the beginning of the Web page
Ctrl+End	Moves to the end of the Web page
Backspace	Deletes the character to the left of the cursor; on a blank line, deletes the blank line
Del	Deletes the character to the right of the cursor; on a blank line, deletes the blank line
Ctrl+Z	Undoes your last editing change
Ctrl+C	Copies your selected text to the Windows Clipboard
Ctrl+X	Copies your selected text to the Windows Clipboard and removes the text from your document
Ctrl+V	Pastes the contents of the Windows Clipboard into your document, starting at the cursor position
Ctrl+B	Boldfaces your selected text; if the text is already boldfaced, removes boldfacing (or click the Bold button on the Character Format Toolbar)
Ctrl+I	Italicizes your selected text; if the text is already italicized, removes italics (or click the Italic button on the Character Format Toolbar)
Ctrl+K	Removes all formatting (such as boldface, italics, and underlining) from your selected text

3 **Press Enter to end your page heading.**

You move to a new paragraph. Notice that the Editor leaves a little extra space between paragraphs.

4 **Type a paragraph describing yourself. Press Enter only when you get to the end of the paragraph.**

heads up

Don't press Enter at the end of every line. Like all word processors, the Editor *word wraps,* which means that when a line of text goes past the right margin, the Editor automatically wraps the text down to the beginning of the next line.

For your personal description, you can write about your work, your family, your hobbies — whatever makes you you! Don't limit yourself to one paragraph if you get the urge to write more. If you'd like to get feedback from the people who eventually view your page, add a last line with your name and e-mail address.

5 **Press Ctrl+Home to return to your heading.**

The heading you typed is nice, but it needs some oomph, don't you think? So far, all the text you've typed has been in the *Normal* style, which is the most common format for Web text. You can make your top line stand out by marking it as a first-level heading, or *Heading 1,* which is one of HTML's built-in formats. (Other HTML formats include Heading 2, Heading 3, and so on for less prominent headings.)

press Enter only at the end of each paragraph

Heading 1 = HTML's format for first-level headings

Figure 9-2: This Web page has a heading and one paragraph of text — a good start.

Figure 9-3: Where do you want to store your Web page, and what do you want to name it?

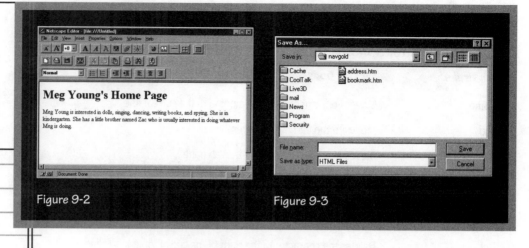

Figure 9-2

Figure 9-3

Paragraph style box

to save your Web page, click the Save button, press Ctrl+S, or choose File→Save

to close the Editor window, choose File→Close or press Ctrl+W

6 **Click in the Paragraph style box, which is the first item on the Paragraph Format Toolbar and currently says** `Normal`**.**

A box pops down, listing a dozen different styles that you can assign to your text.

7 **Click the Heading 1 option.**

Your selection is instantly applied to the paragraph you're on, displaying your heading in huge letters. Your document should now look something like the one in Figure 9-2.

Saving your Web page

You should always save your documents frequently so that, if your keyboard suddenly freezes up or your cat pulls out the power plug, you don't lose more than a few minutes of work. To save your current Web page as an HTML file on your hard disk, follow these steps:

1 **Choose File⇨Save from the menu, press Ctrl+S, or click the Save button (the File/Edit Toolbar's third button, which has a picture of a disk on it).**

The Save As dialog box appears, as shown in Figure 9-3, and prompts you to supply a name for your Web page.

2 **Click in the File name box and type the appropriate drive letter, folder name, and filename for your Web page.**

For example, if you placed your folder for storing Web pages on drive C and named it *WebPages,* and you want to name your current file *HomePage,* you type **C:\WebPages\HomePage**.

3 **Press Enter or click the Save button.**

Your file is saved under the name you typed and the extension *htm* (which is short for *HTML*). For example, if you named your file *HomePage,* it was saved under the filename HomePage.htm.

4 **Exit the Editor window by choosing File⇨Close (or by pressing Ctrl+W).**

The Editor window closes, leaving Netscape running with whatever other Netscape windows you happen to have open.

Congratulations! You created your first Web page!

Ideas for Web pages

In this lesson, you created a personal home page with a little information about yourself, which is fun for your friends and family to see. But what about making Web pages that are of interest to a broader audience? Here are some ideas for other types of Web pages:

▶ **Charitable organizations:** If your church, synagogue, school, club, or other nonprofit organization needs publicity, a Web site is a good way to supply it. Be sure to include information that is of interest to outsiders, like who the organization is open to, when meetings take place, who to contact for more information, and so on. You can include mission statements, text from a recent newsletter, pictures of buildings and people — you name it. (You learn how to place pictures on Web pages later in this unit.)

▶ **Family tree:** Make a Web page for each person in your extended family, with links to spouses, parents, siblings, and children. (You learn how to insert links in Web pages in the next lesson.) Each person's page can contain a photo, vital statistics (birthdate, birthplace, current address), interests, hobbies, and reminiscences.

▶ **Show off your expertise:** Is there something that you know a lot about, like antique beer cans or comic books or independent telephone companies? If so, consider creating a Web page about the subject. Include your personal knowledge, relevant pictures, references to appropriate books and magazines, and links to other Web sites on the topic (which you can find by using search programs such as Yahoo! and AltaVista).

☑ **Progress Check**

If you can do the following, you've mastered this lesson:

❏ Open Netscape's Editor window.

❏ Create a new Web page.

❏ Type text in your Web page.

❏ Format a paragraph as a heading.

❏ Save your Web page.

❏ Close the Editor window.

Recess

After all that typing, you probably need to limber up. Go lie in the sun and stretch your arms, flex your fingers, wiggle your toes, and relax. When you're sufficiently loose, set your sights on the next lesson, which tells you how to liven up your page with pictures.

Editing Your Web Page

Lesson 9-2

You've already made a good start on your Web page. In this lesson, you spiff it up with links to other nifty pages (which is a standard courtesy provided by virtually all Web pages) and with a bulleted list (which is a great format for spotlighting important information).

Retrieving a Web page

As you learned in the preceding lesson, you start a Web page from scratch by choosing File⇨New Document⇨Blank from the Netscape browser window. After you create a Web page, however (or when you want to edit a Web page that's been created by someone else), you reopen it by using the menu command File⇨Open File in Editor. You then can revise the page's contents.

Notes:

Follow these steps to retrieve the Web page you created in the preceding exercise:

1 **Run Netscape (if it isn't already running), but don't bother to connect to the Internet.**

You're going to continue working on the Web page you created in the preceding lesson. Make sure that you're in the Netscape browser window (as opposed to the Mail or News window).

2 **Choose File⇨Open File in Editor from the menu.**

You see the Open dialog box, shown in Figure 9-4.

3 **Click in the File name box and type the appropriate drive letter, folder name, and filename to retrieve your Web page.**

For example, if you placed your folder for storing Web pages on drive C and named it *WebPages,* and you named your HTML file *HomePage,* you type **C:\WebPages\HomePage.htm** (remember to include the *htm* extension!).

4 **Press Enter or click the Open button.**

An Editor window opens and displays your Web page.

You're now ready to make some more changes!

Adding Web page links

Wouldn't it be nice to include a list of your favorite Web pages and allow readers of your page to jump to each site you mention with a mouse click? You can do so by inserting *links* (which you learned about in Lesson 1-2). After you do so, anyone viewing your page can move to a site you recommend by simply clicking its link.

Adding a link is easy. First, you click the Make Link button (which is on the Character Format Toolbar and has a picture of chain links on it), choose Insert⇨Link, or press Ctrl+L to bring up a Link Properties dialog box. You then enter two bits of information into the dialog box:

> ♦ The text that you want readers of your Web page to see (which will be displayed in blue and underlined).

> ♦ The URL of the Web page you want the link to represent. Be sure to type **http://** at the beginning of the URL. (In this book, we omit *http://* in our URL listings because Netscape fills it in for you automatically, but not all Web browsers are as smart as Netscape, and you want your links to work no matter which browser someone is using to look at your Web page.)

The following steps take you through adding links to your page. We suggest a couple of links related to this book, but you can create links to your favorite Web sites instead.

1 **Press Ctrl+End to move to the bottom of your page.**

You should be on a blank line. If you aren't, press Enter to create a blank line.

2 **Type My Favorite Web Pages (but don't press Enter).**

This line is the heading for your list of Web sites. Because it's a subtopic under your main heading, make it a level 2 heading.

to insert a link, click the Make Link button, choose Insert→Link, or press Ctrl+L

type complete URLs when creating links

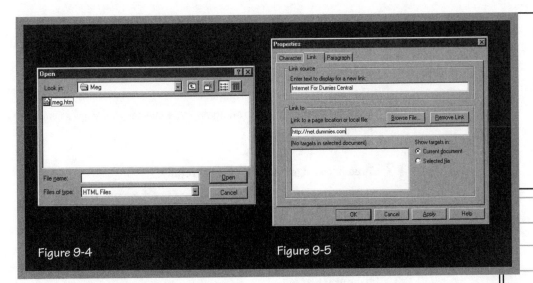

Figure 9-4

Figure 9-5

Figure 9-4: Which Web page do you want to edit?

Figure 9-5: To create a link, fill in the Link source box (which sets the link's displayed text) and the Link to box (which sets the URL the link represents).

3 **Click in the Paragraph style box again (the first item on the Paragraph Format Toolbar, with the word** Normal **in it) and click the Heading 2 option from the drop-down list.**

Now your line is boldfaced and large, though not as large as the heading at the top of the page. Looks good!

4 **Press Enter to start a new line.**

You're automatically switched back to the Normal paragraph style for the new line, as you can tell by looking at the Paragraph style box. The Editor figures that after a heading you want to type some normal text — good guess!

You're now ready to add a link to a Web page. How about this book's home page at net.dummies.com/netscape101?

5 **Click the Make Link button (the button on the Character Format Toolbar with a chain links icon), press Ctrl+L, or choose Insert➪Link.**

A Properties dialog box appears (as shown in Figure 9-5). This box has tabs along the top that enable you to format characters, adjust paragraphs, and insert links — which is the current selection. Your cursor starts off in a Link source box, which establishes the name of the link people see when they view your Web page.

Make Link button

6 **Type** Dummies 101: Netscape Navigator **(the name of the site you visited in Units 2 and 3) as the name for your link. When you're done, press Tab to move to the next text box.**

The cursor jumps to the Link to box. This box lets you enter the URL of the Web page that your link represents.

7 **Type** http://net.dummies.com/netscape101 **very carefully.**

That is, type **http**, a colon, two slashes, **net.dummies.com**, another slash, and **netscape101** (with no spaces in any part of the URL).

That's all the Editor needs to know to create the link!

8 **Press Enter or click OK.**

Your *Dummies 101: Netscape Navigator* link appears on your Web page. Cool!

9 **Place your mouse pointer anywhere on the link you just created.**

The message bar at the bottom of the window displays the URL you set for the link, confirming that you created the link successfully.

Notes:

10 **Press Enter to move to a new line.**

Now create a second link, this time to the *Internet For Dummies Central* home page (which you visited in Unit 4).

11 **Click the Make Link button again, type** Internet For Dummies Central, **and press Tab.**

You move to the Link to box.

12 **Type** http://net.dummies.com **very carefully.**

That is, type **http**, a colon, two slashes, and **net.dummies.com** (with no spaces in any part of the URL).

13 **Press Enter or click OK.**

The link Internet For Dummies Central is displayed on your Web page. As before, if you point to the link, the URL you assigned it should appear in the message bar.

14 **Repeat Steps 10 through 13 to add additional links for Web pages that you like.**

If you don't remember the exact names or URLs of certain Web pages, connect to the Internet and use the Netscape browser window to cruise to those pages for the information you need. Be creative and have fun! And see the sidebar "Dragging links from the browser" for ways to make links with no typing.

15 **When you're done, press Ctrl+S to save your page to your hard disk.**

Saving your page every five minutes or so is a good idea. As we noted previously, doing so ensures that you don't lose more than a few minutes of work if a software problem or power outage occurs.

Your page is starting to look really professional!

Note: You can edit the text of the link simply by clicking in the text and typing. If you need to change the URL of a link, you can click in the link and then click the Make Link button or press Ctrl+L. Or you can right-click the link (click with your *right* mouse button) and choose Link Properties from the menu that appears.

extra credit

Dragging links from the browser

If you keep the Netscape browser and Editor windows open side by side, you can add links to your Web page by using your mouse! To do so, first set the browser window to display the Web page for which you want to create a link. Next, click the chain icon to the left of the Location box and, while holding down your mouse button, drag your mouse pointer to the spot in the Editor window where you want to insert the link. Finally, release your mouse button. A link that points to the Web page in the browser window is added to your Web page!

Making a link to a Web page that you have added to your bookmarks is also easy: Choose Window➪Bookmarks from the menu to open the Bookmarks window, select a bookmark, and drag the bookmark onto the Web page. Netscape creates a link to the bookmarked Web page — quick and easy, with no typing!

Making a bulleted list

Your list of Web pages is already attractive. However, it would look even better if each entry were indented with a little bullet to its left. Follow these steps to create just such a bulleted list:

1 **Select all your links. Specifically, click in front of your first link, hold down your left mouse button, and (while keeping the button pressed) drag down until you reach the end of your last link. When all your links are highlighted, release the mouse button.**

You're now ready to choose a new format, which will be applied to all your selected text.

2 **Click the Bullet List button, which is the second button on the Paragraph Format Toolbar and has a picture of three little bullets on it.**

Your selected text — in this case, your links — is instantly reformatted as items in a bulleted list. We feel that this is an improvement, but if you don't care for it, simply click the Bullet List button again to return the links to their previous format.

3 **Click anywhere outside your selected text to make the highlighting go away.**

The links are no longer selected.

4 **Save your work by pressing Ctrl+S.**

Your page is saved to your hard disk.

You can follow similar steps to apply any other kind of formatting to a section of your text. For example, try highlighting your links again and clicking other buttons on the Paragraph Format Toolbar, such as the Numbered List, Increase Indent, and Center buttons. (Remember, if you aren't sure what a particular button does, you can simply rest your mouse pointer on the button for about a second to display its name.)

Bullet List button

☑ **Progress Check**

If you can do the following, you've mastered this lesson:

❑ Open an existing Web page.

❑ Add links to a Web page.

❑ Format Web page text as a bulleted list.

---

extra credit

Other ways to spruce up your Web pages

Here are some other formatting tricks you can use when editing a Web page:

▶ To center a line of text, click anywhere on the line and click the Center button (the second-to-last button on the Paragraph Format Toolbar). The line is centered between the page's left and right margins.

▶ To insert a horizontal line, move your cursor to the beginning of the line over which you want the horizontal line to appear and then click the Insert Horizontal Line button (the third-from-last button on the Character Format Toolbar).

▶ To make your words appear in a different color, select the text you want to affect and then click the Font Color button (the multicolored squares button in the middle of the Character Format Toolbar). When you see the Color dialog box, click the color you want and click OK. (This option doesn't work with links, only standard text.)

▶ To reverse a change you've just made, press Ctrl+Z or choose Edit⇨Undo.

Lesson 9-3

Adding Pictures to Your Web Page

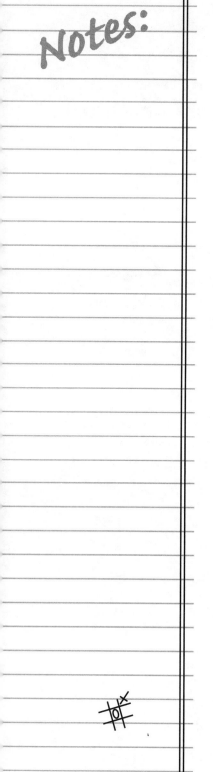

Formatting text is fine, but to *really* dress up your Web pages, you should insert a few colorful pictures (which, as the saying goes, are worth a thousand bulleted lists). On the Net, such electronic pictures are also referred to as *graphics files* or *clip art*.

In this lesson, you learn how to obtain such pictures, pick out the best ones for use on a Web page, revise unsuitable pictures to make them useable, and then add the pictures you select to Web pages.

Getting electronic pictures

You can obtain graphics files in many ways. For example, you can find thousands of public domain images on the Internet by using a search program such as Yahoo! or AltaVista (see Unit 3). You can also get a list of top Web sites that offer such graphics files by going to this book's home page at `net.dummies.com/netscape101` and clicking the link named *Clip Art on the Web.*

When you find a picture that you want in a Web graphics library, you can download it by following the instructions in Lesson 3-2. Alternately, you can download *any* image displayed on a Web page by clicking the picture with your right (*not* left) mouse button, choosing the Save Image As option from the menu that appears, typing the folder name and filename under which you want to store the image, and pressing Enter to copy the picture to your hard disk. (You can even just *drag* a picture from the browser window to the Editor window; for details, see the sidebar at the end of this lesson.)

On the other hand, if you have images that you'd like to use but that happen to be on paper, you can feed them into a PC device called a *scanner* that can copy them to disk as electronic pictures. If you don't want to buy a scanner, you may be able to rent one by the hour at a local photocopying shop or computer store.

Another possibility is to take photographs and then get them in disk form at the same time they're being developed. Some photo shops now offer this option along with their standard service of providing negatives and prints.

Finally, if you have artistic talent and a lot of patience, you can try drawing your own electronic pictures. A fine program you can use for this purpose is Paint Shop Pro, which is included on the CD-ROM at the back of this book.

Choosing and preparing your pictures

In addition to finding electronic images, you need to decide which ones you should use. Your decision should be based mostly on whether you like particular pictures and feel that they work well with the other elements of your Web pages. However, you should also keep in mind some technical issues.

Painting pictures with Paint Shop Pro

If you want to create, edit, convert, or just look at pictures for your Web page, consider the excellent shareware program Paint Shop Pro. As just mentioned, Paint Shop allows you to create pictures from scratch (if you've got more artistic abilities that we do). In addition, you can use it to convert graphics files from one format to another; for example, if you have a picture in PCX format (which is a common format, but one not typically used on the Web), you can save it in GIF format (which is the usual Web picture format). You can also crop pictures (that is, delete unnecessary parts of the image), resize pictures, or reduce the number of colors in a picture, which are all great ways to reduce a picture's file size.

Paint Shop Pro is stored on the *Dummies 101* CD-ROM that comes in the back of this book. For information about installing Paint Shop Pro, see Appendix B. If you decide to use Paint Shop Pro past your 30-day trial period, be sure to follow the instructions to register and pay for your copy.

For example, you have to be legally entitled to use the images. If you created the pictures yourself, if the pictures are from a collection of public domain clip art, or if you paid for permission to use the pictures, then you're set. Otherwise, you should make sure that using the graphics you want for your Web page doesn't violate anyone's copyright ownership of those graphics — that is, only use art that you created, that isn't copyrighted, or for which you have permission from the copyright holder.

You should also verify that the pictures are in the appropriate file format. Electronic pictures come in dozens of different formats, but only two formats are capable of being displayed by virtually all Web browsers: *GIF* (short for *Graphics Interchange Format*) and *JPEG* (short for *Joint Photographic Extensions Group*). You can recognize these files by their three-letter filename extensions, which are, respectively, gif and jpg. If you have a picture in a different file format, you don't have to give up on it, though; you can try turning it into a gif or jpg file by using a format conversion feature that's built into the Paint Shop Pro program.

> use graphics files
> with gif or jpg
> extensions

Lastly, you need to keep your picture files relatively small. That's because all graphics take a long time to be transferred over the Web, but large graphics seem to take *forever*. If you want people to visit your page, be sensitive to how long it takes them to view it. There are always exceptions, but as a rule of thumb we recommend that you stick to pictures that are about 50K or less in file size. (You can check a file's size by listing it in a program such as My Computer, Windows Explorer, or the Windows 3.1 File Manager.)

If you have a huge picture file that you really like, however, you can try reducing it by using a graphics editor such as Paint Shop Pro. For example, you can crop out less important parts of the image, and/or you can reduce the number of colors used in the image. In many cases, putting a graphic through such a "quick-loss diet" doesn't seriously hurt the quality of the picture.

Placing a picture on your Web page

> to add a picture,
> click the Insert Image
> button or choose
> Insert→Image

After you pick out and (if necessary) revise the graphics you want to use, you're ready to put them on your Web page. To add a picture, you simply click in the spot on your page where you want the image to be displayed, click the Insert Image button or choose Insert⇨Image, type the name of the graphics file in the dialog box that appears, and press Enter.

Figure 9-6: What's the name of the graphics file you want to place on your Web page?

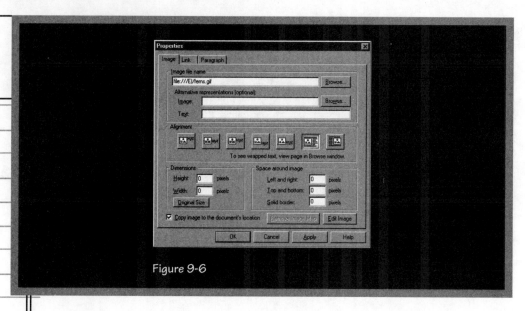

Figure 9-6

Notes:

Insert Image button

Try out the process by placing a restful picture of distant mountains from this book's CD-ROM onto your Web page:

1 **If the Web page you worked on in the preceding lesson isn't still open, open it now.**

You should be in the Netscape Editor window with your Web page displayed.

2 **Insert the CD-ROM that came with this book into your CD-ROM drive.**

If a window that offers to install the CD-ROM's contents to your hard disk appears, click the window's Exit button; you can get the graphics file yourself directly from the CD-ROM.

3 **Place your cursor in the spot on your Web page where you want the picture to appear.**

For example, if you want to place the image at the bottom of your page, press Ctrl+End to move to the bottom and press Enter to create a blank line.

4 **Click the Insert Image button (the fourth-to-last button on the Character Format Toolbar) or choose Insert⇨Image from the menu.**

The Properties dialog box appears with the Image file name box selected, as shown in Figure 9-6. You're now ready to type the name of the graphics file, which in this case is **Mounts.gif**.

5 **Type the letter of your CD-ROM's drive, a colon (:), a backslash (\\), and the filename** Mounts.gif. **For example, if your CD-ROM is drive D (which is typical), type** D:\Mounts.gif. **When you're done, press Enter.**

The dialog box goes away . . . and the picture you specified appears on your Web page!

6 **Click the Center button (the next-to-last button on the Paragraph Format Toolbar).**

The picture is centered on the page. You can perform a number of formatting tricks with images by using the buttons on the Paragraph Format Toolbar. Covering them all is beyond the scope of this book, but you can experiment with the buttons on your own.

7 **Double-click the picture (that is, click it twice in rapid succession).**

Or right-click the image and choose Image properties from the menu that appears. Either way, the Image Properties dialog box appears again. This box offers several options for fine-tuning the appearance of your picture, including adjusting its size, the amount of space around it, and the width of the border around it. Again, discussing these options is beyond the scope of this book, but we recommend that you experiment with them on your own.

8 **Click Cancel to close the dialog box and press Ctrl+S to save your revised page.**

The Properties dialog box disappears, and your page — which now includes the mountain image — is saved to disk.

If you'd like to continue practicing with pictures, you can repeat Steps 3 through 5 using two other files on the CD-ROM named Ferns.gif and Rainbow.gif. If you decide that you don't like a picture, you can delete it at any time simply by clicking it and pressing the Del key.

When you're done using Netscape Navigator, choose File➪Exit from the menu and click the Yes button on the dialog box that appears. All Netscape windows close, and the program exits.

extra credit

Taking a different view

The Editor window doesn't always accurately show exactly where a picture will appear on your Web page. To be certain of what your page looks like in a browser window, click the View in Browser button (the fourth button on the File/Edit Toolbar) or choose File➪Browse Document from the menu. A new Netscape browser window opens that displays your Web page precisely as it will appear to your fellow cruisers on the Web.

extra credit

Dragging pictures from the browser

If you keep the Netscape browser and Editor windows open side by side, you can add pictures to your Web page by using your mouse! To do so, first set the browser window to display an image you want to copy. Next, click the picture and, while keeping your left mouse button held down, drag your mouse pointer to the spot in the Editor window where you want to insert the image. Finally, release your mouse button. A copy of the picture is added to your Web page!

You can also drag graphics files from My Computer and Windows Explorer (in Windows 95) or File Manager (in Windows 3.1) to the Editor window. Drag only gif or jpeg files, which Netscape and most other browsers can display. When you drag a graphics file to the Editor window, the picture appears in your Web page.

☑ **Progress Check**

If you can do the following, you've mastered this lesson:

❏ Understand how to locate, select, and prepare pictures for a Web page.

❏ Add a picture to a Web page.

Lesson 9-4

Publishing Your Web Page

Notes:

Well, you made a lovely Web page. You can continue to expand it and spiff it up by using the Editor window. But unless you share files with other people on a local area network, you're probably the only person who can look at it right now. What if you want to go public?

What's a Web server?

To make a Web page available to the rest of the world, you must store the file that contains the page's text and HTML tags, as well as all related files (such as the picture files that appear on the page) on a *Web server,* which is a computer that communicates with Web browsers over the Internet and sends out the Web pages that they request.

For example, we store the Web pages for this book on a Web server named `net.dummies.com`. When your Netscape browser asks for the Web page at `net.dummies.com/netscape101` (the URL of this book's home page), the server sends back the file containing the text and HTML codes that make up the page, along with the graphics files that contain the pictures on the page. (The picture of the cover of this book is stored in one graphics file, the little blue lines that run down the left margin of the page are stored in another graphics file, and the cute little arrow buttons at the very bottom of the page are stored in a third graphics file.) After your browser receives all these files, it can display them on your screen.

Getting your Web pages onto a Web server

Here are some ways to find a server that can play host to your Web pages:

☑ Progress Check

If you can do the following, you've mastered this lesson:

❑ Find a Web server to play host to your Web pages.

❑ Gather the information you need to upload your Web page files to the Web server.

❑ Upload your Web page files to the Web server.

❑ Jump on the Web to check out your cool new pages.

◆ Ask your Internet provider or online service whether it provides disk space for Web pages to its subscribers; many do so at no extra charge.

◆ If you use America Online, go to keyword **HTML** or keyword **Personal Publisher** to find out how to create personal Web pages on this service.

◆ If you use CompuServe, go to **HPWIZ** to learn about CompuServe's Home Page Wizard, which gives you Web server space.

◆ If you use Prodigy, jump to keyword **PWP** or keyword **Personal Web Pages** to discover how to take advantage of the Web space that comes with your Prodigy account.

◆ If you're affiliated with an organization that's hooked up to the Net, check whether you can get space on its Web server for your Web pages.

◆ Look for some outside group to host your Web pages, especially if your pages are related to a nonprofit organization. To find such groups, go to the Yahoo! search page at `www.yahoo.com` and poke around — we found a list by choosing Business and Economy, then Companies, then Computers, then Internet Services, and then Web Presence Providers.

When you find a Web server that can house your Web pages, you need the organization that runs it to tell you the user name and password you must type to access the server and the URL of the area on the Web server that's assigned to storing your files. The latter typically begins with *ftp://* or *http://* and is followed by the name of the Web server and the name of your file area on the server. (For example, the URL for your Web pages section on America

Online might be `ftp://ftp.aol.com/docs/yourname/index.html`, while the URL for your Web pages section on a server using the HTTP standard might be `http://servername.com/docs/yourname/index.html`.) In addition, you should find out the URL that the general public needs to use to access your Web pages. (For example, in contrast to the URL for an America Online file storage area, the public URL for personal Web pages on America Online is in the format `http://home.aol.com/yourscreenname`.)

After you have all the necessary information, you're ready for the big step: copying your files to the server so the rest of the world can see your Web pages.

Copying your Web pages to a Web server

After you're set up with a Web server, you can copy, or *upload,* your Web page files to it by using the Netscape Editor's Publish command.

To begin, open one of your Web pages in the Editor window and then click the Publish button (the last button on the File/Edit Toolbar) or choose File⇨Publish. Doing so displays a Publish Files dialog box that lets you type the URL of the Web server, your user name, and your password. (To learn more about options in the dialog box, click the box's Help button.) When you're done entering your information, click the box's OK button. The Editor uploads all the files associated with your page to the Web server.

Publish button

When the copying is complete, switch to Netscape's browser window, click in the Location box, type the public URL for your Web page, and press Enter. You should see the page you created up on the Web and available to the millions of people on the Net. Totally cool!

If you later decide to make changes to your Web page, simply revise the page in the Editor window and then use the Publish button to upload the changed files.

Finally, if your Web pages are of general interest, don't hesitate to publicize them! You can do so by going to the Submit It! Web site at `www.submit-it.com` and following the instructions to get listed on AltaVista, Yahoo!, Excite, and other Web directories. All this work may not make you rich; but, if you create a popular Web site, it *may* make you moderately famous!

publicize your Web page at
`www.submit-it.com`

Unit 9 Quiz

For each of the following questions, circle the letter of the correct answer or answers. Remember, there may be more than one right answer for each question.

1. **Web pages are written in:**

    A. The Netscape Editor window.

    B. A language called HTML (Hypertext Markup Language).

    C. Netscape-ese.

    D. Haste.

Notes:

2. **To add a link to your Web page, you can:**

    A. Click the chain-like Make Link button on the Character Format Toolbar.

    B. Click the Glue Pages button.

    C. Choose Insert⇨Link from the menu.

    D. Press Ctrl+L.

3. **Pictures for Web pages are stored in:**

    A. Html files (*Hint:* This is wrong!).

    B. Graphics files.

    C. Air conditioned vaults.

    D. gif or jpg files.

4. **To create a bulleted list:**

    A. Type an asterisk (*) at the beginning of each paragraph.

    B. Select the paragraphs that make up the list and click the Bullet List button.

    C. Select the paragraphs that make up the list and choose Properties⇨Paragraph⇨List Item from the menu. (Try it!)

    D. Shoot the beginning of each paragraph with your Smith & Wesson .45.

5. **Ways to get graphics files to put on your Web pages include:**

    A. Drawing pictures by using Paint Shop Pro or another graphics program.

    B. Downloading graphics files from Web sites.

    C. Turning paper images into electronic ones by using a scanner.

    D. Taking photographs and having them developed as electronic pictures.

Unit 9 Exercise

1. Make a Web page for each member of your immediate family. Store each Web page in a separate file.

2. If you have a way to scan in pictures, add a picture of each person to that person's page.

3. Create links from each person's page to the person's mother, father, siblings, children, or other relations. Make the link display the page for that relative.

4. Show off your pages to your family and friends.

    Extra Credit: If you have access to a Web server, upload the pages to the Web server. Send the URLs of the resulting pages to all your friends who have e-mail addresses.

Part III Review

Unit 8 Summary

▶ **Helper applications, plug-ins, and Java applets:** Helper applications are stand-alone programs that run when Netscape encounters information that it can't handle by itself. Plug-ins are programs that "plug in" to Netscape and expand Netscape's capabilities, such as displaying new types of information in the Netscape window or adding new commands to Netscape's browser, Mail, and News menus. Java applets are little programs written in the Java programming language and included as part of Web pages.

▶ **Installing plug-ins:** The *Dummies 101* CD-ROM contains a bunch of plug-ins you can install by running the *Dummies 101* Installer program (see Appendix B) and clicking the Install Plug-ins button. You can also download plug-ins from the Web — look at the Tucows (www.tucows.com), Consummate WinSock Applications (www.cwsapps.com), and Netscape (home.netscape.com) Web sites. Always install one plug-in at a time, and try Netscape and the new plug-in to make sure that it works and doesn't conflict with another plug-in.

▶ **Types of plug-ins:** Plug-ins fall into these categories: audio players, video players, 3D and virtual reality viewers, document viewers, and other plug-ins.

▶ **Displaying a list of installed plug-ins:** Choose Help⮕About Plug-ins from the menu bar. The standard version of Netscape Navigator comes with several plug-ins, including LiveAudio, LiveVideo, Live3D, and QuickTime.

▶ **Listening to audio files:** The LiveAudio plug-in lets Netscape play sound files in several standard formats, including AIFF, AU, MIDI, and WAV. The RealAudio plug-in can play RealAudio (RA) format files and starts to play sound clips before the file is completely downloaded. To play sound files, you need a sound card and speakers.

▶ **Watching video files:** The LiveVideo plug-in displays AVI video files; the QuickTime plug-in displays QuickTime files; Shockwave displays a variety of audio and video files; and VDOLive plays VDO files. An advantage of VDOLive is that it plays video clips while the video file is still downloading, adjusting the video quality to the speed of your Internet connection.

▶ **Exploring virtual worlds:** The Live3D plug-in displays virtual worlds, or 3D virtual reality objects on Web pages. By using the mouse, you can move around inside the world, changing your point of view. Virtual worlds are created by using a programming language called VRML (Virtual Reality Modeling Language).

▶ **Displaying documents:** Several plug-ins let you display other types of information in the Netscape window. Some let you view files from your own hard disk: For example, the Word Viewer plug-in lets you open Microsoft Word documents in Netscape. Other plug-ins let you view Web pages that include other types of information: ASAP WebShow allows Web pages to include slide show presentations, and Formula One/NET lets Web pages include spreadsheets in which you can type information and see the results of calculations.

▶ **Interactive chat plug-ins:** The Ichat plug-in lets Web pages include live chats, in which participants can type messages that other participants can see.

▶ **Adding a spell-checker to Netscape:** The CyberSpell plug-in adds a Spelling command to the Message Composition window you use to compose e-mail messages and newsgroup articles. After you type the text you want to send, choose Spelling⮕Quick Spell to check for spelling and capitalization errors and doubled words. Choose Spelling⮕Power Spell to check for number format, date format, and punctuation errors.

▶ **Uninstalling plug-ins:** If you don't plan to use a plug-in, or if a plug-in causes trouble with your version of Netscape or with other plug-ins you plan to use, uninstall it. If the plug-in comes with an uninstall program, run the uninstall program. If not, Windows 95 users can click the Start button on the Taskbar, choose Settings⮕Control Panel from the menu that appears, double-click the Add/Remove Programs icon, select the name of the plug-in you want to remove, and click the Add/Remove button. If all else fails, you can delete the DLL file from the Plugins subfolder in the Netscape Program folder. Also delete any folders or program groups that have names similar to the plug-ins.

Part III Review

Unit 9 Summary

▶ **Netscape Editor window:** Netscape Navigator Gold includes an Editor window you can use to create and edit Web pages. To open the Editor window, choose File⇨Open File in Editor from the menu bar. If you're already looking at the page you want to edit, click the Edit button on the Toolbar or choose File⇨Edit Document from the menu.

▶ **Where to store Web pages:** You can create Web pages and store them on your own hard disk. However, to make your pages visible on the Web, you must store them on a *Web server,* a computer that is in constant communication with the Internet and that sends Web pages in response to requests from other people's Web browsers. Whether you plan to store your Web pages only on your own computer or on a Web server, create a new folder to store them in on your computer.

▶ **Anatomy of a Web page:** Web pages are text files encoded by using HTML (HyperText Markup Language) codes. The pictures on Web pages are stored in separate graphics files, in either GIF or JPEG format. You can create Web pages by using any text editor (such as Windows Notepad) or word processor that can store files in plain-text format. However, you may prefer to use a Web page editor such as the Netscape Editor window to avoid having to learn HTML.

▶ **Creating a new Web page:** To create a new Web page from scratch, choose File⇨New Document⇨Blank from the menu bar. You see an Editor window with a blank Web page.

▶ **Editing an existing Web page:** Choose File⇨Open File in Editor from the menu bar in the Netscape browser window. Netscape opens the Editor window and displays the Web page.

▶ **Using the Editor window's three toolbars:** The Netscape Editor window has three Toolbars: the Character Format Toolbar (at the top in Windows 95, but at the bottom in Windows 3.1), with buttons to italicize and boldface your text and change your text's size and color; the File/Edit Toolbar (in the middle in Windows 95, but at the top in Windows 3.1),

with buttons to open, edit, search, print, and save your Web page; and the Paragraph Format Toolbar (at the bottom in Windows 95, but in the middle in Windows 3.1), with buttons to create bulleted or numbered lists, indent text, and align text.

▶ **Adding text to your Web page:** To include text in your Web page, just type! Then format headings by using the Paragraph style box on the Paragraph Format Toolbar, choosing one of the Heading styles. You can create a bulleted list by selecting the paragraphs to include in the list and then clicking the Bullet List button (on the File/Edit Toolbar).

▶ **Adding links to your Web page:** With your cursor on the Web page in the position where you want a link to appear, click the Make Link button on the Character Format Toolbar, press Ctrl+L, or choose Insert⇨Link from the menu bar. When you see the Link Properties dialog box, type the text you want readers of the Web page to see and the URL of the Web page you want the link to represent. To edit an existing link, double-click the link.

▶ **Adding pictures to your Web page:** Move your cursor to the place on your Web page where you want the picture to appear. Then click the Insert Image button on the Character Format Toolbar or choose Insert⇨Image from the menu. You can also drag pictures from your Netscape browser window to the Editor window to add them to your page. To edit the placement of an existing picture, double-click the picture.

▶ **Finding art for your Web page:** Graphics files for use on Web pages should be in the GIF or JPG graphics file format. You can find art to use on your Web page in various clip art collections on the Web — take a look at the clip art on the Web page at net.dummies.com/ netscape101/clipart.htm. Don't use copyrighted artwork in your Web pages unless you have permission from the copyright owner.

Part III Review

♦ **Saving your Web page:** Choose File⇨Save from the menu, press Ctrl+S, or click the Save button (on the File/Edit Toolbar). When Netscape saves a Web page, it uses the filename extension *htm* (short for HTML).

♦ **Publishing your Web page:** To make your Web page visible to the rest of the Internet, you store the files that make up your Web page on a Web server. Your Internet provider or online service may let you use its Web server, or you can sign up with a commercial Web service. You need to know the URL to use when transferring Web page files from your computer to the Web server, and the URL to use when you or other people want to look at your Web pages.

To transmit the files that make up your Web page to a Web server, click the Publish button on the File/Edit Toolbar or choose File⇨Publish from the menu. When you see the Publish Files dialog box, type the URL of your Web server, your user name, and your password. When you click OK, Netscape transmits the files to your Web server. When your Web page is ready for prime time, publicize it at the Submit-It Web page at www.submit-it.com.

Part III Test

The questions on this test cover all the material presented in Part III, Units 8 and 9.

True   False

T F 1. Plug-ins are created only by the company that created Netscape Navigator itself.

T F 2. Netscape plug-ins let you display new kinds of information in the Netscape window.

T F 3. You can listen to National Public Radio over the Internet at the www.npr.org Web site.

T F 4. You always have to download the entire audio or video file before Netscape can begin to play it.

T F 5. You can create Web pages by using Windows Notepad.

T F 6. All the information on a Web page is stored in one file.

T F 7. To create a Web page, you must learn HTML, the language in which Web pages are encoded.

T F 8. You can create your own graphics for your Web page by using Paint Shop Pro or (if you have a scanner) scanning in your own photos or drawings.

T F 9. To create a link on your Web page, you have to know the URL of the Web page you want to link to.

T F 10. After you create a Web page and store it on a Web server, it's still not an *official* Web page.

Part III Test

Multiple Choice

11. **The best way to find out what plug-ins are installed is to:**

    A. Choose Help⇨About Plug-ins from the menu bar.

    B. Try looking at Web pages that display a variety of types of information handled by plug-ins, and see which types work.

    C. Call up Netscape and ask. (**Hint:** This is wrong.)

    D. Click the Plug-in button on the Toolbar.

    E. Choose Plug-ins⇨Which Ones Do I Have, Anyway? from the menu bar.

12. **To install a plug-in that you have downloaded from the Internet:**

    A. Call up Netscape and ask how to do it. (**Hint:** This is still wrong.)

    B. Click the Plug-in button on the Toolbar.

    C. Choose Plug-in⇨Install from the menu bar.

    D. Exit Netscape and then double-click the plug-in filename in My Computer, Windows Explorer, or File Manager.

    E. Click in the Location box in the Netscape browser window, type **install the stupid plug-in!**, and press Enter.

13. **VRML stands for:**

    A. Virtual Reality Modeling Language.

    B. Virtual Reality Markup Language.

    C. Virtually Real Markup Language.

    D. Very Realistic Means of Living.

    E. Nothing.

14. **Using Live3D to enter a virtual world, you can:**

    A. Move around.

    B. Turn your head.

    C. Grab objects.

    D. Talk to people you meet.

    E. Crash Netscape.

15. **To make your Web page accessible to anyone on the Internet:**

    A. Click the Publish button on the File/Edit Toolbar.

    B. Submit your Web page to Internet Galactic Central.

    C. Store the files that make up the Web page on a Web server.

    D. Buy your own Web server computer, install it in your attic, install a special high-speed dedicated phone line attached to the Web server, install Web server software, sign up for a dedicated-line Internet account, leave your Web server computer up and running 24 hours a day, 7 days a week, and store your Web page files on the Web server's hard disk.

    E. Send e-mail to everyone on the Internet, telling them about your Web page and telling anyone interested in seeing the page that you can e-mail the files in which the Web page is stored.

16. **Who developed HTML, the language in which Web pages are written?**

    A. Tim Berners-Lee, a researcher at CERN, the European Particle Physics Lab in Geneva, Switzerland.

    B. A group of programmers at Netscape.

    C. Microsoft, of course.

    D. IBM, of course.

    E. HTML wasn't developed; it was discovered.

Part III Test

17. **Which body of water is at the east end of the Panama Canal?**

    A. Gulf of Mexico

    B. Caribbean

    C. Bay of Panama

    D. Gulf of Panama

    E. Pacific Ocean

    F. Atlantic Ocean

18. **To create a link in your Web page:**

    A. Choose the File➪Make a Link command.

    B. Click the Make Link button on the Character Format Toolbar.

    C. Choose the Insert➪Link command from the menu bar.

    D. Press Ctrl+L.

    E. Type **<A HREF="url">text</A>** in your Web page.

Matching

19. **Match the plug-ins with the types of files they can display:**

    A. Word Viewer   1. Spreadsheets

    B. Formula One/NET   2. Audio and video files

    C. LiveVideo   3. Video files

    D. VDOLive   4. Word documents

    E. Shockwave

20. **Match the plug-ins with their home pages on the Web:**

    A. VDOLive   1. www.macromedia.com

    B. CyberSpell and Word Viewer   2. www.realaudio.com

    C. Shockwave   3. www.vdo.net

    D. LiveVideo, LiveAudio, and Live3D   4. www.inso.com

    E. RealAudio   5. home.netscape.com

21. **Match the buttons and boxes on the Netscape Editor window toolbars with their Names:**

    A.   1. Insert Image

    B.   2. Bullet List

    C.   3. Publish

    D.   4. Make Link

    E.    5. Paragraph style

22. **Match the commands with what they do in the Netscape Editor window:**

    A. File➪Save   1. Insert a picture in your Web page

    B. File➪Close   2. Save your Web page

    C. File➪Publish   3. Insert a link in your Web page

    D. Insert➪Image   4. Transmit your Web page to a Web server

    E. Insert➪Link   5. Close the Netscape Editor window

Part III Lab Assignment

Step 1: Run Netscape and open the Web page you created in Lessons 9-1 through 9-3.

You're going to create a new Web page.

Step 2: Add a paragraph in which you describe your favorite hobby or sport.

Or you can describe your favorite computer book (hint, hint).

Step 3: Save the Web page.

Step 4: View your Web page in the Netscape browser window.

Hint: Click the View in Browser button (the fourth button on the File/Edit Toolbar) or choose File➪Browse Document from the menu.

Looks pretty good, doesn't it?

Answers

Part I Test Answers

Question	Answer	If You Missed It, Try This
1.	False	Review Lesson 1-1.
2.	False	Review Lesson 1-1.
3.	True	Review Lesson 1-2.
4.	False	Review Lesson 1-2.
5.	True	Review Lesson 1-3.
6.	True	Review Lesson 2-1.
7.	True	Review Lesson 2-5.
8.	True	Review Lesson 4-1.
9.	False	Review Lesson 4-1.
10.	True	Review Lesson 4-2.
11.	E	Review Lesson 1-1.
12.	D, E	Review Lesson 1-2.
13.	B, D	Review Lessons 1-2 and 1-3.
14.	E	Review Lesson 2-5.
15.	A, B, C	Review Lesson 3-1.
16.	A, B, C, D	Review Lesson 3-2.
17.	D	Review Lesson 4-2.
18.	E	It's a wonderful world we live in.
19.	A, 4	Review Lessons 1-3, 2-4, 3-1, 4-1, and 4-2.
	B, 3	
	C, 2	
	D, 5	
	E, 1	

20.	A, 3	Review Lessons 1-3, 2-4, 3-1, and 4-2.
	B, 4	
	C, 5	
	D, 1	
	E, 2	
21.	A, 3	Review Lessons 1-3, 2-1, and 3-1.
	B, 5	
	C, 4	
	D, 2	
	E, 1	
22.	A, 4	Review your grade-school geography notes.
	B, 3	
	C, 5	
	D, 2	
	E, 1	

Part II Test Answers

Question	Answer	If You Missed It, Try This
1.	True	Review Lesson 5-2 for what it's like to send e-mail, and Lesson 6-2 for how to save messages for future reference.
2.	True	Review Lesson 5-2 for how to send e-mail, and Lesson 5-5 for rules of e-mail etiquette.
3.	False	Review Lesson 5-2. E-mail addresses contain only one at-sign (@) between the user name and the computer name.
4.	True	Review Table 5-2 in Lesson 5-2.
5.	False	Review Lesson 5-5.
6.	False	Review Lesson 6-3.
7.	True	Review Lesson 6-3.
8.	True	It depends on how you define *largest*, but the Amazon has the most water flowing through it.
9.	False	Review Lesson 7-1.
10.	True	Review Lesson 7-4. Never post test messages to other newsgroups, because you'll just make people mad!
11.	B, C, D	Review Lesson 6-1.
12.	C, D, E	Review Lesson 5-4.
13.	A, B, D, E	Review Lesson 5-2.
14.	E	Review Lesson 6-2.

15.	A, B, C, E	Review Lesson 6-2.
16.	A, B, D	C and E are used only with printed messages, not e-mail messages. Review Lesson 6-3.
17.	A, C	Review Lesson 6-3.
18.	A, B, E	Review Lesson 7-2. The other newsgroups might be educational if you're interested in the sociology and psychology of strange newsgroups!
19.	A, 2	Review Lessons 5-2 and 5-4, and remember that the Close button always closes the window.
	B, 1	
	C, 4	
	D, 3	
	E, 3	
20.	A, 3	Review Lesson 7-1.
	B, 1	
	C, 5	
	D, 4	
	E, 2	
21.	A, 5	Find an atlas or a fifth grader.
	B, 4	
	C, 2	
	D, 1	
	E, 3	
22.	A, 1	Review Lesson 7-4.
	B, 3	
	C, 2	
	D, 4	

Part III Test Answers

Question	Answer	If You Missed It, Try This
1.	False	Dozens of companies have created plug-ins that work with Netscape Navigator. Review Lesson 8-1.
2.	True	Review Lesson 8-1.
3.	True	Review Lesson 8-3.
4.	False	Review Lessons 8-3 and 8-4.
5.	True	Review Lesson 9-1.
6.	False	Review Lesson 9-1.

7.	False	Review Lesson 9-1.
8.	True	Review Lesson 9-3.
9.	True	Review Lesson 9-2.
10.	False	There's nothing "official" about most Web pages — anyone can make one. Review Lesson 9-4.
11.	A	Review Lesson 8-2.
12.	D	Review Lesson 8-2.
13.	A	Review Lesson 8-5.
14.	A, B	Review Lesson 8-5.
15.	A, C, D	Review Lesson 9-4. Note, however, that answer D is a big pain in the neck (not to mention expensive) and not recommended for the faint of heart.
16.	A	Tim now works at the World Wide Web Consortium (W3), whose home page is at www.w3.org.
17.	C, D, E	Trick question! The Panama Canal actually runs from northwest to southeast. The Caribbean is at the northwest end, while the Bay of Panama (part of the Gulf of Panama, which empties into the Pacific) is at the southeast end.
18.	B, C, D	Review Lesson 9-2.
19.	A, 4	Review Lessons 8-1, 8-4, and 8-6.
	B, 1	
	C, 3	
	D, 3	
	E, 2	
20.	A, 3	Review Lessons 8-3, 8-4, 8-5, 8-6, and 8-7.
	B, 4	
	C, 1	
	D, 5	
	E, 2	
21.	A, 4	Review Lessons 9-2, 9-3, and 9-4.
	B, 2	
	C, 3	
	D, 1	
	E, 5	
22.	A, 2	Review Lessons 9-1, 9-2, 9-3, and 9-4.
	B, 5	
	C, 4	
	D, 1	
	E, 3	

Using the Programs on the Dummies 101 CD-ROM

This appendix tells you how to install, use, and get more information about the programs and other files on the *Dummies 101: Netscape Navigator* CD-ROM. The programs discussed are

- **AT&T WorldNet Service:** AT&T WorldNet signup software with Netscape Navigator.

- **Adobe Acrobat Reader:** A free document-reader program that lets you view documents with full formatting (as opposed to plain-text files that don't let you see fonts, boldfacing, and so on). You can use the Acrobat Reader to view some additional material that we wrote for this book.

- **WinZip:** A shareware compression/decompression program that you can employ to make compressed files useable again (an invaluable feature, because many files on the Internet are compressed to save storage space and reduce downloading time).

- **Paint Shop Pro:** A shareware graphics program that you can use to view virtually any picture file.

The CD-ROM Installer program includes buttons for installing all the preceding programs. The program detects whether you're running Windows 95 or Windows 3.1 and installs the appropriate versions of the programs you select. In addition, the Installer includes seven plug-in programs for Netscape Navigator 2.0 and higher. (See Unit 8 for how to use these plug-ins.) The Exit button closes the *Dummies 101* Installer program.

A few words about shareware: As explained in Lesson 3-2, shareware programs are available to you for an evaluation period (typically, anywhere from 30 to 90 days). If you decide that you like a shareware program and want to keep using it, you're expected to send a registration fee to its author or publisher, which entitles you to technical support and notifications about new versions. (Doing so also makes you feel good.)

Most shareware operates on an honor system, so the programs continue working even if you don't register them. However, supporting the shareware concept and encouraging the continued production of quality low-cost software by sending in your payment for the programs you use is a good idea. For more information about paying for your shareware, see the last section that appears under each shareware program description.

If you don't know the letter of your CD-ROM drive: Most PCs assign the letter D to a CD-ROM drive. Here's how to find out which letter your CD-ROM drive uses:

- If you use Windows 95, double-click the My Computer icon on your Windows 95 desktop. A window appears that lists all your drives, including your CD-ROM drive (which is usually represented by a shiny disc icon), and shows you the letter of each drive. When you're done examining the My Computer display, exit by clicking the window's Close button in its upper-right corner or by choosing File⇨Close from its menu.

- If you use Windows 3.1, double-click the File Manager icon in Program Manager. In the File Manager window, you see a row of disk icons. The CD-ROM drive is the one with the little CD-ROM sticking out of it.

Running the Dummies 101 Installer Program

If you're using Windows 95, the Installer window should appear automatically when you insert the CD-ROM into your CD-ROM drive. If you later exit the window, you can bring it back simply by ejecting the CD-ROM and then reinserting it. Alternately, you can bring up the window by double-clicking the My Computer icon (which is typically in the upper-right corner of your desktop) and then double-clicking the 101NETSCAPE icon.

If you're using Windows 3.1, however, the Installer window won't pop up by itself. Similarly, if you're using Windows 95 but your CD-ROM drive's software doesn't support the *autorun* feature, the Installer window won't appear automatically. In these cases, you can always run the Installer manually by clicking either the Windows 3.1 File menu or the Windows 95 Start button and then clicking Run, typing d:\install (with *d* being whatever is the appropriate letter for your CD-ROM drive), and pressing Enter. However, you'll probably find it more convenient to run the Installer by using an icon. To create a *Dummies 101* Installer icon, follow these steps:

1 **Insert the *Dummies 101* CD-ROM into your CD-ROM drive. Be careful to touch only the edges of the CD-ROM and to insert the disc label side up.**

If the Installer window pops up automatically, simply close the window for now by clicking its Exit button.

2 **If you're using Windows 95, click the Start button (located in the bottom-left corner of your screen) and choose the Run option. If you're using Windows 3.1, click the File menu from the Program Manager and choose Run.**

3 **In the Run dialog box that appears, type d:\icons (that is, the letter d, a colon (:), a backslash (\), and the word *icons*). If your CD-ROM isn't drive D, type the letter appropriate for your drive instead of D.**

If you're not sure what letter to type, see the "If you don't know the letter of your CD-ROM drive" paragraphs earlier in this appendix.

4 **Press Enter or click OK.**

A dialog box appears telling you that icons are about to be created.

5 **Click OK.**

After a few moments, a folder (under Windows 95) or Program Group (under Windows 3.1) is created that contains an icon that looks like a CD-ROM disc and is named *Dummies 101 - Netscape Navigator Installer*. Double-clicking this icon runs the Installer program.

You should also see an icon that looks like a trash can and is named *Uninstall Dummies 101 - Netscape Navigator Installer*. After you're done installing everything you need from the *Dummies 101* CD-ROM, double-click this icon to remove the icons you just created.

6 **Click OK in the dialog box that says that the icons have been successfully created.**

A final dialog box appears asking whether you want to run the Installer now. If you do, click Yes; otherwise, click No.

After you create the *Dummies 101* Installer icon, you can run the Installer at any time simply by double-clicking the icon. If you're using Windows 95, you can alternately run the Installer by clicking the Start button and choosing Programs⇨Dummies 101⇨Dummies 101 - Netscape Navigator Installer from the menus that appear.

When you're done with the Installer window, click its Exit button.

To examine the *Dummies 101* CD-ROM's contents: You can use the *Dummies 101* Installer program to install all the programs and data on your CD-ROM. However, if you're simply curious about the CD-ROM and want to examine its contents, Windows 95 users can do so by opening a Windows Explorer window (as opposed to a My Computer window) and double-clicking the CD-ROM's icon. Windows 3.1 users can look at the CD-ROM contents by double-clicking the CD-ROM's icon in File Manager.

Unit 1: Using the AT&T WorldNet Software

AT&T WorldNet Service is an Internet provider with telephone access numbers throughout the U.S. The software that comes with the service includes a customized version of Netscape Navigator. The Windows 3.1 version of the software also comes with a telephone dialer and TCP/IP (Internet connection) program; the Windows 95 version does not, because Windows 95 itself includes these programs.

The *Dummies 101* CD-ROM contains both the Windows 95 and Windows 3.1 versions of the AT&T WorldNet Service 2.0 software. If you do not yet have an Internet account, you may want to consider using it to sign up with AT&T WorldNet Service. If you do, you'll find instructions for installing the AT&T WorldNet Service software and signing up for an AT&T WorldNet account in two Acrobat pdf files on the CD-ROM: Wnet95.pdf (for Windows 95) and Wnet31.pdf (for Windows 3.1).

To read these files, you can use the Adobe Acrobat Reader, described in the section "Unit 1: Using Acrobat Reader" in this appendix. After you install the software and sign up for an AT&T WorldNet Service account, you can upgrade your Netscape Navigator program to the latest version by following the instructions in Lesson 1-1.

Unit 1: Using Acrobat Reader

Acrobat Reader from Adobe Systems Inc. is a free program that displays Portable Document Format (or *pdf*) files on almost any personal computer. Many programs include documentation on disk. Rather than being stuck using text files with no formatting, Acrobat Reader lets you see formatted documents that include different fonts, boldfacing, graphics, and so on. The *Dummies 101* CD-ROM contains three pdf files with additional explanations that we couldn't fit into this book.

Installing Acrobat Reader

To install Acrobat Reader, start the *Dummies 101* Installer program by following the steps in the section "Running the *Dummies 101* Installer Program" earlier in this appendix. When you click the Adobe Acrobat Reader button, installation of the program begins. Follow the prompts that appear on-screen to complete the installation. When the installation of Acrobat Reader is complete, click the Installer box's Exit button. The Installer program exits.

Windows 95 users: You can now run Acrobat Reader at any time by clicking the Start button and choosing Programs➪Adobe Acrobat➪Acrobat Reader from the menus.

Windows 3.1 users: You can now run Acrobat Reader at any time by double-clicking the Acrobat Reader icon in the Adobe Acrobat Program Group in Program Manager.

Reading documents with Acrobat Reader

When you run Acrobat Reader, an Open dialog box appears asking which pdf file you want to see. Move to the drive and folder that contains the pdf file you want to see, and then double-click the pdf file to open it. The document appears in the Acrobat Reader window. (Yay!) You can now read it at your leisure.

If you want to view other pdf documents, choose File➪Open from the menu bar to display the Open dialog box.

You can use the VCR-style buttons on the Toolbar to move forward one page, back one page, to the beginning of the document, or to the end of the document.

If the type looks small, click the Fit Width button on the Toolbar (the button with a little piece of paper in a box). Acrobat Reader expands the page to take up the full width of the window.

If you can't find what you're looking for, click the Find button (the button with the binoculars) or press Ctrl+F. When you see the Find dialog box, type a word or phrase in the Find What box and then click the Find button. Acrobat Reader finds the next occurrence of the word in the document and highlights it.

You can print part or all of the file by choosing File➪Print from the menu bar or pressing Ctrl+P. The Acrobat Reader lets you print the whole document, the current page, or a range of pages.

When you're done using Acrobat Reader, choose File➪Exit from the menu. All your pdf documents close, the Acrobat Reader window closes, and the program exits.

Getting more information about Acrobat Reader

To learn more about using Acrobat Reader, choose Help➪Acrobat Reader Help from the menu bar. You can also get more information, and possibly a newer version of the Acrobat Reader program, by visiting the Adobe Systems Web site at www.adobe.com.

Acrobat Files on the CD-ROM

The *Dummies 101* CD-ROM contains the following Acrobat pdf files, which you can read by using the Acrobat Reader described in the preceding section:

- **Wnet95.pdf:** Instructions for Windows 95 users for installing the AT&T WorldNet Service software and signing up for an AT&T WorldNet Service account

- **Wnet31.pdf:** Ditto, for Windows 3.1 users

- **Maillist.pdf:** A bonus unit titled "Joining Discussions by E-Mail" that tells you how to participate in ongoing discussions on any of thousands of different topics via mailing lists. This is a companion unit to Unit 7, "Joining Discussions via Newsgroups."

These Acrobat pdf files are stored in the root folder of the CD-ROM (for example, in d:\ if your CD-ROM drive is drive D).

Unit 2: Installing the Dummies 101 Bookmarks

In Unit 2, you display pages from the World Wide Web in the Netscape browser window. To spare you from typing dozens of mind-numbing Web page addresses, we have created *bookmarks* (predefined addresses) that lead you to the Web pages we want you to look at.

To install the bookmarks in your copy of Netscape Navigator, first make sure that you aren't running Netscape — that is, if Netscape is open, exit it. Next, start the *Dummies 101* Installer program by following the steps in the section "Running the *Dummies 101* Installer Program" earlier in this appendix.

When the Installer window appears, click its Bookmarks button. The Installer searches for a file named Bookmark.htm on your hard disk and then asks you to verify that it's located the folder that contains your Netscape program. Accept its suggestion or, if the program guessed wrong, select the folder that contains the version of Netscape you're using with this book. After you tell the Installer to proceed, it renames your old *Bookmark.htm* file as *Bookmark.old* and then copies the new *Bookmark.htm* file to the same folder. Follow any other instructions that appear on-screen until the bookmarks installation is completed. Finally, run Netscape, click its Bookmarks menu, and examine your new bookmarks!

Note: Instead of using the Installer program, you can insert the bookmarks manually, which allows you to combine your current bookmarks with the new bookmarks. To do so, first make sure that the *Dummies 101* CD-ROM is in your CD-ROM drive. Next, run Netscape, press Ctrl+B to open the Bookmarks window, choose File⇨Import, and type **d:\bookmark.htm** — that is, the letter of your CD-ROM drive (which is typically the letter *d*), a colon (:), a backslash (\), the word *bookmark*, a period, and the letters *htm*. When you're done, press Enter. The bookmarks on the CD-ROM are copied to your Bookmarks window.

Of course, you can also use the File⇨Import command to copy bookmarks from any other bookmark file. For example, if you used the Installer to replace your current bookmarks with the ones on the CD-ROM, you can get your old bookmarks back by opening the Bookmarks window, choosing File⇨Import, and typing the drive and name of your Netscape folder followed by a backslash and the filename *bookmark.old* (for example, **C:\Netscape\bookmark.old** or **C:\Program Files\Netscape\Navigator\bookmark.old**). When you press Enter, the bookmarks are copied into your Bookmarks window.

Unit 3: Using WinZip

As you learn in Lesson 3-2, you need an unzipping program to deal with compressed files, specifically those files with the file extension *zip* (these files are called, amazingly, *zip files*). Zip files are especially useful on the Internet, because compressed files take up less space and take less time to download. You may receive zip files as e-mail attachments, or you may download them from Web pages.

A Connecticut programmer named Nico Mak wrote a nice little Windows shareware program called WinZip that can both unzip and zip things for you. Copies of WinZip Version 6.1's installation files are on your *Dummies 101* CD-ROM. You may also have a more current version as a result of following the directions in Lesson 3-2 and downloading the program from the Web site www.winzip.com.

Installing WinZip from the CD-ROM

If you did *not* download WinZip from the Web, you can install it from your *Dummies 101* CD-ROM. First, follow the steps in the section "Running the *Dummies 101* Installer Program" earlier in this appendix. When you click the WinZip 6.1 button, installation of the program begins. Follow the prompts that appear on-screen to finish the installation. When the installation of WinZip is complete, click the Installer box's Exit button. The Installer program closes.

Installing WinZip manually

If you downloaded WinZip from the Web, you now have a compressed file named something like Winzip95.exe or Winzip61.exe. How can you decompress a program when you don't have a decompression program yet? Simple: The file is a *self-extracting file,* which means that it can decompress itself. (What will they think of next?)

The directions that follow apply to WinZip Version 6.1. If you have a newer version, the installation instructions may not be exactly the same, but these will probably still be useful as guidelines.

Here's how to decompress and install WinZip:

1 **Run Windows Explorer or My Computer (in Windows 95) or File Manager (in Windows 3.1), open the folder you used to store the file you downloaded, and double-click its filename.**

A dialog box asks whether you want to go ahead and set up WinZip.

2 **Click the Setup button.**

The setup program asks what folder you want to put the program into. The program suggests C:\WinZip, but you can change the folder name if you want to put the file somewhere else.

3 **When the folder name is to your liking, click the OK button.**

Follow the directions on-screen. WinZip displays information about the program.

4 **Click Next.**

WinZip asks you to agree to its license agreement, which is only fair.

5 **Click Yes to agree.**

The program asks what kind of installation you want. We recommend that you use the WinZip "classic" interface. The Wizard is so friendly that we can't figure out how to get it to do what we want!

6 **Click Start with WinZip Classic and then click Next.**

7 **If WinZip suggests an Express setup option, accept the recommendation by clicking Next.**

WinZip installs itself.

8 **Click Finish to end the setup and run WinZip.**

WinZip is installed and running.

9 **Choose File⇨Exit from the menu bar to exit WinZip. If necessary, also click an OK button to close a message box about registering WinZip.**

Don't worry — you'll be back! Windows 95 users should see a WinZip folder on the Windows 95 desktop, with several icons. (If you don't, open a My Computer or Windows Explorer window and then open the folder you selected to store the WinZip files.) Windows 3.1 users see a new WinZip Program Group in Program Manager, with several icons.

10 **Windows 95 users only: To make a WinZip icon on your Windows 95 desktop, click the WinZip32.exe filename in the WinZip folder to select the program. While holding down your mouse button, drag the icon to the desktop, and then release the mouse button.**

The program is unaffected, but Windows 95 creates a shortcut icon on your desktop. You can now run WinZip by double-clicking the icon.

You're ready to unzip programs that you download from the Internet!

Running WinZip

To run WinZip, Windows 95 users can click the Start button and choose Programs⇨WinZip⇨ WinZip 32-bit from the menus that appear. Alternately, if you've created a WinZip icon on your desktop, simply double-click the icon. Windows 3.1 users just double-click the WinZip icon in the WinZip Program Group in Program Manager.

The first time you run WinZip, it may display a bunch of messages and configuration questions (as well as a question about your intention to register your shareware copy). After you answer all the questions, WinZip is ready to go.

Viewing the contents of a zip file

To open a zip file and view the files it contains, follow these steps:

1 **Click the Open button on the WinZip Toolbar, press Ctrl+O, or choose File⇨Open Archive from the menu bar.**

You see an Open Archive dialog box. (The WinZip folks call zip files *archives*.)

2 **Move to the drive and folder that holds your file and then double-click the name of the zip file you want.**

WinZip opens the zip file and displays information about the files it contains. For each file, you see the filename, date, time, size when decompressed, and how much WinZip was able to compress the file.

Extracting the contents of a zip file

After a zip file is open, you can copy decompressed versions of its files to any folder you specify. The zip file itself remains unchanged.

To extract the files from a zip file and make them useable, follow these steps:

1 **Open the zip file you want to work with by using the instructions in the preceding exercise.**

The files in the zip file should be displayed in the WinZip window.

2 **To select one file to decompress, simply click its name. To select more than one file, click each file's name while holding down the Ctrl key. To select all the listed files, choose Actions⇨Select All from the menu bar.**

Each file you select is highlighted.

3 **Click the Extract button on the Toolbar.**

An Extract dialog box appears. Notice that the Extract To box is selected, as indicated by a text cursor blinking in it. This box lets you specify where you want to store the decompressed files.

4 **In the Extract To box, type the name of the folder you want to use to store the extracted files.**

For example, if you want to store the decompressed files in a folder named MyData on drive C, you type **C:\MyData**. Your text replaces the highlighted text in the Extract To box.

5 **Press Enter or click Extract.**

The files you selected are decompressed and copied to the folder you specified, and the zip file remains unchanged.

You can make your own zip files, too: Click the New button on the WinZip Toolbar, type the zip file's location and name, and press Enter. Then click the Add button on the Toolbar to add files to your new zip file.

WinZip is close friends with Windows Explorer, My Computer, and File Manager. If you drag a zip file from any of these programs to the WinZip window, WinZip automatically opens the file. If you drag another kind of file, or a group of files, to WinZip, the file(s) is added to the current zip file.

Note: If you ever decide that you don't want to use WinZip, you can uninstall it from your system, a process that deletes all its program and data files. To remove WinZip, Windows 95 users click the Start button on the Taskbar and then choose Programs⇨WinZip⇨Uninstall WinZip. Windows 3.1 users double-click the Uninstall WinZip icon in Program Manager.

Getting more information about WinZip

To learn more about WinZip's features while the program is running, press the F1 key or click Help from the program's menu bar and click one of the options that appear. Alternately, Windows 95 users can click the Start button and then choose Programs⇨WinZip⇨Online Manual to get detailed information about using WinZip.

Registering WinZip

Now that you know how to use WinZip, you'll probably find it invaluable. (We certainly do!) To order your own legal copy, choose Help⇨Ordering Information from the WinZip menu. Go ahead and register the shareware programs you use — you'll feel positively noble after you do!

Unit 3: Using Paint Shop Pro

Netscape can display picture files (also called *graphics files* or *image files*) that happen to be in gif or jpg format. However, there are dozens of additional graphics formats that Netscape *can't* handle. To view these files, you can use the shareware program called Paint Shop Pro.

Paint Shop Pro is a powerful graphics program that lets you display virtually any picture file. In addition, it lets you manipulate pictures in a variety of ways, convert pictures from one file format to another, and even create your own pictures from scratch.

Installing Paint Shop Pro

To install Paint Shop Pro, start the *Dummies 101* Installer program by following the steps in the section "Running the *Dummies 101* Installer Program" earlier in this appendix. When you click the Paint Shop Pro button, installation of the program begins. Follow the prompts that appear on-screen to complete the installation. When the installation of Paint Shop Pro is complete, click the Installer box's Exit button. The Installer program exits.

You can now run Paint Shop Pro at any time. Windows 95 users can click the Start button and choose Programs⇨Paint Shop Pro⇨Paint Shop Pro on the menus that appear. Windows 3.1 users can just double-click the Paint Shop Pro icon in Program Manager.

Viewing picture files with Paint Shop Pro

To examine a graphics file by using Paint Shop Pro, follow these steps:

1 Run Paint Shop Pro as described in the preceding section.

A dialog box appears, informing you that the program is shareware and that you should register it if you decide to keep it.

2 Click the OK button.

The dialog box disappears, and you see the Paint Shop Pro window.

3 Choose File⇨Open from the menu bar.

An Open Image dialog box appears.

4 Move to the drive and folder that contains the image you want to see.

The files in the folder are displayed in the box on the left. If you want to narrow down your choices, click in the List Files of Type box to specify the type of graphics file you're looking for. Otherwise, accept the default of displaying All Files.

5 **Scroll through the list of files until you find the one you're after. When you locate the file, double-click it.**

The file appears in the Paint Shop Pro window. (Yay!) You can now examine it at your leisure.

6 **If you want to view other picture files, repeat Steps 3 through 5 for each file.**

Each picture opens in its own window. You can switch to any picture by clicking the window it's in or by clicking the <u>W</u>indow menu and then clicking the name of the file you want (which is listed near the bottom of the menu).

7 **When you're done using Paint Shop Pro, choose <u>F</u>ile⇨E<u>x</u>it.**

All your picture windows close, the Paint Shop Pro window closes, and the program exits.

Getting more information about Paint Shop Pro

Paint Shop Pro can do a great deal more than simply display picture files. To learn about the program's many features, press the F1 key or choose <u>H</u>elp⇨<u>C</u>ontents from the menu bar. You can also get more information by visiting the program's Web site at www.jasc.com/psp.html.

Registering Paint Shop Pro

Paint Shop Pro is shareware. Every time you run the program, it reminds you that if you decide to keep it, you have to pay for it. For more information about registering, click the <u>H</u>elp button on the program's initial message box or choose <u>H</u>elp⇨<u>P</u>urchasing from the program's menu bar.

Unit 6: Exercise File

The *Dummies 101* CD-ROM contains a file in the root folder named Meg.gif. You use this file in Lesson 6-3 when you learn to attach files to e-mail messages. This file is not copied to your computer's hard disk. When you follow the steps in the lesson, you read the graphics file directly from the CD-ROM. (Why clutter up your hard disk with files you don't need?)

Unit 8: Installing Netscape Plug-ins

Important: You can use the plug-ins available from the *Dummies 101* CD-ROM with Netscape Navigator Versions 2.0 and higher. If you chose to use the Windows 3.1 version of AT&T WorldNet Service, you received a special version of Netscape Navigator 1.22, which can't use plug-ins. See Unit 1 for how to download the latest version of Netscape Navigator.

Netscape plug-ins are add-on programs that extend the capabilities of Netscape Navigator 2.0 and higher. A number of plug-in programs are included on the *Dummies 101* CD-ROM. Unit 8 describes plug-ins in general and the plug-ins on the CD-ROM in particular. Refer to Lesson 8-2 for the general procedure for installing the plug-ins on the CD-ROM and Lessons 8-3 through 8-7 for details on installing each plug-in.

Note: Install one plug-in at a time, and make sure that Netscape and your other plug-ins still work. See Lesson 8-8 for how to uninstall plug-ins that cause trouble or aren't useful to you.

The plug-in programs included on the CD-ROM are

- **Shockwave:** A plug-in for playing audio and video files (see Lesson 8-4)
- **VDOLive:** A plug-in for playing video files (see Lesson 8-4)
- **ASAP WebShow:** A plug-in for playing slide shows (see Lesson 8-6)
- **Word Viewer:** A plug-in for displaying Microsoft Word documents (see Lesson 8-6)
- **Formula One/NET:** A plug-in for displaying spreadsheets in Web pages (see Lesson 8-6)
- **Ichat:** A plug-in for participating in live chats (see Lesson 8-7)
- **CyberSpell:** A plug-in that adds a spelling checker to Netscape (see Lesson 8-7)

Unit 9: Exercise Files

In Unit 9, you learn to create your own Web pages by using Netscape Navigator Gold. The CD-ROM contains three graphics (gif) files for use in creating sample Web pages. You copy these files to your hard disk when you include them in your Web pages, as described in Lesson 9-3. The names of these exercise files are

- **Mounts.gif:** Restful photo of distant mountains
- **Ferns.gif:** Photo of green ferns
- **Rainbow.gif:** Photo of a rainbow

Index

, *O* ,

, *P* ,

Y

Z

Notes

Notes

Notes

Introducing
AT&T WorldNet^{SM} Service

A World of Possibilities...

With AT&T WorldNet^{SM} Service, a world of possibilities awaits you. Discover new ways to stay in touch with the people, ideas, and information that are important to you at home and at work.

Make travel reservations at any time of the day or night. Access the facts you need to make key decisions. Pursue business opportunities on the AT&T Business Network. Explore new investment options. Play games. Research academic subjects. Stay abreast of current events. Participate in online newsgroups. Purchase merchandise from leading retailers. Send e-Mail.

All you need is a computer with a mouse, a modem, a phone line, and the software enclosed with this mailing. We've taken care of the rest.

If You Can Point and Click, You're There.

Finding the information you want on the Internet with AT&T WorldNet Service is easier than you ever imagined it could be. That's because AT&T WorldNet Service integrates a specially customized version of the popular Netscape Navigator™ software with advanced Internet directories and search engines. The result is an Internet service that sets a new standard for ease of use — virtually everywhere you want to go is a point and click away.

We're With You Every Step of the Way.
24 Hours a Day, 7 Days a Week.

Nothing is more important to us than making sure that your Internet experience is a truly enriching and satisfying one. That's why our highly trained customer service representatives are available to answer your questions and offer assistance whenever you need it — 24 hours a day, 7 days a week. To reach AT&T WorldNet Customer Care, call **1 800 400-1447**.

Safeguard Your Online Purchases

By registering and continuing to charge your AT&T WorldNet Service to your AT&T Universal Card, you'll enjoy peace of mind whenever you shop the Internet. Should your account number be compromised on the Net, you won't be liable for any online transactions charged to your AT&T Universal Card by a person who is not an authorized user.*

*Today cardmembers may be liable for the first $50 of charges made by a person who is not an authorized user, which will not be imposed under this program as long as the cardmember notifies AT&T Universal Card of the loss within 24 hours and otherwise complies with the Cardmember Agreement. Refer to Cardmember Agreement for definition of authorized user.

Minimum System Requirements

To run AT&T WorldNet Service, you need:

- An IBM-compatible personal computer with a 386 processor or better
- Microsoft Windows 3.1*x* or Windows 95
- 8MB RAM (16MB or more recommended)
- 11MB of free hard disk space
- 14.4 Kbps (or faster) modem (28.8 Kbps is recommended)
- A standard phone line

Installation Tips and Instructions

- If you have other Web browsers or online software, please consider uninstalling them according to vendor's instructions.
- At the end of installation, you may be asked to restart Windows. Don't attempt the registration process until you have done so.
- If you are experiencing modem problems trying to dial out, try different modem selections, such as Hayes Compatible. If you still have problems, please call Customer Care at **1 800 400-1447**.
- If you are installing AT&T WorldNet Service on a PC with Local Area Networking, please contact your LAN administrator for set-up instructions.
- Follow the initial start-up instructions given to you by the vendor product you purchased. (See Unit 1 of *Dummies 101: Netscape Navigator.*) These instructions will tell you how to start the installation of the AT&T WorldNet Service Software.
- Follow the on-screen instructions to install AT&T WorldNet Service Software on your computer.

When you have finished installing the software, you may be prompted to restart your computer. Do so when prompted.

Setting Up Your WorldNet Account

The AT&T WorldNet Service Program group/folder will appear on your Windows desktop.

- Double-click on the WorldNet Registration icon.
- Follow the on-screen instructions and complete all the stages of registration.

After all the stages have been completed, you'll be prompted to dial into the network to complete the registration process. Make sure your modem and phone line are not in use.

Registering With AT&T WorldNet Service

Once you have connected with AT&T WorldNet online registration service, you will be presented with a series of screens that will confirm billing information and prompt you for additional account set-up data.

The following is a list of registration tips and comments that will help you during the registration process.

I. Use the following registration codes, which can also be found in Appendix B of *Dummies 101: Netscape Navigator*. L5SQIM631 if you are an AT&T long-distance residential customer, and L5SQIM632 if you use another long-distance phone company.

II. We advise that you use all lowercase letters when assigning an e-Mail ID and security code, since they are easier to remember.

III. Choose a special "security code" that you will use to verify who you are when you call Customer Care.

IV. If you make a mistake and exit the registration process prematurely, all you need to do is click on "Create New Account." Do not click on "Edit Existing Account."

V. When choosing your local access telephone number, you will be given several options. Please choose the one nearest to you. Please note that calling a number within your area does not guarantee that the call is free.

Connecting to AT&T WorldNet Service

When you have finished registering with AT&T WorldNet Service, you are ready to make online connections.

- Make sure your modem and phone line are available.
- Double-click on the AT&T WorldNet Service icon.

Follow these steps whenever you wish to connect to AT&T WorldNet Service.

Choose the Plan That's Right for You.

If you're an AT&T Long Distance residential customer signing up in 1996, you can experience this exciting new service for 5 free hours a month for one full year. Beyond your 5 free hours, you'll be charged only $2.50 for each additional hour. Just use the service for a minimum of one hour per month. If you intend to use AT&T WorldNet Service for more than 5 hours a month, consider choosing the plan with unlimited hours for $19.95 per month.*

If you're not an AT&T Long Distance residential customer, you can still benefit from AT&T quality and reliability by starting with the plan that offers 3 hours each month and a low monthly fee of $4.95. Under this plan you'll be charged $2.50 for each additional hour, or AT&T WorldNet Service can provide you with unlimited online access for $24.95 per month. It's entirely up to you.

*The 5 free hours is limited to one AT&T WorldNet Account per residential billed telephone presubscribed to AT&T for "1+ area code + number" long distance dialing. Unlimited usage offers limited to one logon per account at any time. Other terms and conditions apply. Prices quoted are current as of 4/22/96 and are subject to modification by AT&T at any time. Local, long distance, or 800 number access charges and additional access charges and/or taxes that may be imposed on subscribers or on AT&T WorldNet Service will apply to all usage.

Explore our AT&T WorldNet Service Web site at:
http://www.att.com/worldnet

Over 200 local access telephone numbers throughout the U.S.

IDG BOOKS WORLDWIDE, INC.
END-USER LICENSE AGREEMENT

<u>Read This.</u> **You should carefully read these terms and conditions before opening the software packet included with this book ("Book"). This is a license agreement ("Agreement") between you and IDG Books Worldwide, Inc. ("IDGB"). By opening the accompanying software packet, you acknowledge that you have read and accept the following terms and conditions. If you do not agree and do not want to be bound by such terms and conditions, promptly return the Book and the unopened software packet to the place you obtained them for a full refund.**

1. <u>License Grant.</u> IDGB grants to you (either an individual or entity) a nonexclusive license to use one copy of the enclosed software programs (collectively, the "Software") solely for your own personal or business purposes on a single computer (whether a standard computer or a workstation component of a multiuser network). The Software is in use on a computer when it is loaded into temporary memory (i.e., RAM) or installed into permanent memory (e.g., hard disk, CD-ROM, or other storage device). IDGB reserves all rights not expressly granted herein.

2. <u>Ownership.</u> IDGB is the owner of all right, title, and interest, including copyright, in and to the compilation of the Software recorded on the CD-ROM. Copyright to the individual programs on the CD-ROM is owned by the author or other authorized copyright owner of each program. Ownership of the Software and all proprietary rights relating thereto remain with IDGB and its licensors.

3. <u>Restrictions on Use and Transfer.</u>

   (a) You may only (i) make one copy of the Software for backup or archival purposes, or (ii) transfer the Software to a single hard disk, provided that you keep the original for backup or archival purposes. You may not (i) rent or lease the Software, (ii) copy or reproduce the Software through a LAN or other network system or through any computer subscriber system or bulletin-board system, or (iii) modify, adapt, or create derivative works based on the Software.

   (b) You may not reverse engineer, decompile, or disassemble the Software. You may transfer the Software and user documentation on a permanent basis, provided that the transferee agrees to accept the terms and conditions of this Agreement and you retain no copies. If the Software is an update or has been updated, any transfer must include the most recent update and all prior versions.

4. <u>Restrictions on Use of Individual Programs.</u> You must follow the individual requirements and restrictions detailed for each individual program in Appendix A of this Book. These limitations are contained in the individual license agreements recorded on the CD-ROM. These restrictions may include a requirement that after using the program for the period of time specified in its text, the user must pay a registration fee or discontinue use. By opening the Software packet, you will be agreeing to abide by the licenses and restrictions for these individual programs. None of the material on this disc or listed in this Book may ever be distributed, in original or modified form, for commercial purposes.

5. <u>Limited Warranty.</u>

   (a) IDGB warrants that the Software and CD-ROM are free from defects in materials and workmanship under normal use for a period of sixty (60) days from the date of purchase of this Book. If IDGB receives notification within the warranty period of defects in materials or workmanship, IDGB will replace the defective CD-ROM.

(b) IDGB AND THE AUTHORS OF THE BOOK DISCLAIM ALL OTHER WARRANTIES, EXPRESS OR IMPLIED, INCLUDING WITHOUT LIMITATION IMPLIED WARRANTIES OF MERCHANTABILITY AND FITNESS FOR A PARTICULAR PURPOSE, WITH RESPECT TO THE SOFTWARE, THE PROGRAMS, THE SOURCE CODE CONTAINED THEREIN, AND/OR THE TECHNIQUES DESCRIBED IN THIS BOOK. IDGB DOES NOT WARRANT THAT THE FUNCTIONS CONTAINED IN THE SOFTWARE WILL MEET YOUR REQUIREMENTS OR THAT THE OPERATION OF THE SOFTWARE WILL BE ERROR FREE.

(c) This limited warranty gives you specific legal rights, and you may have other rights which vary from jurisdiction to jurisdiction.

6. **Remedies.**

   (a) IDGB's entire liability and your exclusive remedy for defects in materials and workmanship shall be limited to replacement of the Software, which may be returned to IDGB with a copy of your receipt at the following address: Disk Fulfillment Department, Attn: Dummies 101: Netscape Navigator 3.0, IDG Books Worldwide, Inc., 7260 Shadeland Station, Ste. 100, Indianapolis, IN 46256, or call 1-800-762-2974. Please allow 3-4 weeks for delivery. This Limited Warranty is void if failure of the Software has resulted from accident, abuse, or misapplication. Any replacement Software will be warranted for the remainder of the original warranty period or thirty (30) days, whichever is longer.

   (b) In no event shall IDGB or the author be liable for any damages whatsoever (including without limitation damages for loss of business profits, business interruption, loss of business information, or any other pecuniary loss) arising from the use of, or inability to use, the Book or the Software, even if IDGB has been advised of the possibility of such damages.

   (c) Because some jurisdictions do not allow the exclusion or limitation of liability for consequential or incidental damages, the above limitation or exclusion may not apply to you.

7. **U.S. Government Restricted Rights.** Use, duplication, or disclosure of the Software by the U.S. Government is subject to restrictions stated in paragraph (c) (1) (ii) of the Rights in Technical Data and Computer Software clause of DFARS 252.227-7013, and in subparagraphs (a) through (d) of the Commercial Computer — Restricted Rights clause at FAR 52.227-19, and in similar clauses in the NASA FAR supplement, when applicable.

8. **General.** This Agreement constitutes the entire understanding of the parties and revokes and supersedes all prior agreements, oral or written, between them and may not be modified or amended except in a writing signed by both parties hereto which specifically refers to this Agreement. This Agreement shall take precedence over any other documents that may be in conflict herewith. If any one or more provisions contained in this Agreement are held by any court or tribunal to be invalid, illegal, or otherwise unenforceable, each and every other provision shall remain in full force and effect.

Dummies 101 CD-ROM
Installation Instructions

The CD-ROM in the back of this book contains the AT&T WorldNet Service software, which comes bundled with the Netscape Navigator program that you use throughout the lessons in this book. It also contains other useful programs, Netscape plug-ins, and exercise files that are described in Unit 8 and Appendix B. You can easily install all these files by using the special *Dummies 101* Installer program that's also stored on the CD-ROM.

Follow these steps with Windows running:

1 Insert the *Dummies 101* CD-ROM into your CD-ROM drive. Be careful to touch only the edges of the CD-ROM.

If your CD-ROM drive requires a caddy (a protective plastic holder), insert the CD-ROM into an empty caddy and then place the caddy into your drive. Otherwise, simply insert the CD-ROM directly into the holder provided by your drive. In either case, be sure to insert the CD-ROM with its printed side up.

If you're a Windows 95 user, the Installer may start running automatically a few moments after you insert the CD-ROM into the drive. For now, close the Installer window by clicking the Exit button at the bottom center of the Installer window.

2 Windows 95 users: Click the Start button (located in the bottom-left corner of your screen) and choose Run.

Windows 3.1 users: From the Program Manager, choose File⇨Run.

A Run dialog box appears.

3 In the Run dialog box, type d:\icons (that is, the letter d, a colon (:), a backslash (\), and the word *icons*). If your CD-ROM isn't drive D, type the letter appropriate for your drive instead of D.

4 Press Enter or click OK.

In a few moments, a message asking whether you want to run the Installer appears. Click OK to begin, and follow the on-screen prompts to complete the installation.

5 When you're asked if you'd like to start the *Dummies 101* Installer now, click Yes.

The Installer appears. Use this program to install the various programs and files on the CD-ROM. When you're done with the Installer, close it by clicking the Exit button in the bottom center of its window.

To run the Installer program in the future, simply double-click the *Dummies 101* Installer icon you created. If you're using Windows 95, you can alternately click the Start button in the bottom-left corner of your screen and then choose Programs⇨Dummies 101⇨Dummies 101 - Netscape Navigator Installer from the menus that appear.

If you have problems with the installation process, you can call the IDG Books Worldwide, Inc., Customer Support Number: 800-762-2974 (outside the U.S.: 317-596-5261).

For more information about installing and using the AT&T WorldNet Service software, see Unit 1 and the files Wnet31.pdf and Wnet95.pdf on the CD-ROM. For more information about installing and using all the other programs on the CD-ROM, see Unit 8 and Appendix B.

When you're done with the *Dummies 101* CD-ROM, store it in a safe place.

RETURN THIS REGISTRATION CARD FOR FREE CATALOG

IDG BOOKS WORLDWIDE REGISTRATION CARD

Title of this book: Dummies 101™ : Netscape Navigator™

My overall rating of this book: ❏ Very good [1] ❏ Good [2] ❏ Satisfactory [3] ❏ Fair [4] ❏ Poor [5]

How I first heard about this book:

❏ Found in bookstore; name: [6]

❏ Advertisement: [8]

❏ Word of mouth; heard about book from friend, co-worker, etc.: [10]

❏ Book review: [7]

❏ Catalog: [9]

❏ Other: [11]

What I liked most about this book:

What I would change, add, delete, etc., in future editions of this book:

Other comments:

Number of computer books I purchase in a year: ❏ 1 [12] ❏ 2-5 [13] ❏ 6-10 [14] ❏ More than 10 [15]

I would characterize my computer skills as: ❏ Beginner [16] ❏ Intermediate [17] ❏ Advanced [18] ❏ Professional [19]

I use ❏ DOS [20] ❏ Windows [21] ❏ OS/2 [22] ❏ Unix [23] ❏ Macintosh [24] ❏ Other: [25]

(please specify)

I would be interested in new books on the following subjects:
(please check all that apply, and use the spaces provided to identify specific software)

❏ Word processing: [26]

❏ Data bases: [28]

❏ File Utilities: [30]

❏ Networking: [32]

❏ Other: [34]

❏ Spreadsheets: [27]

❏ Desktop publishing: [29]

❏ Money management: [31]

❏ Programming languages: [33]

I use a PC at (please check all that apply): ❏ home [35] ❏ work [36] ❏ school [37] ❏ other: [38]

The disks I prefer to use are ❏ 5.25 [39] ❏ 3.5 [40] ❏ other: [41]

I have a CD ROM: ❏ yes [42] ❏ no [43]

I plan to buy or upgrade computer hardware this year: ❏ yes [44] ❏ no [45]

I plan to buy or upgrade computer software this year: ❏ yes [46] ❏ no [47]

Name: _____ Business title: [48] _____ Type of Business: [49]

Address (❏ home [50] ❏ work [51]/Company name: _____)

Street/Suite# _____

City [52]/State [53]/Zipcode [54]: _____ Country [55]

❏ **I liked this book!** You may quote me by name in future
IDG Books Worldwide promotional materials.

My daytime phone number is _____

IDG BOOKS
THE WORLD OF COMPUTER KNOWLEDGE

❏ YES!

Please keep me informed about IDG's World of Computer Knowledge.
Send me the latest IDG Books catalog.